The Business of the Metaverse

The metaverse is the future of business applications and models, and this ground-breaking book points and details a complete and clear picture of how the metaverse can impact the various business segments and how the human element will be maintained within the evolutionary change. This book serves as a guide for those planning to implement and expand the metaverse in their business as well as those already using it on limited levels. Simulated intelligence innovation can reveal intricate and significant examples in robust and information-rich situations that posture difficulties for human insight. In addition, similar to other burgeoning advancements, the experience and aptitudes accumulated by vendors and consumers, alongside the steady analysis of interactions and information, empower metaverse calculations to be refined and improved. This book illustrates the current advancements and results and expands the analysis of human-centric metaverse applications to business segments and their future effects on overall enterprise management. Essentially, this book elaborates on the impact of the metaverse across business sectors through the use of case studies.

The Business of the Metaverse
How to Maintain the Human Element
Within This New Business Reality

Edited by
Hemachandran K. and Raul V. Rodriguez

Routledge
Taylor & Francis Group

A PRODUCTIVITY PRESS BOOK

First published 2024
by Routledge
605 Third Avenue, New York, NY 10158

and by Routledge

4 Park Square, Milton Park, Abingdon, Oxon, OX14 4RN

Routledge is an imprint of the Taylor & Francis Group, an informa business

ISBN: 9781032594798 (hbk)
ISBN: 9781032594781 (pbk)
ISBN: 9781003454878 (ebk)

DOI: 10.4324/b23404

Typeset in Garamond
by KnowledgeWorks Global Ltd.

Contents

Preface

The convergence of technology and business has ushered in a new era of innovation, with the metaverse and artificial intelligence (AI) at the forefront of this revolution. As we navigate through the digital landscape, the impact of the metaverse and AI on various industries cannot be overstated. From business applications and marketing strategies to supply chain management and entertainment, the metaverse and AI are transforming the way we conduct business and interact with the world.

This book delves into the multifaceted aspects of the metaverse and AI in business and beyond, exploring their applications, implications, and future possibilities. Each chapter takes a deep dive into a specific industry or sector, analyzing the current landscape, evaluating the impact of the metaverse and AI, and showcasing innovative strategies and practices being employed by businesses to stay ahead in the rapidly changing digital world.

The book begins with an introduction to the metaverse in business applications, discussing its evolution, potential, and implications for various industries. It further examines how the metaverse is being leveraged for re-wilding natural habitats, operations management in sports like football, and brand management in the virtual world. The role of AI in consumer decision-making and the interplay of AI and the metaverse in human resources, recruitment, and the fintech industry are also explored in detail.

The book explores the impact of the metaverse and AI in traditional industries such as supply chain, logistics, and manufacturing, showcasing how businesses are leveraging these technologies to streamline operations and enhance efficiency. It also delves into the applications of the metaverse and AI in the public sector, automobile industry, and education, discussing the potential for innovation and transformation in these domains.

Furthermore, the book explores the influence of AI on human cognizance, the emerging trends of AI and digital transactions in the financial sector, and the use of the Indian Premier League (IPL) as a marketing platform. It also delves into the pursuit of keeping the human element intact in the media and entertainment industry, showcasing the role of AI in decision-making and future innovations.

The chapters in this book are authored by experts and practitioners who bring a wealth of knowledge and insights into the topic. They share their experiences, case studies, and best practices, providing readers with valuable perspectives and practical guidance.

The metaverse and AI are driving a digital revolution, transforming the way we live, work, and perform business. The book provides a comprehensive overview of the current landscape and future possibilities of the metaverse and AI in various industries, serving as a valuable resource for business leaders, entrepreneurs, researchers, and anyone interested in the intersection of technology and business. We hope that the insights shared in this book will inspire and inform readers as they navigate the exciting and ever-evolving landscape of the metaverse and AI in the business world and beyond.

Contributors

Maddu Sai Adarsh
Woxsen University
Hyderabad, Telangana, India

V. Vikram Adithya
Woxsen University
Hyderabad, Telangana, India

Geddam Annirudh
Woxsen University
Hyderabad, Telangana, India

Ezendu Ariwa
University of Wales Trinity Saint
    David
Wales, UK

Kondisetti Venkata Bhavana
Woxsen University
Hyderabad, Telangana, India

Keerthi Boddapati
Woxsen University
Hyderabad, Telangana, India

Channabasava Chola
Department of Electronics and
    Information Convergence
    Engineering
College of Electronics and
    Information, Kyung Hee
    University
Suwon-si, South Korea

Hitesh Kumar Devaki
Woxsen University
Hyderabad, Telangana, India

Divya Dwivedi
The Supreme Court of India,
Woxsen University
Hyderabad, Telangana, India

Chinna Swamy Dudekula
Northumbria University
Newcastle, UK

Máté Farkas-Kis
Corvinus University of Budapest
Budapest, Hungary

Sanjeev Ganguly
Woxsen University
Hyderabad, Telangana, India

Rekulakunta Greeshma
Woxsen University
Hyderabad, Telangana, India

Boggarapu Sudeep Gupta
Woxsen University
Hyderabad, Telangana, India

Diya Gupta
Woxsen University
Hyderabad, Telangana, India

Shashank Raj Gupta
Woxsen University
Hyderabad, Telangana, India

Kaushik Gurram
Woxsen University
Hyderabad, Telangana, India

Divya Gutti
Woxsen University
Hyderabad, Telangana, India

Krishna Hitesh
Woxsen University
Hyderabad, Telangana, India

Anurag Jain
School of Business
Woxsen University
Hyderabad, Telangana, India

Dr. Hemachandran K.
Woxsen School of Business,
    Woxsen University
Hyderabad, Telangana, India

Gabriel Kabanda
UNOPS – United Nations Office for
    Project Services
New York, NY

Sai Kiran Kadari
Woxsen University
Hyderabad, Telangana, India

Harshitha Kaja
Woxsen University
Hyderabad, Telangana, India

Saransh Kalambele
School of Business
Woxsen University
Hyderabad, Telangana, India

Harshita Kallem
Woxsen University
Hyderabad, Telangana, India

Vishwa K.D.
Woxsen University
Hyderabad, Telangana, India

Hridya Koduri
Woxsen University
Hyderabad, Telangana, India

Madhuri Kompelly
Woxsen University
Hyderabad, Telangana, India

Jai Kothari
Woxsen University
Hyderabad, Telangana, India

Markus Krebsz
University of Stirling, Woxsen
    University
Hyderabad, Telangana, India

Kritika Kulkarni
Woxsen University
Hyderabad, Telangana, India

Pokala Pranay Kumar
MPS Data Science
University of Maryland
Baltimore County, MD

Neelam Kumari
Dublin Business School
Dublin, Ireland

Rajesh Kumar K.V.
Woxsen University
Hyderabad, Telangana, India

Shiva Lagishetty
Woxsen University
Hyderabad, Telangana, India

Swagatika Mohapatro
Woxsen University
Hyderabad, Telangana, India

Prasad Moligari
Woxsen University
Hyderabad, Telangana, India

Sanjay M.S.
Woxsen University
Hyderabad, Telangana, India

Sudhakar Reddy Nalamalapu
Woxsen University
Hyderabad, Telangana, India

Kundu Varshini Naidu
Woxsen University
Hyderabad, Telangana, India

Tanveer Nayak
School of Business,
Woxsen University
Hyderabad, Telangana, India

Shaik Nouman
Woxsen University
Hyderabad, Telangana, India

Zita Zoltay Paprika
Corvinus University
Budapest, Hungary

Anil Audumbar Pise
University of the Witwatersrand
Johannesburg, South Africa

Kalluri Poorvaj
Woxsen University
Hyderabad, Telangana, India

P. Baby Priya
Woxsen University
Hyderabad, Telangana, India

Charan P.V.
Woxsen University
Hyderabad, Telangana, India

D. Prithvi Raj
Woxsen University
Hyderabad, Telangana, India

C.V. Sai Supraja Reddy
Woxsen University
Hyderabad, Telangana, India

Guda Vineeth Reddy
Woxsen University
Hyderabad, Telangana, India

Priyanka Reddy
Woxsen University
Hyderabad, Telangana, India

Pulivendula Preethi Reddy
Woxsen University
Hyderabad, Telangana, India

R. Ramakrishna Reddy
Woxsen University
Hyderabad, Telangana, India

S. Veena Reddy
Woxsen University
Hyderabad, Telangana, India

Yamasani Keerthi Reddy
Woxsen University
Hyderabad, Telangana, India

Shiva Rohit
Woxsen University
Hyderabad, Telangana, India

Noyonika Sahoo
Woxsen University
Hyderabad, Telangana, India

Jeevan Venkata Sai Gollapalli
Woxsen University
Hyderabad, Telangana, India

P. Sanjna
Woxsen University
Hyderabad, Telangana, India

Krishna Saraf
Woxsen University
Hyderabad, Telangana, India

Bhavika Saraswat
Woxsen University
Hyderabad, Telangana, India

Kakoli Sen
Woxsen University
Hyderabad, Telangana, India

Delukshi Shanmugarajah
Middlesex University
London, UK

Devarasetty Sujith
Woxsen University
Hyderabad, Telangana, India

B. Vasavi
Woxsen University
Hyderabad, Telangana, India

K. Vinodh
Woxsen University
Hyderabad, Telangana, India

Goda Vardhini Yadav
Woxsen University
Hyderabad, Telangana, India

Chapter 1

Introduction to the Metaverse in Business Applications

Shiva Rohit, C. V. Sai Supraja Reddy,
and Rekulakunta Greeshma
Woxsen University, Hyderabad, Telangana, India

Pokala Pranay Kumar
MPS Data Science, University of Maryland, Baltimore County, MD, USA

1.1 Introduction to the Metaverse

The metaverse is a virtual world that is intertwined by physical, augmented, and virtual reality (VR) in a shared space over the internet (TechAhead, n.d.). The word *metaverse* first appeared in the 1982 novel, *Snow Crash*, written by Neil Stevenson, where the characters could go to escape dreary reality. In 2011, Ernest Cline released his book called *Ready Player One*, which has given a sneak peek into the world of VR, the book was an instant success and showed an ambitious route to VR and it was later made into a movie under the same name (Marr, 2022). The metaverse is a combination of the word "meta" and "universe," a space where the virtual avatars interact with each other to have all kinds of social conversations and meet people across the world in the virtual world and indulge in social, economic, and psychological conversations (Wikipedia, 2021). The idea of the metaverse hass been around for decades, but it waited for the technology to catch up and recent developments have shown that the world of the metaverse has been ready to interact with the users or among the users in the digital space. As technology is growing rapidly, it now has the biggest potential for

DOI: 10.4324/b23404-1

making a stand-alone technology. The metaverse is not just an application, but a concept that encompasses various technologies.

Imagine yourself sitting at home shopping for groceries and the application interface you have is very flat, simple, and non-interactive on your phone beyond the basic information; the metaverse helps you have an actual shopping experience, walk through the aisle, pick up and compare the items you require, or experience a big theatrics experience, or understand the concepts of space. All of this is now made possible by the growing influence of the metaverse across various domains, leading to significant investments by many platforms. Consequently, numerous companies have started pivoting towards the concept of the metaverse.

1.2 History of the Metaverse in Business

The concept of the metaverse was during the early science fiction days. Still, the idea of a metaverse in the gaming and entertainment environment has grown massively over the last decade and it has been a tool for business applications that involve virtual meetings, collaboration, and multiple screens in a work environment, etc.

One of the earliest examples of business applications in the metaverse comes from "Second Life," which launched in the year 2003; it is a virtual world where users can create their avatars and subsequently interact among them in a virtual world. Companies have also used Second Life for their virtual meetings. Many businesses have realized the potential of this metaverse and some companies have started using this as a market tool; companies such as Adidas, IBM, and Toyota are one of the initial storefronts in this digital space. In the long run, "Second Life" has failed to become a top platform in the metaverse space.

In 2007, IBM has launched its simulator for creating virtual worlds. In 2023, they are fulfilling the demand for stores and space innovation in the virtual world. In the metaverse, businesses look forward to creating new designs and prioritize the navigation in the metaverse to seamlessly work across the spectrum. IBM quotes, "They see the potential value in both Micro and Macro level of store and space design" (Castellano, 2022).

One of the key pillars in the metaverse is blockchain technology and it is highly business faced, which is decentral, and launched in the year 2017. This allows users to monetize their content. It has attracted many companies in due course, and also a few companies want to build the biggest casino in the virtual world (Wilser, 2022).

In 2014, Oculus VR was acquired by Facebook (which was later renamed Meta in 2021), which has shown its interest in the metaverse all along and remarked on its transition of becoming a metaverse company from its existing social media company. Other companies, such as Microsoft, have actively pushed their R&D to create more rampant growth in the meta space. Epic Games and Fortnite have already been active in creating a metaverse as an experience for their users.

While the concept of a metaverse for business applications is still in its early stages, it has the potential to transform how businesses collaborate and interact with customers. As more businesses investigate the potential of these platforms, we can anticipate an increase in the number of use cases.

1.3 Concept of the Metaverse

Metaverse's VR headsets, which have been in development for over a decade now, have been a center of the ecosystem, and as people are playing virtual games with more customized characters, they are becoming an integral part of the metaverse, and these features are further connected with blockchain technology. The metaverse is not just a game in reality but a gamified experience that will help imagine, create, co-create, and fully own the digital experience in the ecosystem.

1.3.1 Infrastructure

The common misconception around the metaverse is about how it looks and what is its functionality; in layman's terms, it is a digital world with the traits of the physical world but is present in the digital space, and we can simply access it through the internet. The majority of the early metaverse apps were focused on games with tokenized rewards. *Sandbox* is an open-world game that is not just restricted by gaming space, but has developed into something bigger with users able to buy land in the metaverse, create shops, and make brand awareness; further, users can buy non-fungible token (NFT) from the same space (Bartolo, 2022).

1.3.2 Digital Economy

Since 2021, Meta changed its name from Facebook Inc. and they are rapidly investing in making this technology relevant and introducing it to users.

Brands have started advertising themselves in the metaverse. Gucci has started advertising in the metaverse through the virtual space of *Sandbox*, and Burberry has introduced itself to users and made it available free for users to download. Gucci has made their handbag available for users for about $5, and it is easy for users to acquire a Gucci product that is highly expensive in the real world. Users can customize their avatars in the virtual world, which the brand can monetize through their shops and brands in their virtual plane (Anderrson, 2023).

1.3.3 Integration of the Physical and Digital World

The most important part of the metaverse is navigating the metaverse across the physical and virtual domains. Users can experience and feel the effect of brands, and own the digital assets in the metaverse. To materialize the metaverse and integrate it effectively with technologies like 5G, sophisticated, virtual, and augmented tools are essential for further evolution. Additionally, the integration of blockchain technology will play a crucial role in advancing the reality of the metaverse. The most difficult part of the metaverse is the integration of the physical and digital worlds.

1.4 The Emergence of the Metaverse

The term "metaverse" refers to a collective virtual, shared area that is often accessed through the internet and allows users to engage in real time with both a computer-generated environment and other users. The metaverse has attracted a lot of interest recently, especially as technological developments have made it more and more conceivable. The metaverse will soon become a reality, according to several experts, as virtual and augmented reality, blockchain technology, and advances in artificial intelligence all grow in popularity (Bojic, 2022).

The emergence of VR and augmented reality (AR) technology, as well as the rise in popularity of social media and online gaming, all contributed to the metaverse's emergence. Users have a rare chance to participate in immersive activities in the metaverse, such as exploring imaginative settings or interacting with virtual things, that aren't possible in the real world. In addition to being a source of entertainment and social engagement, the metaverse has the potential to be a substantial economic force. Businesses can establish a presence in the metaverse and engage in virtual commerce with customers. While offering people new ways to learn, receive medical care, and make purchases, the metaverse has the power to transform industries like education, health care, and retail.

The metaverse has the potential to alter a variety of industries, including those in entertainment, gaming, education, and health care. Users will be able to create their avatars in the metaverse and interact with virtual worlds without any glitches. In this virtual setting, there will be many chances for interaction, research, and creative expression. The metaverse will be used by businesses to develop new revenue streams and marketing opportunities. But the rise of the metaverse also prompts significant moral and social issues. How, for instance, would safety and privacy be guaranteed in this virtual world? However, if access is restricted to those who can afford the requisite technology or if specific groups are disenfranchised within the virtual world, the metaverse could exacerbate already existing inequities and foster the emergence of new ones. Furthermore, it's unclear how the metaverse will affect people's physical and mental health because extended contact with virtual worlds could have unintended implications (Boulben, 2023).

1.5 Growth

Over the past ten years, the metaverse has expanded dramatically, yet it still only makes up a small portion of daily life. Many uses of the metaverse have already been made this year, including virtual shopping and medical diagnosis. Since its inception, the metaverse has gradually expanded thanks to the addition of new platforms, the development of fresh methods of engagement, and the rising popularity of the metaverse as a whole.

One element encouraging the growth of the metaverse is the popularity of AR and VR technology. Users can enter fully immersive digital worlds that either replicate real-world experiences or build entirely new ones using these technologies. It is projected that more people will engage with the metaverse as technology advances and expenses decline. Another factor supporting metaverse expansion is the advancement of blockchain technology. Blockchain can make it possible for secure transactions to take place in the metaverse and decentralized digital economies, allowing users to monetize and do business there.

According to predictions, the metaverse market would expand significantly between 2021 and 2027, with a CAGR ranging from 39.8% to 47.2%. In 2021, the market was estimated to be worth USD$22.79 billion, and by 2027, it is anticipated to be worth USD$426.9 billion.

The surge in popularity of online gaming and commerce, the increasing convergence of the digital and real worlds, and increased spending on VR and AR technology are all factors that have contributed to this expansion. Companies have a lot of interest in the metaverse, since it has the potential to generate up to $5 trillion in value by 2030 (Mileva, 2023).

VR is now used often by millions of individuals as a result of the rising interest in technology. Also, we are witnessing a shift away from traditional gaming and towards more engaging, captivating, and interactive activities, such as social networking sites and video games with VR capabilities. Businesses are building new channels for the sale of goods and services, including online stores and marketing campaigns, as a result of the metaverse's influence on commerce.

1.6 Advantages

The next incarnation of the internet is the metaverse, a collective virtual shared environment that enables deep digital interaction (Pratt, 2022). The following are a few advantages of the metaverse.

1.6.1 Experience Affordability

The metaverse will make experiences more accessible, giving people access to chances and skills they have never had before.

1.6.2 Digital Communication That Is Fully Immersed

The metaverse's main advantage is that it enables fully immersed human connection with digital media.

1.6.3 Overcoming Difficulties

The metaverse can assist with difficulties like limitations that hinder people from doing anything in real life.

1.6.4 Parallel Setting

The metaverse is intended to develop into a setting where people may communicate, collaborate on projects, build professional networks, and exchange things.

1.6.5 New Possibilities

People will have access to hitherto unexplored possibilities and powers thanks to the metaverse.

1.6.6 Improving Education

By offering engaging and immersive learning opportunities, the metaverse can improve education.

1.7 Limitations

1.7.1 Privacy Issues

As our lives become more and more digital, the metaverse, or the future internet, raises privacy issues, with immense tracking and sometimes constant recording of overheard information that can be often used for commercial purposes by organizations.

1.7.2 Technological Prerequisites

Fiber-based connections, 5G wireless networks, and faster, more consistent internet rates are needed for the metaverse. VR or MR headsets are also essential conditions to provide users with a fully immersive experience.

1.7.3 Lack of Common Protocols and Standards

For the metaverse to develop correctly, the main players in the VR space must work together to establish common protocols and standards for building virtual worlds.

1.7.4 Addiction and Problems with Mental Health

Spending too much time in VR can hurt one's mental health, resulting in addiction, social isolation, and other issues.

1.7.5 Effect on the Real World

The metaverse may be given priority over problems and issues in the real world that call for immediate response. It could exacerbate already-existing social and economic inequality since those who are more affluent in the real world might also benefit there (Agbaghe, 2022).

1.8 Key Industries for the Metaverse

The metaverse is a virtual world where people may engage with one another, work, play games, shop, and socialize. It is a completely new plane of existence that will fundamentally change the way we live. The ability to create, invent, and design will be made available to more people thanks to the metaverse. The industrial metaverse is a continuously evolving environment that contains mirror images of real-world equipment, factories, buildings, cities, grids, and transportation systems. The metaverse may have an impact on many industries, including retail, banking, advertising, architecture, engineering, and manufacturing. The market for the metaverse is projected to be worth $800 billion in 2024 (Adair, 2022). Some of these industries include the following.

1.8.1 Gaming

It makes sense that the gaming sector was among the first to embrace the concept of the metaverse. The metaverse offers the potential for fully immersive gaming experiences by allowing players to interact with virtual environments and other players in ways that are not possible with traditional games. Undoubtedly, other game companies will adopt the popular metaverse-like experiences created by companies like Roblox and Fortnite.

1.8.2 Social Media

Online communities like Facebook and Twitter are already exploring the potential of the metaverse as a fresh forum for communication. Imagine having access to a completely realistic virtual world where you could attend virtual events, interact with colleagues, and hang out with friends.

1.8.3 Real Estate

The metaverse has the potential to radically alter the real estate market. Before choosing to purchase or rent a home, think about having access to a virtual tour of it. Meetings with real estate agents and home tours that are performed online might become more available shortly.

1.8.4 Education

The metaverse can significantly transform our perspective on education. Think about being able to take part in virtual lectures, collaborate with other students online, and even conduct experiments virtually. Immersive, fascinating education is available in a variety of ways.

1.8.5 Culture and the Arts

For musicians, designers, and other creatives, the metaverse might offer fresh studio spaces. In a fully immersive virtual environment, people could create, exchange, and enjoy art, music, fashion, and culture. Virtual worlds as a medium for art that could be created by artists. New types of virtual innovation, self-expression, and cultural encounters might be made possible by the metaverse.

1.9 Significance of the Metaverse

The potential uses and applications of the metaverse include the following.

Based on blockchain technology, it delivers digital experiences as an alternative to, or a duplicate of, the actual world, replete with social interactions, money, trade, the economy, and property ownership, as well as all of the key features of a developed society. It could displace current methods of earning a living, working, having pleasure, and engaging with others in virtual environments.

It is far away from an all-encompassing VR, even though people utilize it for entertainment and games. It is a discipline with unique applications. It can be also used for a variety of enterprises and procedures, including internet transactions, due to its procedural and industry neutrality.

It grants users total creative control over their virtual universes, allowing them to construct anything from mansions with river views to space stations where they may collaborate, talk to friends, or even do their schoolwork. It is a network of three-dimensional virtual worlds where social interaction is the main focus (XR Today, 2022).

1.10 Technology in the Metaverse

1.10.1 Virtual Reality

The term "virtual reality" refers to a computer-generated simulation of a three-dimensional environment that enables interaction and experience by the user. To enter and interact with the virtual environment, which can include visual, auditory, and even haptic (touch-based) feedback, the user often dons a head-mounted display (HMD) or makes use of a VR device such as gloves or motion sensors. Oculus Rift and HTC Vive are two common VR headsets (Joe, 2019).

A VR experience can be extremely immersive, giving the impression that (Corporation, 2021) and it is increasingly prevalent across various industries, including entertainment, education, healthcare, and training. It enables the development of convincing simulations that are entertaining and useful for a range of applications, including training, gaming, and therapeutic.

VR has been a notion since the middle of the 20th century, but recent developments in computer technology and graphics have made it more usable and convincingVR is utilized in a wide range of applications today, including video games, virtual tours, virtual meetings, and even telepresence, which uses it to give remote users a sensation of presence.

1.10.2 Augmented Reality

AR is a technology that overlays digital data or virtual objects onto the real environment in real time. AR can be accessed using devices like a smartphone, tablets, or AR headsets. Users can view and engage with digital content while in their real-world surroundings thanks to technology that combines the digital and physical worlds (Corporation, 2021).

In contrast to VR, which fully immerses the user in a digital environment, AR adds digital material to the real world. AR technology works by detecting and tracking the user's surroundings with the help of the device's camera and sensors and then superimposing digital objects, text, or pictures over the user's surroundings.

AR can be used in advertising and retail to give consumers a virtual try-on experience or to provide more details about goods and services. Google Glass and Microsoft HoloLens are two common AR gadgets.

With many smartphones and tablets now being able to run AR apps, AR technology is growing in popularity and accessibility. Wearable gadgets like smart glasses and headsets are also incorporating technology to create more realistic, hands-free AR experiences.

In the metaverse, AR and VR can be combined to create immersive and dynamic virtual experiences that merge the virtual and real worlds and take users to completely different places and settings.

These technologies can be used in several ways in the metaverse. For example:

- It can be used to create virtual storefronts or showrooms within the metaverse, allowing users to browse and purchase products in a fully immersive and interactive virtual environment.
- can be used to create virtual fitting rooms or virtual try-on experiences within the metaverse.
- can be used to create interactive advertising experiences within the metaverse.
- can be used to enhance social interactions within the metaverse. Users can see virtual avatars or information about other users overlaid onto their real-world view, providing additional context and information (Manasa, 2022).

1.10.3 Artificial Intelligence (AI)

The creation of computer systems that are capable of doing activities that traditionally require human intelligence, such as sensing, reasoning, learning, and decision making, is known as artificial intelligence (AI). The creation of algorithms and models for AI entails the ability to process massive volumes of data and make predictions or judgments based on that data (Haenlein, 2019).

Natural language processing, computer vision, robotics, and machine learning are a few of the many uses for AI technology. AI may be utilized to create speech recognition and language translation systems for natural language processing. AI can be used to evaluate and interpret visual data, such as pictures or videos, in computer vision. AI can be applied to robotics to create intelligent, self-aware robots. Large data sets can be used to train AI algorithms for machine learning so they can use the data to make predictions or judgments.

Virtual assistants, self-driving cars, and medical diagnostic systems are just a few of the goods and services that are incorporating AI technology, which is developing quickly. Although AI has numerous advantages, such as greater effectiveness and precision, there are also worries about its possible effects.

AI can be employed to generate and power the virtual worlds and characters within the metaverse. Users can interact with one another and with virtual objects or environments in the metaverse, a shared virtual world. AI can be used to construct and manage virtual settings, create and control virtual characters, and offer users individualised recommendations and experiences to create a realistic and immersive metaverse experience (Huynh-The, 2023).

AI algorithms, for instance, can be utilized to develop intelligent, autonomous, virtual characters that can communicate realistically and naturally with users and one another. AI can also be used to create and modify virtual environments, including landscapes, buildings, and objects, in real time based on user input and other factors.

1.10.4 Cloud Computing

The deployment of computing services, such as software, storage, and processing power, through the internet is referred to as cloud computing. Cloud computing enables users to access resources from a remote server or network of servers situated in data centres all over the world, as opposed to storing and accessing data and programmes on a local computer or server (Tyagi, 2017).

Since cloud computing resources can be swiftly and inexpensively scaled up or down, organizations may readily change their computing requirements to meet shifting demands. As resources are offered on a pay-as-you-go basis, it reduces the need for enterprises to invest in expensive hardware and infrastructure. Collaboration and remote work are made easier thanks to cloud computing, which enables users to access their data and applications from any location with an internet connection.

The production, rendering, and delivery of virtual material in the highly immersive and interactive metaverse require a sizable computing infrastructure. The computational power and storage required to enable expansive virtual worlds and experiences can be provided through cloud computing in the metaverse (Dheer, 2022).

1.10.5 Blockchain

Blockchain technology is a distributed ledger that is decentralized and allows secure transactions without the use of middlemen like banks or other financial institutions. A blockchain, put simply, is a digital ledger that securely and openly records transactions.

A network of computers that collaborates to validate and log transactions maintains the blockchain. Each transaction is represented by a block, which cannot be changed or removed once it has been put into the chain.

Blockchain technology is not just for financial transactions; it has many other uses as well. Secure voting platforms, the tracking of the origin of goods and services, and even smart contracts—self-executing contracts—can all be made using it.

Blockchain technology can be utilized in the metaverse to manage virtual assets and transactions securely and openly. Users can build and trade digital assets including virtual money, virtual homes, and virtual commodities in the metaverse, a virtual environment.

Users will be able to transfer virtual goods and money between various environments thanks to blockchain technology's ability to promote interoperability between various metaverse platforms and virtual worlds.

The metaverse's creation and exchange of virtual assets could be completely transformed by blockchain technology, which offers a safe, open, and effective mechanism for managing virtual goods and services (TPPTechnology, 2020).

1.10.6 3D Modeling and Animation

3D modeling and animation are techniques used to create digital content with depth, realism, and movement. With specialist software, 3D modeling entails building a virtual 3D environment or object. The object can have its shape, color, texture, and lighting altered as well as be constructed from scratch or based on pre-existing designs (Martin, 2023).

On the other hand, 3D animation entails giving 3D figures or objects movement. This is accomplished by modifying the 3D models that were produced during the modeling phase, controlling movement with keyframes, and using animation tools to produce intricate movement sequences. Depending on the intended usage, the animation can either be rendered in real time or as a recorded sequence.

The generated 3D models and animations can be applied to a variety of fields, such as architecture, product design, video games, movies, television, and VR. They produce immersive and interesting digital content for a variety of sectors and consumers by adding a level of depth and realism that is impossible with conventional 2D graphics and animation.

The creation and animation of avatars and virtual worlds in the metaverse heavily rely on 3D modeling and animation. By using animation and interactive features, these approaches are utilized to produce lifelike 3D models of virtual settings, objects, and characters (Ripert, 2022).

With 3D modeling tools, users can design unique avatars that represent them in the virtual world. Virtual environments are created using 3D modeling, including towns, landscapes, and buildings.

Character motions, item interactions, and environmental effects are all made possible in the virtual world using 3D animation. Particle effects, weather effects, and other special effects are produced using 3D modeling and animation.

1.11 Business Models of the Metaverse

The metaverse has witnessed the emergence of numerous business models. Some of the popular models are listed below.

1.11.1 Virtual Land

Businesses provide customers with virtual land so they can create their virtual worlds or experiences on it. Companies like Decentral, The Sandbox, and Somnium Space are currently selling virtual land. Sales of real estate and virtual goods inside those worlds are two possible revenue sources (DiLella & Day, 2022).

1.11.2 Virtual Goods and Services

Organizations like Roblox, Second Life, and IMVU provide digital items including furniture, clothing, and pets. Users can purchase these things from the corporation for real money or digital currency, resulting in money for the business (Wu, 2007).

1.11.3 Sponsorship and Advertising

In the metaverse, businesses can fund virtual activities or places while also promoting their goods and services to consumers. For marketers aiming to reach younger audiences, in particular, this can be a profitable source of income (Glaveski, n.d.).

1.11.4 Subscription-Based Model

This model provides access to premium features or content, such as exclusive virtual goods or improved customizability, to the subscribers by some metaverse businesses (Chambers, 2021).

1.11.5 Gaming and E-sports

Game developers have incorporated metaverse components into their gameplay in games like *Fortnite* and *Roblox*, enabling users to explore virtual worlds and communicate with other players. These businesses can make money by selling items in-game and by sponsoring e-sports events (Breia, 2022).

1.11.6 Social Media and Networking

Some metaverse businesses provide social networking and virtual hangout experiences, such VRChat and AltspaceVR. These businesses can make money by selling virtual products, running ads, and doing sponsored events (XR Today, 2021).

1.11.7 Education and Training

Virtual training and educational experiences are provided by certain metaverse businesses, including Engage and Educators in VR. Via subscriptions, sponsorships, and joint ventures with educational institutions, these businesses can make money (ViewSonic, 2022).

1.11.8 Virtual Currency and Blockchain

Blockchain technology is used by several metaverse businesses like Decentral and The Sandbox to make it possible to create, own, and exchange virtual assets. transaction fees, and the selling of virtual currency can generate revenue (Abrol, 2023).

1.11.9 Virtual Tourism and Experiences

Several metaverse businesses, like Sansar and High Fidelity, provide virtual vacation spots and experiences for consumers to explore. These businesses can make money by selling virtual items, running advertisements, and forming alliances with travel agencies (ZohaIslands, 2018).

The above-mentioned business models are just a handful of the many commercial prospects that the metaverse has to offer. There are likely to be new business opportunities as the metaverse develops and evolves.

1.12 Conclusion

This chapter discusses the history and concept of the metaverse from its inception. It further assesses the technology used in the metaverse and its applications in real time and gives a perspective on the growth and limitations of the metaverse.

References

Abrol, A. (2023, January 17). *Metaverse Blockchain and Crypto Projects*. Retrieved February 24, 2023, from https://www.blockchain-council.org/metaverse/metaverse-blockchain-and-crypto-projects/

Adair, M. (2022, March 22). *Five Industries That Will Be Transformed By The Metaverse*. Retrieved from Forbes: https://www.forbes.com/sites/forbestechcouncil/2022/03/22/five-industries-that-will-be-transformed-by-the-metaverse/?sh=6c623b364e40

Agbaghe, O. (2022, February 10). *The Metaverse: 5 Disadvantages and Challenges*. Retrieved from Metarficial: https://metarficial.com/challenges-disadvantages-metaverse/

Anderrson, S. (2023, March 02). *Gucci to Join Metaverse: What's New and What Do Consumers Get*. Retrieved March 03, 2023, from https://www.thecoinrepublic.com/2023/03/02/gucci-to-join-metaverse-whats-new-and-what-do-consumers-get/

Bartolo, T. D. (2022, October 5). *The 3 Phases of the Metaverse*. Retrieved Februrary 27, 2023, from https://www.forbes.com/sites/forbesbusinesscouncil/2022/10/05/the-3-phases-of-the-metaverse/?sh=2adda7b11de6

Bojic, L. (2022). *Metaverse through the Prism of Power and Addiction: What Will happen When the Virtual World Becomes More Attractive Than Reality?*. *European Journal of Futures Research*, 10(1), 1–24. https://doi.org/10.1186/s40309-022-00208-4

Boulben, F. (2023, January 14). *The Emergence and Staying Power of the Metaverse*. Retrieved from Venture Beat: https://venturebeat.com/virtual/the-emergence-and-staying-power-of-the-metaverse/

Breia, R. (2022, November 16). *Esports and the Metaverse*. Retrieved March 2, 2023, from https://sensoriumxr.com/articles/esports-and-the-metaverse

Castellano, J. (2022). *Beyond the Hype*. Retrieved from https://www.ibm.com/thought-leadership/institute-business-value/en-us/report/enterprise-metaverse

Chambers, P. (2021, December 1). *Metaverse & Subscriptions: Entering the Virtual Reality World of the Future*. Retrieved February 25, 2023, from https://subta.com/metaverse-subscriptions-entering-virtual-reality-world-future/

Corporation, M. (2021). *What Is Augmented Reality or AR | Microsoft Dynamics 365*. Retrieved February 25, 2023, from https://dynamics.microsoft.com/en-us/mixed-reality/guides/what-is-augmented-reality-ar/

Dheer, P. (2022). *Metaverse and Cloud Computing: Future of Technology*. Retrieved March 1, 2023, from https://www.testpreptraining.com/blog/metaverse-and-cloud-computing-future-of-technology/#:~:text=The%20metaverse%20and%20cloud%20computing,cloud%20computing%20applications%20and%20services

DiLella, C., & Day, A. (2022, January 12). *Investors Are Paying Millions for Virtual Land in the Metaverse*. Retrieved February 24, 2023, from https://www.cnbc.com/2022/01/12/investors-are-paying-millions-for-virtual-land-in-the-metaverse.html

Glaveski, S. (n.d.). *6 Ways to Advertise Your Brand in the Metaverse*. Retrieved February 28, 2023, from https://www.collectivecampus.io/blog/6-ways-to-advertise-your-brand-in-the-metaverse

Haenlein, M. A. (2019). A Brief History of Artificial Intelligence: On the Past, Present, and Future of Artificial Intelligence. *California Management Review.*

Huynh-The, T., Pham, Q. V., Pham, X. Q., Nguyen, T. T., Han, Z., & Kim, D. S. (2023). Artificial Intelligence for the Metaverse: A Survey. *Engineering Applications of Artificial Intelligence. 117*, 105581.

Joe, B. (2019, March 26). *What Is Virtual Reality | 3D Cloud by Marxent*. Retrieved February 25, 2023, from https://www.marxentlabs.com/what-is-virtual-reality/

Manasa. (2022, January 12). *R and VR Technologies Are Revolutionizing Metaverse. Here's How*. Retrieved February 26, 2023, from https://www.analyticsinsight.net/ar-and-vr-technologies-are-revolutionizing-metaverse-heres-how/

Marr, B. (2022, March 21). *A Short History of the Metaverse*. Retrieved February 22, 2023, from https://www.forbes.com/sites/bernardmarr/2022/03/21/a-short-history-of-the-metaverse/?sh=64dc4a8a5968

Martin, J. (2023, August 19). *How Is 3D Modeling Used in Animation?* Retrieved March 1, 2023, from https://usv.edu/blog/how-is-3d-modeling-used-in-animation/

Mileva, G. (2023, January 4). *52 Metaverse Statistics | Market Size & Growth* (2023).

Pratt, M. K. (2022, November 8). *Metaverse Pros and Cons: Top Benefits and Challenges.*

Ripert, D. (2022, May 24). *The Pathway to the Metaverse Begins with 3D Modelling*. Retrieved February 25, 2023, from https://www.entrepreneur.com/science-technology/the-pathway-to-the-metaverse-begins-with-3d-modelling/425643

TechAhead. (n.d.). *Top Business Applications of Metaverse That Will Change the Future Forever*. Retrieved February 20, 2023, from TechAhead: www.techaheadcorp.com/knowledge-center/business-applications-of-metaverse

TPPTechnology. (2020). *Why Blockchain Is a Key Technology for The Metaverse.* Retrieved February 28, 2023, from https://www.tpptechnology.com/en/blog/why-blockchain-is-a-key-technology-for-the-metaverse/

Tyagi, A. (2017). A review paper on cloud computing. *International Journal of Engineering Research & Technology, (IJERT),* 2278-0181.

ViewSonic. (2022, November 22). *Metaverse Education: What's Next for Virtual Learning?* Retrieved February 26, 2023, from https://www.viewsonic.com/library/education/metaverse-education-whats-next-for-virtual-learning/#:~:text=In%20general%2C%20education%20in%20the,within%20a%20virtual%20learning%20environment

Wikipedia. (2021, December 4). *Metaverse - Wikipedia.* Retrieved February 21, 2023, from https://en.wikipedia.org/wiki/Metaverse

Wilser, J. (2022, August 29). *The Metaverse Casino That Wasn't.* Retrieved February 26, 2023, from https://www.coindesk.com/layer2/sinweek/2022/08/29/the-metaverse-casino-that-wasnt/

Wu, S. (2007, June 20). *Virtual Goods: The Next Big Business Model.* Retrieved February 25, 2023, from https://techcrunch.com/2007/06/20/virtual-goods-the-next-big-business-model/

XR Today. (2021, November 5). *AltspaceVR vs VRChat: Competing VR Worlds.* Retrieved February 27, 2023, from https://www.xrtoday.com/mixed-reality/altspacevr-vs-vrchat-competing-vr-worlds/

XR Today. (2022, March 11). *Why is the Metaverse Important?* Retrieved from XR Today: https://www.xrtoday.com/virtual-reality/what-can-you-do-in-the-metaverse-2/

ZohaIslands. (2018, December 31). *Virtual Worlds: High Fidelity vs Sansar.* Retrieved February 27, 2023, from https://blog.zoha-islands.com/virtual-worlds-high-fidelity-vs-sansar/

Chapter 2

Evaluation and Future Impact of a Metaverse in Business

Shaik Nouman, Shiva Lagishetty, and Pulivendula Preethi Reddy
Woxsen University, Hyderabad, Telangana, India

Channabasava Chola
College of Electronics and Information, Kyung Hee University, Suwon-si, Republic of Korea

2.1 Introduction and the Potential Impact of the Metaverse

The metaverse is a digital environment that integrates immersive technologies such as augmented reality (AR), virtual reality (VR), and blockchain to create a three-dimensional (3D) environment that anybody with an internet connection may explore. While it is still in its early stages, the metaverse has the potential to have a substantial impact on business in a variety of ways, from establishing new revenue streams to revolutionizing the way people work and connect. This chapter investigates the metaverse's possible impact on business and its potential to alter the way we work, study, and play. The establishment of new revenue sources is one potential influence of the metaverse on business. Businesses that can generate and commercialize virtual products can sell virtual products and services to a worldwide reach, such as virtual real estate or digital assets. This has the potential to open up new

DOI: 10.4324/b23404-2

markets and revenue streams for virtual-world firms. Companies such as Roblox and Fortnite, for example, have already shown the potential of virtual products and services, earning millions of dollars through in-game transactions (Lawton 2022). The metaverse has the potential to transform the way people operate. Employees can work and cooperate in a virtual environment from anywhere in the world, reducing the requirement for actual office space. This can result in significant cost savings for corporations and enhanced employee flexibility. Furthermore, the metaverse can be used by corporations to hold virtual conferences, trade exhibitions, and other events, avoiding the need for costly travel and venue fees (Marthew 2020). The metaverse has the potential to change the way people learn. The metaverse, with its potential to produce immersive learning experiences, can provide a more engaging and participatory approach for people to learn new skills and knowledge. This might be especially advantageous for organizations that provide employee training and education. Companies, for example, can utilize the metaverse to re-create real-world circumstances and provide hands-on training to staff in a safe and regulated setting (Lawton 2022). The establishment of new business models is another potential impact of the metaverse on business. Businesses that can build and sell virtual products can create new revenue streams and business models that would not be conceivable in the actual world. Businesses, for example, can develop subscription-based services that allow access to virtual goods and services like virtual entertainment or virtual education. Furthermore, the metaverse can be used by businesses to develop and sell digital assets such as virtual real estate or virtual artwork (Marthew 2020). The metaverse, on the other hand, poses possible obstacles and threats. The topic of privacy and security is one of the most difficult. There is a risk of data breaches and cyber assaults with massive volumes of personal data that will be collected and kept in the metaverse. Furthermore, because people will be utilizing their real-world identities in the virtual world, there is a risk of identity theft and fraud (Lawton 2022).

To summarize, the metaverse has the potential to profoundly impact business in a variety of ways, ranging from the creation of new revenue streams to the transformation of how people work and interact. There are, however, significant obstacles and risks that must be handled. As the metaverse evolves, businesses will need to keep aware and adapt to the changes in order to remain competitive.

2.2 Future of the Metaverse in Business: Trends and Predictions

The metaverse, a virtual world where users can interact with one another and digital items, has gained popularity in recent years. With technological improvements and the pandemic hastening the shift to virtual experiences, the metaverse is poised to become a significant business opportunity. We will look at some trends and forecasts for the future of the metaverse in business in this chapter. The emergence of virtual gatherings and conferences is one trend. Traditional in-person gatherings have been supplanted with virtual equivalents as more organizations transition to remote labor. The metaverse provides a more immersive experience, allowing guests to engage more naturally with one another and with the event space. The Cannes Lions Festival of Creativity, for example, conducted a virtual event in the metaverse in 2021, allowing guests to explore a virtual beach and attend virtual seminars and parties (Staff 2021). The usage of the metaverse for marketing and advertising is another trend. Virtual experiences can be created by brands to engage customers and increase brand exposure. Nike, for example, built a virtual store in the video game *Fortnite* where players can purchase real-life footwear with virtual currency (Berthiaume 2022). The metaverse also opens up new avenues for targeted advertising, as users' digital behavior may be tracked to deliver more personalized advertisements (Krotoski 2022). E-commerce has the ability to flourish in the metaverse. With virtual storefronts and interactive product displays, virtual markets can provide a more interesting buying experience. Gucci, for example, opened a virtual store in the game *Roblox,* where players could browse and purchase virtual representations of its products (Hahn 2021). The metaverse also enables more frictionless transactions, with virtual currencies and digital wallets making purchases within the virtual world easier (Krotoski 2022). One forecast for the metaverse's future is that it will become a new social media platform. Users will be able to interact with one another in a more immersive environment, rather than scrolling through feeds. Virtual social networks can provide new avenues for connecting with friends and meeting new individuals. VR Chat, for example, allows users to build their own avatars and explore virtual places with others (Krotoski 2022). Another prediction is that the metaverse will open up new opportunities for employment and education. The metaverse provides new methods to cooperate and learn as remote work and online learning become increasingly common. With tools for virtual whiteboards and presentations, virtual offices and classrooms may provide a more engaging and participatory experience (Krotoski 2022).

Finally, the metaverse provides fascinating new options for organizations to interact with their customers and staff. The metaverse is poised to become a major platform for the future of business, from virtual events to e-commerce and social networking.

2.3 Metaverse Adoption and Implementation Strategies for Businesses

The metaverse is a virtual world that is becoming increasingly important for organizations wanting to remain ahead of the competition. With the emergence of VR and other advanced technologies, businesses are investigating new methods to communicate with their customers, employees, and partners through the metaverse (Hall 2022). This chapter will look at how corporations can use the metaverse to their advantage.

2.3.1 Adoption Strategies

To implement the metaverse successfully, firms need to determine their aims and objectives for employing this technology (Krishnamurthy n.d.). Some of the tactics that corporations can take to adopt the metaverse are as follows:

Identify opportunities: The first stage is to identify the metaverse's opportunities. Companies can use the metaverse to generate new revenue streams, raise brand awareness, and provide customers with immersive experiences. Businesses, for example, can develop virtual showrooms to exhibit their products or host virtual events like conferences, trade shows, and concerts.

Invest in technology: The next stage is to invest in the appropriate technology for creating a metaverse experience. This includes purchasing gear like VR headsets as well as software like game engines and 3-D modeling tools. Companies must assess the cost and technical knowledge required to develop a metaverse experience and ensure that they have the necessary resources.

Collaboration: Collaboration is an important technique for metaverse adoption. Companies can work together to build a common metaverse experience, which can help cut costs and enhance participation. Companies, for example, can work together to establish a virtual environment for a certain industry or a shared virtual event platform.

Develop a strategy: After identifying opportunities, organizations must create a strategy for using the metaverse (Krishnamurthy n.d.). This includes determining the target audience, developing a budget, and establishing success measures. Companies must analyze the metaverse's distinct traits and how they differ from traditional marketing methods.

2.3.2 The Metaverse's Advantages for Companies

The metaverse offers various benefits for firms wishing to exploit this technology (Cowlan 2021). Some advantages include:

Increased engagement: Compared to traditional marketing methods, the metaverse provides a more immersive and engaging experience. Companies can use this to promote consumer, employee, and partner engagement.

New revenue streams: The metaverse provides enterprises with new revenue streams. Businesses, for example, can sell virtual products or charge for admission to virtual events.

Brand awareness: The metaverse provides a new avenue for businesses to raise brand awareness. They can advertise their brand in a fresh and engaging way by building a virtual presence.

Competitive advantage: Companies that adopt the metaverse early on can acquire a competitive advantage over their competitors. Businesses can differentiate themselves and build a unique value offer by embracing this technology.

The metaverse provides a new approach for businesses to interact with their consumers, employees, and partners. Businesses can gain a competitive advantage, enhance engagement, and generate new revenue streams by embracing the metaverse early. Businesses must discover opportunities, invest in technology, engage with others, and build a strategy to successfully integrate the metaverse (Cowlan 2021). Businesses may build immersive experiences that provide a new level of engagement and value to their stakeholders by implementing these tactics.

2.3.3 Metaverse Implementation Strategies

In recent years, there has been a lot of buzz about the metaverse, which is a shared virtual realm where users may interact with each other and digital items in a fully immersive way. As technology progresses, businesses are beginning to investigate methods to use the metaverse to improve their operations and communicate with customers. This post will go through some business metaverse implementation ideas.

Virtual events are one possible application for the metaverse. Businesses can reach a larger audience and create a more immersive experience for guests by conducting virtual conferences, trade exhibitions, and other events. Balenciaga, for example, launched a virtual fashion presentation in 2020 that allowed visitors to explore a digital environment and interact with virtual models dressed in the brand's current creations (Balenciaga 2021). Similarly, in 2021, the Cannes Film Festival launched a virtual version of the event, complete with virtual screenings, conferences, and networking possibilities (Cannes Film Festival 2022).

Virtual product demos are another potential application for the metaverse. VR and AR technology can be used by businesses to create realistic product demonstrations that allow consumers to engage with products in a more realistic way than traditional movies or photographs. IKEA, for example, has created a VR software that allows shoppers to see furniture in their homes before purchasing it (demodern n.d.).

Employee training and collaboration can also be done in the metaverse. Businesses can provide hands-on training to employees in a safe and controlled atmosphere by building virtual environments. Walmart, for example, has developed VR training programs for its employees that imitate real-life circumstances and allow employees to practice their abilities in a risk-free setting. Employees can work on projects and presentations in a virtual place using platforms like Spatial, regardless of their physical location.

Using the metaverse in company operations necessitates significant thought and strategy. Consider the following major strategies:

Establish clear business objectives: Before investing in metaverse technologies, companies should establish clear goals regarding how the technology will be used. This includes determining the target audience, the exact business outcomes to be reached, and the success measures.

Begin small and progressively scale up: It is critical to begin with a small pilot project and gradually build up as the technology and team's skills mature. This enables for testing and improvement of the technology, as well as the identification of potential issues before investing in a full-scale implementation.

Choose the appropriate technology: There are numerous metaverse technologies accessible, each with its own set of advantages and disadvantages. Companies should carefully assess their requirements and choose the technology that best meets their goals and budget.

Ensure user adoption: In order for the metaverse to be successful, user adoption must be ensured. This necessitates investing in user experience design and training programs to assist users in navigating the virtual environment and making the most of the technology.

Businesses can use the metaverse to improve their operations and engage with customers in new and inventive ways. Yet, putting the technology into action needs considerable preparation and study. Businesses can utilize the potential of the metaverse and accomplish their desired outcomes by implementing the above-listed tactics.

2.4 Ethics and Regulatory Implications of the Metaverse in Business

The metaverse is a shared virtual environment where users can interact with one other and digital things. With the development of VR technology and online gaming platforms, the idea of the metaverse has gained popularity recently. There are various ethical and legal repercussions for corporations as the metaverse spreads, though. The possibility of exploitation and abuse within the metaverse is one ethical worry. For instance, in virtual worlds like Second Life, there have been allegations of sexual harassment and other types of abuse (Dibbell 2005). Companies that conduct business within the metaverse must take action to stop such conduct and guarantee that users are secure and safe from harm.

The possibility of addiction and misuse of the metaverse raises further ethical concerns. The metaverse, like any other online platform, has the potential to be addictive, leading users to spend excessive amounts of time there. Companies must take precautions to avoid aggravating this issue and should encourage ethical metaverse usage. The metaverse has regulatory repercussions, including concerns about data privacy and intellectual property. Large volumes of data are produced as users interact with one another and with virtual items in the metaverse. Companies must make sure they abide by data protection rules and take precautions to shield user data from misuse or illegal access. Likewise, when producing content for the metaverse, firms must take care not to violate the intellectual property rights of others. While the metaverse presents fascinating business potential, there are also important ethical and legal ramifications that must be taken into account. To safeguard customers and uphold the integrity of the metaverse, businesses must make sure they conduct their operations in accordance with moral standards and legal requirements (Anshari 2022).

2.5 Evaluation of the Metaverse in the Entertainment Industry

The entertainment business is affected significantly by the idea of the metaverse, and its possible effects have been discussed recently. Offering viewers immersive experiences is one of the metaverse's primary benefits to the entertainment sector. Since the development of VR technology recently, audiences can now interact with information in novel and interesting ways. The metaverse provides a platform for immersive experiences. Users can view movies in virtual theaters; attend virtual concerts; and have real-time conversations with imaginary characters, among other things, in the metaverse (Robertson 2021).

The metaverse's potential to develop new revenue streams is another benefit for the entertainment sector. Content producers can profit from ticket sales, item sales, and other digital transactions by providing virtual experiences. Additionally, because marketers can design virtual experiences for users within the metaverse, the metaverse presents prospects for product placement and sponsorship arrangements (Tucci 2022). The metaverse may have disadvantages for the entertainment sector, though. The possibility of content piracy and illicit distribution within the metaverse is one issue. Companies must take action to safeguard their intellectual property rights and stop information from being distributed without permission. The possibility of metaverse addiction and usage is a further worry. The metaverse, like any other online platform, has the potential to be addictive, leading users to spend excessive amounts of time there. Companies must take precautions to avoid aggravating this issue and should encourage ethical metaverse usage.

The metaverse presents the entertainment sector with intriguing potential, but there are also important issues that need to be resolved. In order to protect users and preserve the integrity of the metaverse, content producers and businesses must weigh the potential advantages of the metaverse against any potential disadvantages. They must also take steps to ensure that they operate in accordance with applicable laws and ethical standards.

2.6 Evaluation of the Metaverse in the Education Industry

The metaverse is a new technology with the potential to change the way we live, work, and learn. While the notion of a metaverse has been around for a while, it has lately gained traction with the popularity of video games like *Fortnite* and *Minecraft*, both of which feature their own metaverses. This has sparked conjecture about the metaverse's possible applications in a variety of industries, including education. In the education business, the virtual world could open up new avenues for students and teachers to interact in a common online environment. One industry where the metaverse has the potential to have a huge impact is education. While the traditional classroom paradigm has served us well for generations, it is becoming increasingly evident that it has limitations (Srivastava 2022). With the advancement of technology comes new chances to create more engaging and immersive learning experiences, and the metaverse is one of them.

The metaverse could be used in education in a variety of ways. One of the most obvious is as a remote learning platform. With the COVID-19 pandemic forcing many schools and institutions to transition to online learning, there has been an increase in demand for more engaging and dynamic virtual learning environments. The metaverse has the potential to provide such an environment, allowing students to engage with one another and with virtual objects in ways that standard online learning platforms do not provide. Another way the metaverse could be used in education is as a tool for experiential learning. Experiential learning is a pedagogical technique that stresses experiential learning over lecture-based instruction. Students could use the metaverse to engage in experiential learning activities such as simulations, role-playing, and virtual field trips (Asad et al. 2021).

There are already some examples of metaverse applications in education. For example, the University of Texas will establish a virtual campus in the game *Minecraft* in 2021. The virtual campus is a duplicate of the physical campus of the institution and is designed to be used as a tool for attracting and engaging students. Similarly, during the COVID-19 epidemic in 2020, a group of instructors developed a virtual classroom in the game *Animal Crossing*, allowing them to continue teaching. While these instances are encouraging, there are several drawbacks to using the metaverse in education. One of the difficulties is ensuring that all students, regardless of background or ability, have access to the virtual environment. This includes making certain that the virtual environment is accessible and compatible with assistive technology such as screen readers.

Another problem is ensuring that students' virtual environments are safe and secure. This involves safeguarding students' privacy and preventing them from being exposed to unsuitable content or behavior. It also entails preventing cyberbullying and other forms of harassment from taking place in the virtual environment (Lin et al. 2022).

Despite these obstacles, there is increasing interest in using the metaverse in teaching. More innovative and interesting learning experiences are likely to be developed as more schools and institutions investigate the potential of the metaverse. It will be fascinating to observe how the metaverse is used to improve students' learning experiences as technology advances.

2.7 Evaluation of the Metaverse in the Retail Industry

One of the most significant advantages of the metaverse for merchants is the ability to provide customers with immersive shopping experiences. Retailers can develop virtual shops and interactive displays in the metaverse, allowing customers to browse and purchase things in a visually stunning setting. This type of purchasing experience has the potential to be significantly more interesting than standard e-commerce, which frequently depends on static images and text descriptions.

Furthermore, the metaverse provides retailers with the possibility to reach a worldwide audience at a minimal cost. Physical storefronts are geographically confined and can only reach clients within a given radius, whereas e-commerce is constrained by the requirement to send tangible things. The metaverse, on the other hand, is accessible to anybody with an internet connection, allowing shops to reach clients all over the world without the need for physical inventory (Bourlakis et al. 2009).

Another potential benefit of the metaverse for retailers is the ability to collect data on customer behavior and preferences. In the metaverse, every action a customer takes can be tracked and analyzed, providing retailers with valuable insights into what products and experiences are most appealing to their customers. This data can be used to personalize the shopping experience and make targeted product recommendations.

Yet, retailers face enormous hurdles as a result of the metaverse. One of the most important is the necessity to produce visually appealing and engaging virtual experiences. This necessitates substantial investments in technology and skill, which may be out of reach for many shops, particularly small ones.

Another issue is the possibility of fraud in the metaverse. Customers may be taken advantage of by unscrupulous retailers or hackers because the metaverse is a relatively new technology. This could harm the reputation of retailers who invest in the metaverse and could lead to customer distrust (Srinivasan 2022).

Despite these obstacles, the metaverse has tremendous potential benefits for the retail business. According to a Goldman Sachs estimate, the metaverse might be worth $12.5 trillion by 2030, including applications in gaming, social networking, and e-commerce. Some stores, such as Nike and Gucci, have already begun to experiment with the metaverse, creating virtual experiences for customers (Wright 2022). It will be interesting to observe how retailers innovate and adapt to this new technology as the metaverse evolves.

2.8 Evaluation of the Metaverse in the Manufacturing Industry

The metaverse has several potential applications, including entertainment, education, and socializing, but one industry that is particularly interested in the metaverse is manufacturing. The metaverse has the potential to alter the way things are created, manufactured, and sold in the manufacturing business.

The capacity to generate and test virtual prototypes is one of the key benefits of the metaverse in the manufacturing industry. Before producing actual prototypes, firms can use virtual prototyping to uncover and address design faults. This method not only saves time and money, but it also lowers waste and increases the design process's efficiency. Virtual prototyping can also be used to model the manufacturing process, allowing producers to optimize production processes and identify potential problems before they exist (Zimmermann 2022).

The ability to construct a digital twin is another advantage of the metaverse in the manufacturing industry. As a virtual counterpart of a physical product or system, a digital twin can be used to monitor and optimize performance. Manufacturers may monitor the performance of their products in real time, discover any flaws, and make improvements as needed by building a digital twin. This strategy has the potential to improve product quality while also increasing efficiency (Kritzinger et al. 2018).

The virtual world also has the potential to increase manufacturing collaboration and communication. Designers, engineers, and manufacturers may collaborate in a virtual environment, independent of their physical location, thanks to the metaverse. This technique has the potential to improve collaboration and communication, leading to faster and more accurate decision making.

Furthermore, the metaverse can enable manufacturers to provide clients with a more immersive and individualized experience. Manufacturers can use the metaverse to construct virtual showrooms and product demonstrations that allow buyers to engage with products in a virtual setting. This technique has the potential to promote customer involvement, product understanding, and sales (Clark 2022).

There are, however, significant hurdles and drawbacks to implementing the metaverse in the industrial industry. The cost and complexity of constructing a virtual environment that accurately mimics the physical world is one of the key problems. Another source of concern is the possibility of cybersecurity risks, as virtual environments are prone to hacking and other unwanted acts.

Finally, the metaverse has the ability to alter the manufacturing business by improving the design process, optimizing production processes, improving collaboration and communication, and offering customers a more immersive and personalized experience. While the adoption of the metaverse may provide some obstacles and inconveniences, these can be avoided with appropriate methods. Ultimately, the metaverse has the potential to disrupt the manufacturing business, and manufacturers should assess the potential benefits and challenges of this developing technology.

2.9 The Metaverse as a Gamechanger for Business

Although the idea of the metaverse has been around for a while, new technological developments have pushed it closer than ever to reality. A metaverse is a virtual environment where users can communicate with each other and other digital entities in real time, adding a fresh level of social and commercial activity. In this chapter, we've spoken about how the metaverse can revolutionize business by opening fresh avenues for interaction and trade. One of the most significant advantages of the metaverse is its ability to create immersive and captivating experiences that are impractical in the real world. Businesses can provide a more personalized and engaging experience for their customers by creating a digital environment in which people can interact with each other and with digital items in real time. A fashion merchant, for example, can create a virtual store that allows buyers to try on clothing and assess how they look before making a purchase. Similarly, a car manufacturer can create an online showroom where customers can browse different models and customize their vehicles. Also, there are new business opportunities in the metaverse. Businesses can reach a worldwide audience and enter new markets by developing a digital marketplace where individuals can purchase and sell goods and services (Kumar 2023). For instance, a musician can skip conventional distribution methods and sell their music straight to listeners in the metaverse. In a similar vein, a tiny company can open a digital storefront in the metaverse and market its goods to clients all over the world.

The ability of the metaverse to develop new sources of income for enterprises is another benefit. Businesses can create income outside of their regular products and services by providing virtual goods and services. For instance, a game creator might produce virtual goods that users can buy with actual money, making income from both the game and the goods. Similar to how a media firm can develop virtual events and experiences that people can pay to attend, ticket sales and advertising money are both sources of income (Boyd 2019). The metaverse, however, also brings with it fresh difficulties for companies. As with any new technology, privacy, security, and regulation are issues that need to be addressed. Companies must make sure that they are collecting and processing personal data in an ethical and responsible manner. Companies must also make sure that their virtual environments are safe from hackers and secure. Finally, they will have to navigate a complicated regulatory environment to make sure they are acting legally. Yet the metaverse also presents new challenges for businesses. Privacy, security, and regulatory concerns must be handled as with any new technology. Businesses must ensure that personal data is collected and processed in an honest and responsible manner. Additionally, businesses must ensure that their virtual environments are secure and safe from hackers. Finally, to ensure that they are doing so legally, they will need to navigate a challenging, regulatory environment.

References

Anshari, Muhammad. 2022. "Ethical responsibility and sustainability (ERS) development in a metaverse business model." *Sustainability*, 14(23), 15805.

Asad, Muhammad Mujtaba, Aisha Naz, Prathamesh Churi, Mohammad Mehdi Tahanzadeh. 2021. "Virtual reality as pedagogical tool to enhance experiential learning: A Systematic literature review." *Education Research International*, *2021*, 1–17.

Balenciaga. 2021. *Dimension.* https://www.dimensionstudio.co/work/ balenciaga-afterworld-age-tomorrow-volumetric.

Berthiaume, Dan. 2022. *chainstoreage.* https://chainstoreage.com/nike-creates-virtual-product-community-metaverse#:~:text=Nike%20is%20continuing%20 to%20expand,swoosh.

Bourlakis, Michael, Savvas Papagiannidis, Feng Li. 2009. "Retail spatial evolution: Paving the way from traditional to metaverse retailing." *Electronic Commerce Research*, *9*, 135–148.

Boyd, D. Eric. 2019. "Virtual reality and its impact on B2B marketing: A value-in-use perspective." *Journal of Business Research*, *100*, 590–598.

Clark, Scott. 2022. "4 Ways the Metaverse Can Enhance the Customer Experience." *CMSWIRE CONNECT.* Austin, TX.

Cowlan, Becky. 2021. *LinkedIn.* https://www.linkedin.com/pulse/metaverse-new-frontier-marketing-becky-cowlan-/.

demodern. n.d. *demodern.* https://demodern.com/projects/ikea-vr-showroom.

Dibbell, Julian. 2005. *The village voice.* https://www.villagevoice. com/2005/10/18/a-rape-in-cyberspace/.

Cannes Film Festival. 2022. *marche du film.* https://www.marchedufilm.com/ programs/cannes-xr/.

Hahn, Jennifer. 2021. *dezeen.* https://www.dezeen.com/2021/03/19/ virtual-25-gucci-wanna-digital-sneaker/.

Hall, Stefan Brambilla. 2022. *World Economic Forum.* https://www.weforum.org/ agenda/2022/02/future-of-the-metaverse-vr-ar-and-brain-computer/.

Krishnamurthy, Rajeshwari. n.d. *California Review Management.* https://cmr. berkeley.edu/2022/12/transforming-your-brand-using-the-metaverse-eight-strategic-elements-to-plan-for/.

Kritzinger, Werner, Matthias Karner, Georg Traar, Jan Henjes, Wilfried Sihn. 2018. "Digital twin in manufacturing: A categorical literature review and classification." *Ifac-Papers Online, 51*(11), 1016–1022.

Krotoski, Aleks. 2022. *sciencefocus.* https://www.sciencefocus.com/future-technology/metaverse/.

Kumar, Prashant. 2023. *Techblocks.* https://tblocks.com/how-the-metaverse-will-transform-retail-experiences/#:~:text=Retailers%20can%20also%20use%20the, demonstrations%2C%20or%20even%20virtual%20events.&text=Augmented%20 reality%20(AR)%20is%20a,objects%20in%20the%20physical%20world.

Lawton, George. 2022. *How will the metaverse affect the future of work?* https://www.techtarget.com/searchcio/tip/How-will-the-metaverse-affect-the-future-of-work.

Lin, Hong, Shicheng Wan, Wensheng Gan, Jiahui Chen, Han-Chieh Chao. 2022. Metaverse in education: Vision, opportunities, and challenges. In 2022 IEEE International Conference on Big Data (Big Data) (pp. 2857–2866). IEEE.

Marthew, Ball. Jan 13, 2020. *The Metaverse: What It Is. Where to Find It, Who Will Build It, and Fortnite. https://www.matthewball.vc/all/themetaverse*

Robertson, Adi. 2021. *theverge.* https://www.theverge.com/22701104/metaverse-explained-fortnite-roblox-facebook-horizon.

Srinivasan, Srii. 2022. *chargebackgurus.* July 07, 2022. https://www.chargebackgurus.com/blog/metaverse-fraud.

Srivastava, Sudeep. *Appinventiv.* March 29, 2023. https://appinventiv.com/blog/metaverse-in-education/#:~:text=Metaverse%20in%20the%20education%20sector, immersive%2C%20engaging%2C%20and%20communicative.

Staff, Ad Age. 2021. "13 Takeaways from the 2021 Virtual Cannes Lions." *Ad Age.* https://adage.com/article/special-report-cannes-lions/13-takeaways-2021-virtual-cannes-lions-including-lots-gripes/2346431.

Tucci, Linda. 2022. *techtarget.* https://www.techtarget.com/whatis/feature/The-metaverse-explained-Everything-you-need-to-know#:~:text=The%20metaverse% 20is%20a%20vision,not%20in%20the%20physical%20world.

Wright, Webb. 2022. *TheDrumb.* June 01, 2022. Accessed. https://www.thedrum.com/news/2022/06/01/5-brands-winning-the-metaverse.

Zimmermann, Katrin. 2022. *Venturebeat.* April 26. https://venturebeat.com/business/how-the-metaverse-could-remake-manufacturing/.

Chapter 3

Re-wilding Natural Habitats with Flying Robots, AI, and Metaverse Ecosystems

Markus Krebsz
University of Stirling, Woxsen University, Hyderabad, Telangana, India

Divya Dwivedi
Supreme Court of India, Woxsen University, Hyderabad, Telangana, India

DEFINITIONS

METAVERSE

We like Matthew Ball's definition of the metaverse, as it captures its meaning well with the context of this book chapter by describing it as follows:

> The **Metaverse** is a massively scaled and interoperable network of real-time rendered 3D virtual worlds and environments which can be experienced synchronously and persistently by an effectively unlimited number of users with an individual sense of presence, and with continuity of data, such as identity, history, entitlements, objects, communications, and payments. (Ball 2021)

DOI: 10.4324/b23404-3

STRUCTURE-FROM-MOTION (SfM) AND PHOTOGRAMMETRY

In general terms, in **photogrammetry**, the exact points on an image and/or the camera position(s) themselves are known, while in **structure-from-motion**, software-specific algorithms are used to estimate camera positions by point-matching multiple images that have been uploaded (Green, Bevan, and Shapland 2014).

UAVs

UAVs are small unmanned aerial vehicles, more commonly known as aerial drones or flying bots.

UMVs

UMVs are small unmanned marine vehicles, more commonly referred to as submarine bots or underwater drones. Due to physical limitations of radio-transmission signals underneath water, these are often "tethered" by controlling them via a controller attached to a long cable connected with the UMV.

WAYPOINTS AND WAYPOINT MISSIONS

A **waypoint** is a term often used by providers of software and/or applications to plan autonomous UAV flights and the term refers to reference points selected and linked to GPS coordinates. A **waypoint mission** is the sequential connection of these points within the software, providing a virtual path whereby the UAVs can then autonomously fly from waypoint to waypoint and execute a series of pre-programmed actions including taking off, hovering, changing the angle of the camera, taking pictures or video footage, correcting the course dynamically, and landing.

3.1 Introduction

Climate change represents a truly big and global strategic challenge that is felt by everyone and everywhere. Given the sheer size of the issue at hand, it can easily overwhelm all of us and make it somewhat difficult to comprehend what it means both at a community level and when considering concrete actions for local habitats.

At the same time, volunteers and citizen scientist around the globe are keen on improving local living conditions both for fellow humans and flora and fauna alike while gathering hugely valuable environmental data and habitat-specific insights.

Such localized data sets are becoming increasingly important from a global perspective for multinational organizations such as the United Nations as part of participatory policy research initiatives as well as an ever more connected network of scientists trying to understand the impact of climate change at a more localized micro level.

This made us think and consider what would happen if we could engage local people by using existing consumer-grade gadgets they already own, enhancing those with some great low-cost or completely free tools readily available to gather localized habitat data with a view of generating digital twins and sharing this information in the metaverse, thereby ultimately helping to protect local habitats.

Since 2020, we have innovated and experimented with a variety of lightweight yet incredibly capable consumer drones that have been supercharged with third-party applications to turning them into flying autonomous robots used to gather localized, geospatial, and environmental data. The information harvested has subsequently been processed within a selection of AI tools, for instance by applying plant health analysis algorithms in order to determine ecosystem health at various points in time throughout the seasons. In addition, matching 3D aerial habitat scans taken at different times were run through software used in the medical world (originally developed to compare MRI scans), allowing plant growth, habitat trend, and vegetation expansion analysis amongst others.

More recently, some of these approaches initially developed in conjunction with the deployment of small unmanned aerial vehicles (UAVs) have since been further experimented with as part of the mapping of coral reefs with small unmanned marine vehicles (UMVs) and/or small unmanned surface vehicles (USVs).

The submarine data gathered, specifically for coral reefs and mangroves, is then expected to be used to develop digital twins of these natural habitats, opening up a variety of use cases for different purposes (more about this in the Scubaverse.xyz case study later in this chapter) including digital twinning, gamification, integration in the metaverse, virtual gaming edutainment experiences, and gathering real-time, localized alerts for environmental warning systems.

Regardless of the environmental setting (e.g., airborne or submarine) and medium-specific adaptations, the underlying approaches for deploying flying (or swimming/diving) robots aimed at gathering environmental data that is then used within digital twinned or metaverse-like platforms aimed at both protecting and re-wilding natural habits is largely the same and we are pleased to be sharing our methods and findings with the readers of this ground-breaking new book.

We hope that you will feel inspired to be using and further developing these methods as part of forthcoming citizen science projects and would love to hear from your experiences and thoughts; you can find the authors' contact details at the beginning of this chapter or reach out to and connect with us on LinkedIn.

3.2 Current Typical Approaches and Soft-Hardware Landscape

The deployment of UAVs (commonly known as drones) for the purpose of photogrammetry, which involves the generation of orthophotos and geospatial models, is not a novel approach. In the references section of this chapter, you can find a considerable number of scientific papers on this topic, some of which date back several years.

That said, until recently, using drones to explore and analyze natural habitats has been a tedious, complex, time-consuming process of intricate individual tasks with many barriers strewn across its path.

First of all, it requires drone operators with advanced skill levels both for flying (larger) UAVs as well as, often, some additional programmatic skills for producing 3D models.

The drone equipment that has typically been deployed for photogrammetric tasks tends to be large and heavy, often weighing in excess of several kilograms and, as a direct consequence of its weight, the operational range is limited due to air space regulations restricting the permissible flying envelope.

Furthermore, the kind of professional UAVs deployed for such tasks are expensive, with costs easily exceeding several thousand US dollars, and that is without the modeling software needed, often adding another few thousand dollars on top.

Additionally, depending on the operational environment, external conditions, and the habitat selected for such geospatial model analysis, traditional methods would traditionally often require the collection of many hundreds or even thousands of photographs naturally posing several additional procedural and data-related challenges.

With typical battery technology subject to environment (e.g., tropical heat and humidity or artic temperatures), yielding around 30 minutes of flight time in an ideal setting, even operating the UAV in a semi-automated or autonomous fashion means potentially a lot of intermittent battery changes for relatively little surface coverage and requiring a lot of time spent in the field, often in challenging environmental conditions.

The huge number of high-resolution photos (or, in some cases, 4K videos, respectively, for structure-from-motion data capture) further requires availability of large data storage capabilities. And it does not stop here: large numbers of photos translate into enormous computational requirements, meaning it can take easily take several hours or even days in order to process the aerial data gathered.

In order to support the computational needs, most photogrammetry software needs suitably powerful and modern computational resources, typically what one may consider a gaming PC machine or setups used by graphic designers, which represents another major expense and potential hurdle for making photogrammetry more widely accessible.

Ultimately, taking all of these individual barriers and restrictions into account, so far this has meant that using drones to observe natural habitats and supporting ecosystem risk analysis, despite the increasing need for more localized research in light of global climate change, to date is still mostly limited to few scientists and researchers.

3.3 The Evolution from Self-Built Drone to Flying Robot

One of the authors started building, programming, and flying drones over 10 years ago, when they were only available as a cheap radio-controlled toy or a kit pack that would include things such as plastic frame, low-quality electronic speed controllers (ESCs), and some brushed electric motors.

This was later surpassed by more expensive quadcopters with equally expensive, large two-axis gimbals to carry a digital camera of some sort. Again, most of this was a combination of individual tech pieces loosely connected together and then deployed to fly, with varying levels of success.

Initially, the author experimented with a small radio-controlled fix-wing foam glider with a tiny keychain HD camera attached to record footage of local parks and nature reserves. This somewhat crude, flying camera then evolved from a lightweight "wood drone" (with an actual wooden frame from balsa, and yes, it did fly), via a composite Acrylonitrile Butadiene Styrene (ABS) plastic and carbon-fiber frame into more sophisticated drones.

Nowadays, consumer drones have turned into widely available and much more affordable off-the-shelf turn-key solutions: they are lightweight, typically carry high-resolution 4K cameras on stabilized three-axis gimbals, and come with an arsenal of built-in sensors as well as, increasingly, on-board Original Equipment Manufacturer (OEM) software with built-in artificial intelligence.

Such AI features may include pre-determined but adjustable flying patterns as well as the ability to track and follow objects often paired with active tracking and dynamic obstacle avoidance features.

Most importantly, within the context of the innovative methodologies presented in this chapter, some of these consumer drones come with an open software development kit (SDK) that now gives drone operators the ability to combine the UAVs with third-party software applications that provide additional features that are not natively included as part of the drone manufacturers originally supplied (OEM) software. It may be somewhat counterintuitive, but newly released UAVs typically do not come with an open SDK and therefore limit the drone's capabilities purely to advertised off-the-shelf and out-of-the-box features and, in this respect, are not that dissimilar to SIM-locked devices and mobile phones.

With this in mind, it is worth researching the consumer drone market closely to identify drones that already have an open SDK and/or where the drone manufacturers have announced a forthcoming introduction of such.

For example, one of the author's preferred UAV of choice for geospatial modeling and digital twinning is currently the DJI Mini 2, which was initially introduced globally in November 2020. It took until December 2021 when the SDK for this drone become available and it is also worthwhile recognizing that it will likely take third-party app developers another month or two for adjusting, beta testing, and integrating such newly released APIs into their own software.

Since the release of this particular UAV model, the manufacturer has also released the DJI Mini 3 Pro (May 2022), the DJI Mini 3 (December 2022), and the DJI Mini 2 SE (March 2023) for none of which, at the time of writing this chapter, a new SDK has been made available yet. In addition, it was initially reported that the manufacturer was not intending to develop a new SDK release to include with this new line of drones. This decision has since been reportedly revised but it will likely take many more months for the release of the new version.

In conclusion, it requires a keen eye for detail and additional research to identify a readily available UAV that is capable of such third-party app enhancements. By utilizing such open SDKs and augmenting the UAVs with third-party apps that increasingly also include AI capabilities, these consumer drones have been turning into very capable mini flying robots and the authors have successfully used those for most of the case studies presented in this chapter.

3.4 Disruptive Flying Bot Innovation: The Workflow and Toolbox

As part of driving disruptive UAV innovation by pairing consumer drones and combining them with readily available third-party apps, the authors have developed a structured workflow approach that considers various stages of the aerial data gathering and 3D model production process and the following sections with a look at practical considerations at different stages and the overall approach taken. Finally, the authors will be sharing with you our flying robot of hard- and software of choice and how they can be combined in a modular fashion for achieving different tasks as part of the digital twinning process.

3.5 Practical Considerations

Regardless of the purpose of any particular flying mission, it is important to start with the end result in mind and envision the various stages this will consequently involve. Typically, at a fairly generic level, those are:

- Pre-flight
- In-flight
- Post-flight

and as you can see for the Scubaverse case study, the aerial data collected may then further yield input parameters for generating the digital twins' informational layer(s) and as such the production process becomes even more detailed and modular.

During those major stages, both the flying mission's overall objectives and desired outputs will naturally influence some high-level decisions, further impacted by externalities and other factors in the flying field, such as regulatory requirements, flying restrictions, weather conditions, etc.

In addition, post-flight objectives and data processing will almost always impact the selection of relevant hardware (drone) and software (flight planning, post-processing) tools, meaning it is equally important to planning every flying mission from front to back before executing it.

For instance, waypoint mission planning tools such as DroneLink assist greatly with mission planning, as they dynamically calculate mission estimates such as flight duration, distance, height, and number of photos taken, etc. In addition, it is possible to simulate the actual flight on the desktop by overlaying a 3D mission path that gives a "drone-eye view," helping to determine the most suitable camera angles and other operational features, etc. overlayed on a Google map view. The following section will provide more details of things that are worthwhile to consider when planning such missions.

3.6 Approach

Our general approach, as shown in Figure 3.1, when using flying robots to monitor and analyze wildlife habitats, regardless of whether they are urban wetlands, dense forests, mangroves, or coastal estuaries with coral reefs is

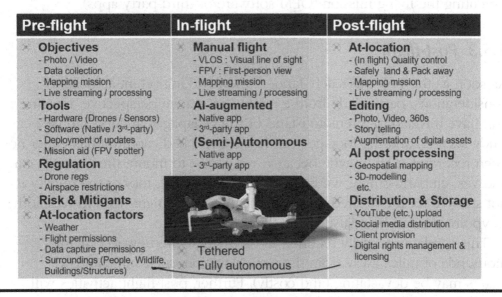

Figure 3.1   Workflow considerations at different stages. (Markus Krebsz.)

the same. That said, it is important to consider the contextual settings as well as any environmental factors such as weather, possible disturbances to animal breeding grounds, and safe mission execution for everyone involved.

3.6.1 Pre-flight

Mission objectives are therefore an important driver for the selection of appropriate UAV tools (see Section 3.7 for more details on both hardware and software) and may range from aerial photography, videography, data collection (photos with a nadir angle), mapping missions, and, in some instances, live streaming of footage.

From a safety perspective, dynamic risk assessments are important and will need to consider at-location factors such as weather, flying permission (and temporary airspace restrictions), data privacy/photographic permissions, and the wider surroundings including people, wildlife, as well as buildings and other infrastructures.

3.6.2 In-flight

The overall purpose of the mission and expected outcomes is also greatly influenced by considerations made during the duration of the flight. This includes the drone operator's chosen flying style (manual vs. AI-augmented vs. autonomous) and the nature of the applications that are used for executing the flying mission (OEM software or third-party apps).

3.6.3 Post-flight

As soon as the UAV has safely landed, there are important at-location considerations, particularly from a quality assurance perspective: imagine you have traveled to a remote island or the Galapagos archipelago (see case study section) and the footage you thought you had captured has either not been recorded at all (maybe because you forgot to mount the microSD card, and yes, embarrassingly, we have made that mistake, too) or the quality is not suitable for the desired purpose, meaning you might need to repeat the waypoint mission by adjusting the flight parameters.

This is relatively easily rectified in the flying field; however, many thousands of miles away from the target location, such sub-standard results may be devastating (and costly). Further, post-flight activities will also influence if/how the drone can best be deployed and that means, for instance, using (or not) ND filters or finding the best balance between height, camera coverage, and available battery life for the drone.

3.7 The Flying Bot Toolbox

The following section lists a selection of tools that are necessary when turning aerial data into 3D scans for digital twinning and, ultimately, making those available as digital assets in gaming environments and the metaverse.

Where applicable, we will also mention our hard- and software tools of choice and, while we have been using those quite happily for a number of years, we also would like to remind the readers that this is a rapidly evolving market and there may be similar and/or better tools out there.

Often, we found, that nothing beats "practice, practice, and practice" and then experimenting with the outcomes. As you can see from the reference section, there is a huge body of knowledge and large number of scientific studies; however, you need to find the set of tools that work best for your given circumstances.

In addition, we have equally been mindful that our approach is as inclusive as possible, meaning excessively high costs for drones and third-party software would mean that this method is not feasible in developing countries, which defeats the objectives from what we set out to do with this method, making it as widely applicable and deployable as possible.

3.7.1 Choice of UAV

One of the key factors in choosing the right UAV for the 3D-modeling task at hand is the availability of a SDK, allowing augmentation with third-party apps.

This is then followed by factors such as weight (lighter means typically less regulatory restrictions, but possibly also less wind resistance), portability (some UAVs are foldable with a smaller footprint, when folded, than a 6-inch screen smartphone), battery life (typically quoted at >30 minutes, in practice often not lasting longer than 20 to 25 minutes), stabilized HD camera (4K is good, but 2.7K may also be also sufficient in some cases), radio controls (most drone controllers attach to a smartphone or tablet that serves as a screen with live-feed of footage from the drone), and built-in safety features (ability to deploy geo-fencing and ability to fly in restricted airspace, subject to explicit permission by air traffic control). Our UAV tool of choice for pre-planned waypoint missions is the DJI Mini 2.

3.7.2 Mission Planning Software

Most lightweight consumer drones do not come with built-in capabilities to pre-plan waypoint missions. Fortunately, for drones with available SDKs, there is a range of third-party applications on the market, enabling pre-planning of flying missions through modern web-browser-based software on laptop or desktop PCs. They usually come with companion apps for smartphones that allow execution of such pre-planned autonomous flying missions while in the flying field. Our software tool of choice for mission planning is DroneLink.

3.7.3 Flight Augmentation Apps

For certain scenarios, it may be desirable to use a third-party app to augment drone flights with AI features such as dynamic active tracking and/or execution of pre-determined, more complex flight patterns that are not included in the OEM software. Our choice of software is either Litchi for DJI Drones or Maven Lite.

3.7.4 Geospatial Modeling Software

The more traditional and established tools for generating 3D scans, geospatial models, and the production of digital assets for metaverse platforms tend to be costly for a variety of reasons, including (i) cost for the application itself, (ii) computational requirements typically need a state-of-the-art gaming computer or high-power graphics processor to run, (iii) energy consumption to compute the models—often over several days, and (iv) data storage space needs to accommodate the many thousands of pictures or lengthy 4K video footage captured as part of the production process.

This made us reconsider the key elements needed in order to produce a 3D scan or geospatial model of a wildlife habitat and then also give thought to whether exact dimensions/surface or volumetric measurements are required.

In addition to this, some software applications provide the ability to produce elevation models, interrogate orthophotos further, and deploy built-in AI algorithms for plant health analysis and vegetation index calculations. The answer to these questions will drive the selection of software needed for the task at hand.

3.7.5 Simple 3D Surface Scans without Animation

Simple 3D surface scans can be relatively easily and quickly produced and often it is even possible to generate a simple 3D surface habitat scan in situ in the flying field, either on a laptop or smartphone, including simple model edits such as cropping or adjusting horizon leveling.

We have two applications of choice depending on the smartphone operating system that is used: For Android—Kiri AI engine and for iOS—Trnio.

Some of these tools permit direct export of the resulting model files into model viewer applications such as Sketchfab (Trnio), whereas others (Kiri AI) will require an export via their PC/laptop-based desktop viewer in order to import the file elsewhere. Both work well for this purpose.

3.7.6 Simple 3D Surface Scans with the Ability to Animate Models

One of the ways of bringing simple 3D surface models to life is by animating them, giving the feel of a virtual fly-through. For instance, if researching habitats of a remote island in the Maldives or hard-to-reach mangroves in Kenya, an animated surface model of such an area can make all the difference in understanding relative features within the flying field as well as enabling a more immersive look and feel.

While there are a lot of expensive software tools available enabling this feature, our choice to produce animated 3D scans is 3DF Zephyr, specifically the Free and Lite versions of this software; while the Free version does not require any registration and can just be downloaded from the company's website, it is also limited to a maximum number of 50 photos. The examples provided in the case study section were all produced with this Free version.

In contrast, there is also a Lite version that will require registration and comes with a one-off license fee cost of €149.00 at the time of writing, allowing processing of a maximum of 500 photos per model.

3.7.7 3D Scans and Geospatial Models with Metrics and AI Plant Health Analysis

Localized wildlife habitat and ecosystem risk analysis will often also require not just a visual and/or 3D representation but also the ability to produce detailed measurements. For instance, in the example of case study 1, the UAV was autonomously deployed in order to produce initially a 2D-orthophoto

Name	Description & usage	Filters	Colours
NDVI	Normalized Difference Vegetation Index shows the amount of green vegetation	3	7
NDVI (Blue)	Normalized Difference Vegetation Index shows the amount of green vegetation	2	7
ENDVI	Enhanced Normalize Difference Vegetation Index to isolate plant health (focus on G+B)	1	7
vNDVI	Visible NDVI is an un-normalized index for RGB sensors using data from citrus/grape/sugarcane	1	7
VARI	Visual Atmospheric Resistance Index shows areas of vegetation	1	7
EXG	Excess Green Index emphasises greenness of leafy crops such as potatoes	1	7
TGI	Triangular Greenness Index performs similarly to EXG but with improvements in certain environments	1	7
BAI	Burn Area Index highlights burned land in the red to near-infrared spectrum	3	7
GLI	Green Leaf Index shows green leaves and stems	1	7
NDVI	Normalized Difference Vegetation Index shows the amount of green vegetation	3	7
GRVI	Green Ratio Vegetation Index is sensitive to photosynthetic rates in forest	3	7
SAVI	Soil Adjusted Vegetation Index is similar to NDVI but removes effects of soil via an adjustment factor	3	7
MNLI	Modified Non-linear Index improves the index algorithm to account for soil areas	3	7
MSR	Modified Simple Ratio is an improvement of the SRI to be more sensitive to vegetation	3	7
RVI	Renormalized Difference Vegetation Index shows areas of healthy vegetation	3	7
TDVI	Transformed Difference Vegetation Index highlights vegetation cover in urban environments	3	7
OSAVI	Optimized Soil Adjusted Vegetation Index is based on SAVI but works better where little vegetation is present	3	7
LAI	Leaf Area Index estimates foliage areas and predicts crop yields	1	7
EVI	Enhanced Vegetation Index is useful in areas where NDVI might saturate, uses blue wavelengths to correct	1	7

Figure 3.2   List of WebODM's built-in vegetation index algorithms, filters, and colors. (Markus Krebsz.)

of the bird sanctuary that was then followed by deploying a series of built-in AI algorithm for plant health analysis, specifically to color in and highlight different areas of the invasive species. Surface areas where the invasive weed could be clearly identified were then measured, giving the local park rangers and specialist teams on the ground an opportunity to develop the best suited and most targeted treatment approach.

Our choice for this more complex activity is WebODM (www.opendronemap.org).

The desktop version comes at a moderate one-off license fee of ca. $60.00 at the time of writing, while including a vast range of built-in tools and features. Initially, it will require a bit of a learning curve as some of the modeling features can be finely adjusted, allowing for greater nuances in the habitat analysis and, as can be seen in Figure 3.2, the software comes with a wide range of built-in vegetations index algorithms as well as the ability to deploy a huge selection of different filters and color variations.

3.8 Case Studies

The innovative conservation methods presented in this chapter, which deploy off-the-shelf consumer drones (UAVs) that are paired with third-party turn-key solutions, originally evolved over a 24-month period from mid-2020. Since then, it has been successfully used multiple times for habitat restoration work as well as the establishment of a new wetlands. The following section details the methods/tools used for those use cases and links to some of the results.

3.9 The Slack (Bird Sanctuary) and River Rom Wetlands

The Slack is a bird sanctuary nestled inside the Chase local nature reserve, considered one of the best urban nature reserves in Essex, covering 48 hectares with a patchwork of habitats including horse-grazed pastures, scrubland, river, woodland, reed beds, and shallow wetlands.

The reserve is an established wildlife habitat with an impressive array of flora and fauna, including one of the United Kingdom's rarest native trees, the Black Poplar. The site and in particular the Slack, is also a haven for birds, with around 200 different species recorded throughout the seasons, including kingfishers, reed warblers, skylarks, little ringed plovers, and lapwings, as well as rare visitors such as pine buntings, great snipe, and spotted crakes.

Over the years, likely to due to locals releasing freshwater fish from their aquariums, the Slack (as well as some of the other lakes nearby) have been plagued by an invasive species, New Zealand pigmyweed (*Crassula helmsii*). Even small pieces of *Crassula* leaves entering the natural habitat and waterways in the United Kingdom have been found to cause huge havoc to local wildlife: The weed grows green carpets with dense coverage across the bird sanctuary's mudflats, both depleting and removing valuable breeding and feeding grounds for waders and many birds relying on these otherwise muddy waters.

The park rangers in conjunction with the local councils and national research institutes has been looking at a variety of treatment methods to removing, or at least heavily restricting the growth, of this invasive weed. As part of this work, the authors have been involved in a longitudinal study investigating and monitoring the spread of the *Crassula* by deploying autonomous UAVs.

The approach used was relatively simple and is replicable for a range of projects:

i. Planning the autonomous UAV mission in DroneLink (or similar third-party software)
ii. Executing the autonomous waypoint drone mission at the flying field

   iii. Using the aerial data collected (in this case, 26 photos) and running it through a geospatial modeling suite of choice. Driven by individual needs, the tool used could be as follows:
      a. Quick production of a 3D model with the capability for basic edits and then exporting this into SketchFab.com: **KIRI AI (web) engine**
      b. Production of a more sophisticated 3D model with the ability for simple measurements, greater flexibility to edit the mesh and point clouds, and built-in features such as an animation tool that allows to generate fly-through views of the 3D model: **3DF Zephyr (Free)**
      c. Detailed production of a 3D geospatial model with the ability to use a variety of built-in AI tools lending themselves to plant health analysis paired further and aided by tools to measure elevation levels, surface spread, volume, and angles of building structures: **WebODM (OpenDroneMap)**
   iv. Using the output(s) of step iii. For a variety of added features, including comparing several orthophotos of the area(s) of investigation taken during different seasons and then comparing the results to determine treatment effectiveness, see Figure 3.3.
   v. In addition, the 3D scans, the geospatial model, as well as the animated version, have been shared via a variety of forums with a multitude of stakeholders including researchers, council and local authority staff, community groups, and also been featured in a recent TEDx talk by one of the authors.

One of the great advantages of using tools such as DroneLink is the ability to be able to re-fly waypoint missions autonomously at different points in time and then compare and contrast the results. Since this is a longitudinal project with funding secured for the next 10 years, we will continue working with the park rangers and local authority to refine this approach further and re-deploy the UAV in a similar fashion during the seasons.

In addition, by making both 3D models and animated 3D scans available to the wider public, the project has been able to generate interest for this otherwise relatively hidden local habitat. Visitors of the habitat's digital twin have been able to explore features of the otherwise mostly inaccessible bird sanctuary while at the same time keeping wildlife disruption to an absolute minimum.

An animated version, using 3DF Zephyr Free, of the Slack Bird Sanctuary is available here: https://youtu.be/CTs7QPA9pgI

Figure 3.3   The Slack (Bird Sanctuary) autonomous waypoint mission plan and mission parameter estimate in DroneLink. (Markus Krebsz.)

An animated version comparing orthophotos before and after restoration is available here: https://youtu.be/61X7sIqhN9E

The software that has been used in this particular example to compare both orthophotos, as shown in Figure 3.4, is often deployed in the medical world to analyze MRI scans. A free tool with similar capabilities is the web-based Image Comparison Slider (https://web-toolbox.dev/en/tools/image-compare-slider).

3.9.1 The River Rom Wetlands

A tributary to the River Thames, the River Rom forms the boundary between two east London boroughs. And sadly, similar to many other of London's rivers, the River Rom has endured substantial environmental damage in recent years: Sewage overflows and misconnections lead to water quality deterioration while adjoining wildlife habitats have also

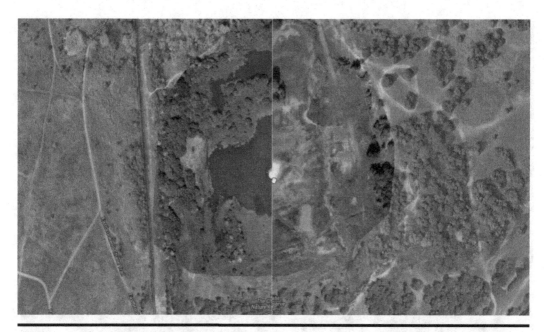

Figure 3.4   The Slack Bird Sanctuary—Orthophoto overlay (before and after habitat restoration). (Markus Krebsz.)

been damaged by dredging of the river channels and straightening and concreting of river banks.

The lower part of this river (commonly known as the River Beam) flows through the eastern section of the Chase Local Nature Reserve, which has been designated a Site of Metropolitan Important for Nature Conservation.

The area for the new River Rom wetlands were previously undeveloped floodplains, which are part of one of the United Kingdom's most neglected wildlife habitats. Typically, in their natural state, such floodplains are known to support a wide range of aquatic and semi-aquatic species as well as helping to fight climate change by locking in carbon. In addition, they also form a physical protection by holding back floodwaters and thereby reducing the flood risk for downstream communities. Sadly, 90% of floodplains in England have been separated from river channels, mostly due to urbanization and artificial flood embankments, meaning they are not capable to project communities any more from devastating floods, and this includes the River Rom floodplain, which has not been able to support the range of flora and fauna it would normally be able to.

Fortunately, in 2021, this area received funding from a partnership scheme, which enabled the establishment of two new wetlands, including

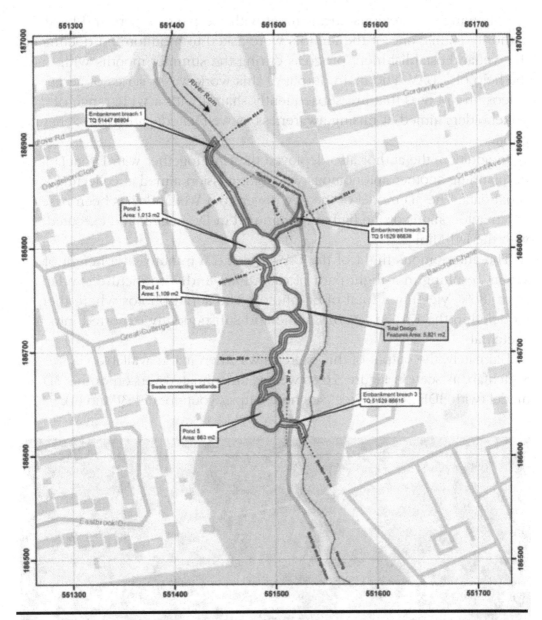

Figure 3.5 **Map showing the new River Rom Wetlands development plan. (https://barkinganddagenhamcountryparks.com/wetland-habitat-creation-at-the-chase-local-nature-reserve-2022/ [Website accessed on 31/03/2023].)**

several embankment breaches and ponds to be built (please see Figure 3.5 for a map plan of this new development), which will be able to trap surplus water during periods of heavy rain and act as important new habitats for wetlands plants, birds, and small mammals.

Following the previous engagement with the park rangers and local authority teams, one of the authors were asked to monitor and document the wetland establishment progress during the summer months with the help of a UAV. The main output of this work was a series of aerial videos and photos that are subsequently shared with a wide range of stakeholders aimed at raising awareness as well as educating the general public.

In addition, the author also deployed the UAV together with DroneLink for planning another autonomous waypoint mission aimed at collecting aerial data. The 3D model of the new River Rom Wetlands has been based on an autonomous drone flight programmed in DroneLink and executed with the DJI Mini 2.

The autonomous flight of the UAV took ca. 6 minutes at a height of 115 m, resulting in a flight path of ca. 1.8 km and with picture overlap of ca. 80%, yielding a total of 66 photos. The aerial photos where then modeled in the Kiri Ai (Web) Engine and subsequently exported into Sketchfab.

Ultimately, the output of this exercise was then made available via Sketchfab, as seen in Figure 3.6 as well as an animated version of this 3D model (with 3DF Zephyr Free, see here: https://youtu.be/0Pe3JMhtvFI).

Figure 3.6   3D model of the River Rom Wetlands on Sketchfab.com. (Markus Krebsz [Model is accessible here: https://skfb.ly/oACuP]. A selection of videos of this project is available at www.drone.consulting and an explanation of the project's purpose, drivers, methodologies, as well as a UAV demonstration and the software deployed is available at Prof. Krebsz's recent TEDx talk:.)

3.10 Iguanas from Above

Iguanas from Above (www.iguanasfromabove.com) is an amazing project on the Galapagos archipelago that uses a combination of consumer drones paired with AI and citizen science to bring wildlife conservation into the digital age. It commenced its fourth expedition in early 2023, going on another month-long voyage to the Galapagos central islands.

The underlying principle is that the Galapagos marine iguanas, exclusive to those islands, are a gravely endangered, unique species threatened with extinction and the team of scientists running this project are keen to better understand how many there are and the marine iguanas' seasonal migration patterns.

They do this by deploying a combination of new hardware (e.g., UAVs), software, AI tools, as well as an army of volunteers revolutionizing conservation approach aimed at increasing effectiveness while keeping habitat disruptions to a minimum.

Prof. Krebsz ('MK') has been able to interview Dr. Amy Mcleod ('AM'), leader and creator of this innovative conservation project, and what follows are selected highlights of this interview.

MK: Amy, can you tell us bit more about the Iguanas from Above project, please?

AM: So, from the initial idea in 2015, it took a while for the technology to develop. [...] The authorities started to see the use of these approaches and, luckily, allowed it so that we actually really started in mid-2020 with getting on board with this. This was a big learning curve because none of us were drone pilots at that time – we were just people interested in conservation that wanted to approach this in a different way [...to] vegetation mapping/terrestrial uses. We actually wanted to launch [UAVs] from small boats which is really pushing the boundaries [...] in some of the conditions that we're flying in.

So, in the video you see here (https://youtu.be/CH1Rt-YPee4) [...] this was actually our first field season so that's Andrea and I on the boat and we're flying the drone which is a Mavic Pro 2 from the small boats approaching the coastline. This is actually a really nice lagoon on San Cristobal where we saw a lot of really cool rays and sharks – and this clip is Santa Fe and you can see the terrain we're dealing with, that it looks very treacherous and how do you access that [...] and here you can see a bit of the rays so it's really good for getting into mangrove so very difficult to approach otherwise and, you know, it's amazing to see this perspective on the place that I already knew quite well.

So, we basically fly the drones over the coastline [and] normally we're flying and facing directly down with the camera like this, we capture photographs and we kind of often fly in a zig-zag [pattern] with an overlap and then we'll stitch those photographs together into a mosaic photo and then we'll cut them up for counting, if we're doing it on Zooniverse (https://www.zooniverse.org/projects/andreavarela89/iguanas-from-above/).

So, we're flying the drones ideally from the boat and we land them on the boat as well, which like in this situation you see is very calm. It's not usual actually, sometimes we're really dealing with a lot of swell, waves and wind and it gets very exciting to say the least.

We're hand-launching [the UAVs] and we're hand-catching them and we have to really train for that and [...] the sea conditions were pretty wild.

We wanted to have two drone teams because boat [rental] times [are] very expensive, we wanted to maximize drone times there. There's real logistical stuff and also the point of a moving home point, if [the drone] loses connection to the remote [...] and if the drone tries to return to the home point it lands in the sea – and that did happen more than once.

Losing drones is the kind of thing that we know is going to happen but [...] we need to try to recover it because we don't want to leave the drones in the sea with the lithium batteries [...], so each time we have managed to recover them but those are always the most tense moments, but still we're getting to places that you just couldn't get otherwise and the risk here is losing a drone instead of having a person swept out to see or smashed on the rock.

You know these [risks] are real, I am not being dramatic like these are real things that happen out there, [which is] why we're trying to develop this method of using the drones because it's just safer for the people but it's also safer for the islands if we can avoid getting on those islands [and] there's no risk of us bringing accidentally a small ant or seed [back]. Invasive species [are] a huge risk and these islands are really pristine and [...] the only way for it to be 100% safe is to just not go there so we're doing this in a very non-invasive way as we're just going there visually.

And the other think I find very cools is that we can [...] take other people online because we have for instance Zooniverse volunteers who are there [and although] it's not like visiting the island but it's an eye on the islands in a really detailed way that they can access from the safety of their house: For instance, during Covid, we have had a lot of volunteers who perhaps otherwise like to have gone and done [...] real field conservation work but since they couldn't, so what they could do was to work with us – we really appreciated the help and it is a kind of win-win. We have had other people who have for instance illnesses or physical disabilities that preclude them from traditional conservation work and they've been able to help us and make a real contribution and I think that's awesome that it's sort of inclusive for all kinds of people and very useful for us [scientists].

MK: The Zooniverse-part of the project you mentioned earlier, which I guess is a combination of innovative crowdsourcing and citizen science, you can probably walk me through [...] ow this works, your experiences and [...] maybe also how are you thinking you could augment this research with machine learning and deploying some AI?

AM: Okay, so first I just talk about how these images were created: we generally were flying the drones from the boats [...] with a zig-zag pattern with a large overlap between the images that allows us to stitch them together to create these mosaics and orthophotos.

We then slice those down for [...] the volunteers to look at a detailed angle because [...] you really have to zoom in to see the iguanas so [...] we present the images at this kind of level already.

We have this quite detailed tutorial to explain workarounds and [...] we're doing in in different phases because ultimately we're going to survey the entire archipelago anywhere where we suspect the iguanas to be found. We did originally want to do the entire coastline but it turns out that it's way too optimistic, so we are focusing on it but it's still much better coverage than we've ever had before for this species, so were taking the images and phases.

It is challenging and the volunteers are going to miss some of [the iguanas] and we would miss some of them as well – that's just the natural part of counting animals: it is never ever perfect, and you get as close to perfect as you can but you have to accept that […] animals […] move and they hide and they camouflage with their environment.

Alongside with the counts we get from the volunteers we're also doing counts in the field to ground truth this and see how realistic it is […], so once we've figured out [how many we missed] we might be able to apply a correction factor and say 'okay, well, we've counted 7,000 marine iguanas here but actually we should add 30' for […] the ones we missed.

We also show each individual photo at least 20 different times [on Zooniverse] to that we're looking on aggregate for an average we don't expect every count to be perfect so not all the pressure is on one person.

MK: How do you envisioning this project to develop over the next few years?

AM: So, we do want to use machine learning, we're still kind of finding the right collaborators for that because it's outside of our network. There are so many commercial applications for machine learning it's sometimes difficult to get the people interested when can't offer any of benefit other than what you're doing.

(The full 52-minute conversation is available here: https://youtu.be/ XgPF3dazm1E)

> *Interview by Prof. Krebsz with Dr. Amy Macleod, Iguanas from Above, https://www.iguanasfromabove.com/*

3.11 Scubaverse

Scubaverse (www.scubaverse.xyz) is a gaming metaverse start-up company developing digital twins of marine life, islands, and coastal areas (e.g., mangroves) for the purpose of solving real-life marine problems by combining youth innovation and science engagement on blue sustainability with gamification.

The idea behind this is that, by using a combination of aerial UAVs, submarine UMVs, and human snorkelers, Scubaverse can gather local real-life and real-time aerial and submarine environmental data. These user-generated data sets can then be merged with other available scientific and

Scubaverse: From Real World Data to Video Game

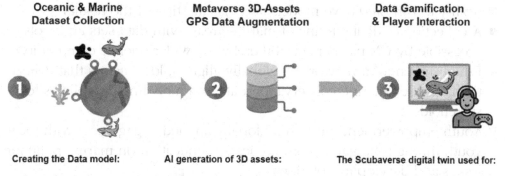

Figure 3.7   **Scubaverse digital twinning & gamification process. (Scubaverse.xyz [Website accessed on 31/03/2023].)**

environmental data that is then turned into 3D models for digital twinning of real location in the metaverse.

But far beyond pure game play, these digital twins of coral reefs or mangroves can also be used to run predictive environmental risk models, develop stress scenarios, suitable mitigants as part of addressing climate change and showcasing regenerative projects while engaging both local communities and global gamers alike, as shown in Figure 3.7.

According to the company, 90% of oceans are still unexplored and could be key for the regeneration of planet Earth, further accelerated by the recent increased use of Blue Bonds by governments and island nation states. Scubaverse's business model is in essence a Free-to-Play PC Game, tapping into a total market of 1.7 billion PC gamers by using Steam as a viable distribution platform with ca. 75% of the global gaming market.

The company expects the following outcomes and is aligning those closely with the United Nation Sustainable Development Goals (SDGs):

■ Provision of both playful and experiential learning on marine life conservation
■ PC-based video game running social "quests" linked to real-life climate events
■ Mobile app suite for fieldwork and data collection with UAVs and UMVs

- Identification and engagement of community-based citizen scientists who can assist with fieldwork-based data collection
- Ability to run predictive models and visualisation of the results
- A collection of digital twins of marine areas, with data sets and tools accessible by UN partners (and thereby the wider science community)
- Establishment of a network of globally aligned, local actors that collect, train, and sell marine conservation data and modeling capabilities to stakeholders
- Youth empowerment through a globally aligned engagement with local youth through the game, communication/education on marine pollution issues and developing solutions
- Close collaboration with and engagement of local stakeholders who want to engage in marine conservation and provide them with opportunities to take action, including provision of digital sandbox tools for the training of local climate actors and aspiring scientists

Figure 3.8 depicts what a pre-planned waypoint mission for a UAV of one of the Maldives' islands for digital twinning in Scubaverse could look like; this would roughly need flying of four maps, with a distance of 35 km, yielding 858 photos taken at approximately 120 m height and would total

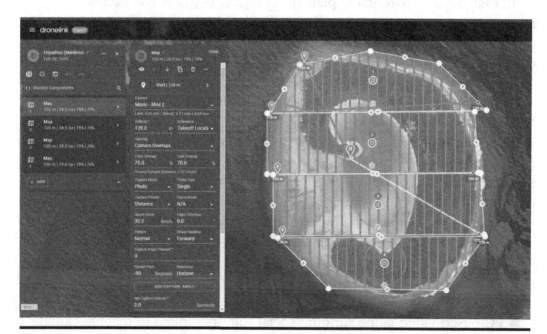

Figure 3.8 Aerial waypoint mission of a Maldives island for the Scubaverse. (Markus Krebsz.)

Figure 3.9   Scubaverse's digital twin of the Maldives Island. (www.Scubaverse.xyz [Website accessed: 31/03/2023].)

around 1 hour 41 minutes (which is roughly akin to four drone batteries). The resulting digital island in the Scubaverse is shown in Figure 3.9.

3.12 Conclusion

Hopefully, it has become evident to the readers that this innovative method deploying flying bots to produce digital assets for the purpose of wildlife habitat analysis and use within a gamified metaverse-like platform, is a very dynamic and evolving field.

This is further exacerbated by the global market penetration with increasingly lighter and more affordable consumer drones and, in the authors' view, represents an unprecedented opportunity for localized environmental and habitat data collection, trend analysis, and digital twining of the real world. If this then also helps encouraging the younger gamer generation to appreciating our amazing planet and mothership, while engaging with globally crowd-sourced citizen scientists either in the metaverse and/or other digitally twinned environments for the purposing of both having fun as well as protecting mothership, then our work is done.

Although we know our innovative and, even somewhat disruptive approach, may not be always perfect, we believe that in at least 80% of use cases this is sufficient to provide good enough quality results that can then be used to that are easily implementable, low-cost, and high-impact develop localized climate change mitigation strategies.

References

Ball, Matthew. 2021. "Framework for the Metaverse." June 29. https://www.matthewball.vc/all/forwardtothemetaverseprimer.

Green, Susie, Andrew Bevan, and Michael Shapland. 2014. "A Comparative Assessment of Structure from Motion Methods for Archaeological Research." *Journal of Archaeological Science* 46 (1): 173–81. doi:10.1016/j.jas.2014.02.030.

Chapter 4

Digitalization Impact of the Metaverse on Humankind

Madhuri Kompelly, Maddu Sai Adarsh,
P. Baby Priya, and Rajesh Kumar K. V.
Woxsen University
Hyderabad, India

4.1 Introduction

Digitalization is the deliberate use of cutting-edge tools for advancing and making sense of digital operations. These activities include the merging of electronic and digital technologies. Hardware can communicate with sensors connected to cloud servers, and data (which comprises information in bits) can communicate with the hardware. This convergence not only supports the significant organizational change and digital innovation, but it also poses a serious threat to the old industrial practices. In addition to technological components, social reactions might be crucial to the success of a digital transition. Competitive advantage depends on digitization, which in turn is driven by customer behavior, which in turn indicates the industrial and research environment connected to market direction.

The digital economy is quite effective at cutting down on costs. The influence of digital transformation on both businesses' and consumers' perceptions of value is substantial. In today's data-driven market, the physical attributes of goods are less important than ever. These days, it's expected that everything is quick and simple to use (IEEE Digital Reality, https://digitalreality.ieee.org/).

DOI: 10.4324/b23404-4

Consider how attitudes regarding the car industry have changed over the last several decades. Prior to recently, an automobile's acceleration and top speed were its only selling advantages. Consumers' priorities are shifting swiftly in response to the rise of ride-sharing services and autonomous cars. Rider comforts will unquestionably outweigh the requirements of the driver. As a result of the COVID-19 epidemic, several businesses have implemented cutting-edge strategies in line with digital innovations. The tense physical exchange abruptly stopped. Only the most robust companies have had the time to investigate effective methods of streamlining their operations. The digital revolution has changed the rules and businesses must adapt. Despite the difficulties brought on by the pandemic, businesses may maintain their lead in new areas and consistently surpass consumer expectations.

4.2 Development in Digital Transformation

The discussions have progressed recently because of the widespread use of digital technologies. Although digital technology has the potential to have a significant impact on every facet of a business, economy, or society (Catlin et al., 2017; Kozarkiewicz, 2020), the focus of this investigation is limited to the repercussions that digital transformation has had on individuals and their communities. The advent of cutting-edge technologies like blockchain, AI, and the IoT has given rise to a plethora of alternate approaches to common problems. Organizations of all shapes and sizes, both public and private, may benefit from digital transformation, especially those that, without it, might go out of business (Siebel, 2019). This trend cannot be disregarded by developing countries, since the influence of digital transformation on all disciplines is already substantial and will grow substantially in the future.

Because digital conversion is so crucial, it is seen as a catalyst for progress (Yoo et al., 2012). Researchers have pointed to the importance of digital transformation in light of the emergence of new technologies and the consequential shifts in the innovative practices of businesses and society (Berghaus & Back, 2016; Warner & Wäger, 2019). Many aspects of modern life have been altered by the rise of digitalization, including the nature of goods, business operations, relationships, and services (Karimi & Walter, 2015). As competition increases, businesses must adapt their strategies (Hartl & Hess, 2017). The term "digital transformation" has not yet been adequately defined. To counter this, digital transformation is frequently cited as a fundamental change-driven organizational shift that is redefining business as usual (Bilgeri et al., 2017).

While terms like *digital innovation* and *digitization* are not mutually exclusive, digital transformation has become the preferred term. Digital transformation, as defined by Osmundsen et al. (2018), involves the integration of software and hardware to provide novel benefits for consumers and society. By changing the business model, digital transformation also means that procedures and the corresponding team may be improved. The impact of digital change on the global economy has been substantial, particularly during the COVID-19 epidemic. Significant developments in the processing, control, and analysis of blocks reflect this tendency.

Big data is not a simple thing to expand (Anh, 2020a). Many nations now devote significant resources to studying and developing digital currencies. Although some Asian governments have explored and tried digital currencies, others are not yet ready to do so. Because digital money operates on a global scale, it is difficult to oppose or restrict it. Instead, governments should work together more closely to research and issue digital money (Nham, 2020). Warnings have been issued, however, against the use of Bitcoin in illegal activities including sponsoring terrorism, money laundering, etc. (Anh, 2020b).

Changes in digital technology and global integration may have varied effects in the future on the tactics that now play a significant part in the accomplishments of many nations. As a result, executives at many public and commercial organizations are making massive investments in digital transformation (Thuong et al., 2019). To keep up with digitization, businesses need to shift their attention to efficiency and enhance the quality of their leadership. Greater leadership satisfaction and productivity may be attributed to enhanced digital leadership (Antonopoulou et al., 2019). Even before the COVID-19 period, public and commercial organizations had plans for digital transformation (Matt et al., 2015).

Governments and organizations had to re-evaluate their strategies as COVID-19 came dangerously close to affecting the whole planet. Digital transformation, which is gradually changing the way governments and businesses provide services like communication, health care, and education, has now reached a tipping point (Ting et al., 2020). Thus, digital transformation is becoming more mainstream, making it impossible for any individual, nation, or organization to ignore it. There's also the matter of addressing the circumstances around digital change (Priyono et al., 2020).

4.3 Changes in Transformation

The integration of digital technologies into existing IT infrastructures, such as cloud computing, social technology, and the Internet of Things (White, 2008), is a key component of the digital transformation process. Occasionally, this idea is expanded to include the possibility of technological novelty and greater functional capability brought about by digital means (Westerman et al., 2014). There are three parts to digital transformation: (1) external (to better serve customers), (2) internal, and (3) organizational leadership. With the advent of digitalization, new models for running organizations have been introduced (Hess et al., 2020).

Leadership settings may be shifted via digital transformation, which uses digital technology to modify or create new practices, encounters, and cultures. This shift is being seen as a digital revolution in the information era (Luong, 2020). It is possible to see digital transformation as the effects of technological advancements brought about by the widespread use of computers and other electronic devices in many facets of modern life (Stolterman & Fors, 2004). Different research points to four aspects of digital transformation: big data, the Internet of Things (IoT), interoperability, and cybernetics (Figure 4.1). In many ways, society stands to benefit from these innovations.

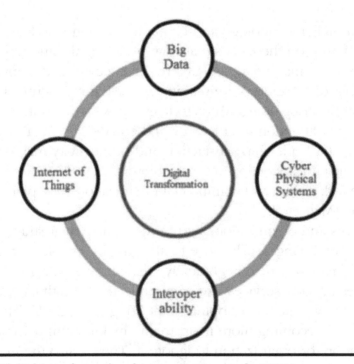

Figure 4.1   Digital transformation factors. (Imran et al., 2018.)

To put it simply, digital transformation is the process by which businesses and other organizations adapt their operations to make better and more efficient use of digital technologies to better serve the public good. Meanwhile, it has a significant impact on how individuals go about their daily lives, careers, relationships, and intellectual and experiential pursuits. In addition, modern technology has caused significant shifts in the delivery of services in the realms of medicine, security, and education. This helps leaders anticipate and prepare for future events so they can accomplish their objectives. The process of digital transformation is complicated by a wide range of circumstances.

This era of digital transformation impacts every facet of a business today (Boulton, 2020). As a result, businesses must adapt to a dynamic environment in which new technologies are always emerging and significantly increasing the company's and society's worth. Increases in value-adding elements and technical development have contributed to a heightened understanding of the need for digital transformation (Shahbaz et al., 2019).

4.4 Impact on Society

With all its beneficial impacts, it is vital to be able to forecast, recognize, and manage unfavorable trends, difficulties, and dangers associated with digital transformation. In particular, knowledge is an important aspect of the economy alongside more conventional economic variables like labor, money, and land. When it comes to establishing a company's competitive advantage and the value of its product, service, and workforce, knowledge is quickly overtaking other economic aspects. The economy and the pace of innovation will both undergo dramatic shifts as a result of digitalization (Gbadegeshin, 2019). By 2035, it is expected that between 50 and 70% of all manufacturing employment would be automated away. Not only does economic prosperity play a role in the ability to actively participate in the process of digitization, but it also contributes to the widening gap between the level of economic and technological development of different countries and between different groups of the population within the same country. The already alarming extent of social disparity is only going to become worse as a result of this. However, at the current time, basic research in this field is not conducted utilizing multidisciplinary techniques, despite the seriousness of the difficulties stated above.

Articles in business periodicals, studies from consulting firms or government regulators and non-governmental organizations (NGOs), and a smattering of practical advice and White Papers predominate, but they lack a solid scientific foundation (Heavin & Power, 2018). The following establishes the critical need of doing empirical research within the framework of sociological science to comprehend the processes of digital transformation of society.

4.5 Digitalization of the Real Sector of the Economy

This is the backbone of the digital economy, and it will be a major component in the expansion of both the economy at large and the digital industry as a whole (and the digital industry in particular, as a producer of technological goods). Digital technology forms the backbone of marketing and production plans in many industries. New goods, services, platforms, and innovations arise as a result of their disruptive power altering established business models, manufacturing chains, and procedures. Businesses, especially smaller and medium-sized ones, and the industry as a whole may benefit from the right setting and the right information marketing and economic incentives. Both the organizational and technical access to the associated digital infrastructures, and the financial and economic perspective, i.e., via the introduction of instruments that will stimulate corporate digitalization, are necessary for the widespread use of digital technologies (Kockmann et al., 2018). The modernization, revival, and competitiveness of the economy will all arise from these efforts.

4.6 Education

Developing and spreading educational resources and digital platforms that can support interactive and communication is necessary that are readily accessible by educational both institutions and students; creating and implementing state-of-the-art laptop, multimedia, and computer-oriented teaching aids and equipment for establishing a digital learner environment.

There can be no advancement in health care or efficient delivery of medical services without the digitization of the industry. In digital medicine, information and communication technologies are used to facilitate interactions between patients, healthcare providers, and organizations (Gbadegeshin, 2019). One of the main goals of digital medicine is the complete digitalization of the medical process. The digitization of medical and associated services and the cooperation of operators in this sector may both benefit from the creation of a comprehensive digital medical platform. When it comes to a patient's medical history, a digital medical platform is a dynamic collection of electronic data that is systematically arranged to ensure privacy and security. This platform facilitates communication and collaboration between various healthcare providers. Despite the progress made in digital health, the implementation of TeleSystems to help rural physicians and provide people with access to distant medical services is still crucial (Denicolo et al., 2016). The Internet of Things (IoT) enables the use of sensors to continually monitor human health, and medical service providers are increasingly taking part in digital platforms. This has the potential to revolutionize medicine. The medical system as a whole is negatively impacted by all of these factors.

4.7 E-democracy

Increasing digital programs has opened up new methods for the public to become involved in democratic institutions (Larsson & Teigland, 2019). The offline democratic procedures may be adapted to the online environment. E-referendums, e-consultations, political events, and online polls are all examples of the many shapes that e-democracy has taken as it has evolved. The most crucial aspect, however, is the use of computerized voting. Although this is the least complex kind of electronic democracy, putting it into practice presents some political and administrative hurdles. This style is also being adopted by a growing number of nations, eventually becoming the norm around the globe. Offering voters a way to cast their ballots electronically requires fine-tuning election technology. Online voting improves the speed and accuracy with which election results may be tallied, allows voters to cast ballots from far away, and expands the number of people who can participate in elections (New Digital Economy, 2011). Developing an electronic voting platform will increase voter turnout, particularly among young generation, improve election representation and quality, and lessen the likelihood of skewed or fraudulent outcomes.

4.8 Ecology and Environmental Protection

Using the digitalization technology has the possibility to greatly improve environmental conditions, lessen emissions from industrial operations, and support long-standing firms' pursuit of sustainable development. Establishing some of the highest-priority initiatives are digitized natural resource registers to aware people and state institutions during discussions and decision making about ensuring environmental sustainability, early intervention, fast response, and emergency recovery (Metallo et al., 2020).

4.9 Is This Transformation Helpful for Society?

In a word, yes, change is good for society. Scarcity in the supply chain is a natural consequence of the depletion of finite resources. On the other side, a digital economy is a prosperous one. Bits in computers can be copied endlessly and with perfect accuracy for pennies. To progress toward a fully digital society, people must have faith in the organizations that are producing and sustaining digital services (Taşaltin, 2019).

4.10 Impact on the Supply Chain

Businesses aim to provide the best possible goods to consumers at the most affordable price. Putting together and selling a product has a monetary and material price tag. However, digital transformation disrupts the established company structure, particularly in manufacturing. Expenses are reduced in a digital economy because of its efficiency. Those cost reductions are then passed on to the customer by the firm. But overall revenue falls as customers pay less (StudyCorgi, 2022).

4.11 Confronting Industrial Disruption

There are disadvantages of a market's maturity. An IEEE Digital Reality white paper from 2019 estimates the 1995 music industry's worth at $21.5 billion, based on the sale of CDs, cassette tapes, and vinyl albums. Industry value as a whole is down by more than 50% since then. The digitalization of music has ushered in a new digital economy.

The newspaper business has also been impacted negatively by the rise of digital media. According to the white paper, print advertising income has decreased from $65 billion in 2000 to less than $15 billion in 2015. Weak gains in digital advertising have not been enough to make up for devastating losses in the print industry (Srai & Lorentz, 2019).

4.12 Scope of the Metaverse

In this day and age, one can easily imagine a virtual world where they can make a whole new environment with their real experiences. The internet became public merely three decades ago and a lot of businesses realized the importance of marketing around two decades ago. There is no need to explain how soon social media has become the part of everyone's life. If VR experts are to be believed, 93.3 million people will use AR and 58.9 million will use VR once in a month in the near future.

The metaverse can definitely be a successor of the modern internet. The emergence of AI, 5G, and edge computing will definitely make it smoother to deliver more fun, smooth, and affordable AR/VR experience in different digital devices. Industry insiders have predicted the metaverse to be the next big thing for marketers. According to Facebook founder Mark Zuckerberg, Facebook is already becoming a "metaverse" giant. The metaverse is well regarded as the beginning of the modern internet that one can be a part of rather than just looking at. It may promise vast digital worlds like the real one. The metaverse has come as an opportunity for digital marketing to engage customers in different ways.

4.13 Evaluation of Worth

The impact of digital transformation extends well beyond specific sectors to how economic value is understood more generally (Alcácer & Cruz-Machado, 2019). Particular qualities of a physical good are less important in a data-driven economy. These days, what counts most are things that are easy to use and don't waste time. Consider how the public's view of the car industry has changed over the last several decades. Historically, automakers have placed a premium on driver-centric metrics like peak speed and acceleration when designing new vehicles. Consumer priorities are shifting as ride-sharing grows in popularity and autonomous vehicles enter the mainstream. Ultimately, a passenger's comfort will take precedence over a driver's requirements.

The vast majority of individuals must also possess enough digital abilities to make autonomous and unrestricted use of e-services in a digital society. This necessitates a solid foundation for educational initiatives and continuous instruction.

Concerns about free speech, as well as the safety and viability of democracy, are warranted in light of the rise of user-specific content-generation platforms like Facebook and Twitter (Antikainen et al., 2018). The effect on elections and referendums of state-sponsored information campaigns must be mitigated.

Like all good technology paradigms, the period of technical creation was followed by one of widespread implementation. Smartphones and internet connectivity have spread at a dizzying rate. The result was the birth of what we now call "big data" and the breakdown of obstacles to global communication across space and time (Paritala et al., 2017). Rather than spreading rapidly via a single social network, a new way of thinking typically spreads slowly but surely throughout several different networks, ultimately dividing the well-off from the poor.

The ambitions of the information economy have put a strain on people's brains, resulting in the all-too-familiar condition known as "information overload." At the same time, it led to the "unreasonable effectiveness of data" in enabling AI systems to unearth previously hidden insights (Bond et al., 2018). Since the world's processing capability has grown at a pace three times faster than our information storage and transmission capacity (about 80% per year), we were able to do an automated analysis of the provided data (Ozdogan et al., 2017). Many experts now consider data-driven machine learning, such as that found in deep learning architectures' neural networks, to be the same thing as artificial intelligence (AI).

The field of artificial intelligence has made tremendous progress recently. AI has not only become an integral cornerstone of the most crucial building blocks of civilization, but it has also largely replaced humans in a wide range of intellectual jobs, such as cancer diagnosis and voice recognition (with the word-error rate of AI falling from 26% to 4% between 2012 and 2016 alone) (Carbó-Valverde, 2017). These days, most people not only trust their lives to AI in the form of autopilots on planes and anti-lock braking systems (ABS) in their cars, but also let AI shape their perspectives on culture, economics, society, and politics. One-third of all weddings in the United States are now planned with the help of AI, and AI is responsible for controlling the nation's power grid and executing seven out of ten deals on financial markets. When biological and AI components are integrated, it's game over for social scientists (OECD Digital Economy Papers 2019). Emerging negative effects of this union include loss of privacy, political division, psychological manipulation, addictive use, social anxiety and distraction, incorrect information, and pervasive narcissism.

4.14 Digital Transformation During COVID-19

There are numerous indications that the COVID-19 crisis has accelerated the global trends toward digital transformation, including the development and maintenance of digital infrastructure, firms' shift to delivering support virtually, and an expansion in the role of electronic innovations in industry Chircu et al., 2017). Even while the epidemic has hurt many companies, it has also created fresh chances for those with an entrepreneurial spirit. Changes in consumer behavior during and after the epidemic have been reflected in the rise of digital entrepreneurship (Neubert, 2018).

Since women have been hit harder than males by the global economic downturn caused by the COVID-19 epidemic, the term "shecession" has come to be used to describe it.

Increased numbers of individuals working from home, and widespread agreement that the COVID-19 epidemic has sped up the process of digitally transforming the workplace (Eurofound 2018). Those who have seen this acceleration may likely picture a future where they do their entire job online. Because of the COVID-19 outbreak, the gain of a standard situation as a reliable source of income has declined, while the value of digitalization forms of labor has soared. A growing number of people in the labor force expect that digital employment will replace conventional occupations as their primary means of financial security in the near future (Latos et al., 2018).

In the era of COVID-19, digital transformation rests on firm ground. As a result of the epidemic, more individuals are now working remotely, and this is being seen as a positive force in the acceleration of the digital transition. In addition, those who believe the epidemic has produced quick change report being more willing to work digitally solely as a result of their own experiences. Additionally, the value of digital labor as a dependable source of income has increased. There is no correlation between working from home and lower job satisfaction; instead, it is the level of personal income that matters most (Kärner, 2017).

Through COVID-19, respondents report a shift in the relative value of various types of employment. More research is needed to demonstrate the long-term validity of the claim that the COVID-19 epidemic has accelerated digital transformation.

4.15 Conclusion

Identifying where various societies are in the technology innovation and adoption cycles is essential for assessing the social and economic effects of digitization across three distinct "waves" of digitization. According to the information provided above, the first wave of digitalization saw increases in productivity, economic development, job creation, and welfare as a consequence of the widespread use of personal computers, broadband Internet access, and mobile phones. High-skilled workers have been drawn to the emerging digital sectors that have emerged as a consequence of the second wave of digitization, which is connected to the widespread use of the internet and its associated platforms like cloud computing. Nonetheless, automation has led to the elimination of positions requiring low to moderate levels of ability. The need for low-skilled employees has increased locally as a result of the rise in high-skilled jobs. As the second wave of digitalization continues, it remains challenging to quantify its associated trends consistently due to the time lag between the adoption of new technologies and the subsequent social and economic effects. Researchers believe that the consequences of automation will significantly alter the occupational profile of labor markets, especially hurting low-skilled individuals. The acceleration of these impacts is caused by the third wave of digital technology's expanding potential and the growing intangible capital of enterprises (organizational shifts, reengineering of business processes). The Metaverse provides a platform to immerse one's mind in the digital world, allowing for an immersive experience in an artificial environment with a physical presence at any place and time. This enables people to feel and see things from all across the world while sitting in one place. Robotics, 3D printing, machine learning, and big data are all examples of technologies associated with the third wave of digitization, although the study of these developments is still in its infancy. Robotics and the increased computing capacity of fields like artificial intelligence and voice recognition are blamed in some studies for the impending extinction of several occupations. However, some scholars argue that not all jobs are replaceable by automation and that the disruptive effects may be mitigated by the development of second-order employment brought about by either new inventions or higher production and expenditure. Nonetheless, these experts agree that if production doesn't rise, neither will living standards and so, second-order effects won't happen. For this reason, governments must create appropriate policy tools that can make the most of the benefits of digitalization while mitigating the dangers of disruption that come with each of its three waves.

References

Alcácer, V., & Cruz-Machado, V (2019). Scanning the industry 4.0: A literature review on technologies for manufacturing systems. *Engineering Science and Technology, an International Journal*, 22(3): 889–919.

Anh, T. (2020a). 5 Digital Transformation Trends - VnExpress. Retrieved 30 December 2022, from https://vnexpress.net/fpt-van-hanh-so/5-xu-huong-chuyen-doi-ky-thuat-so-4127485.html

Anh, V. (2020b). The Era of Digital Money. SGGP. Available online: https://www.sggp.org.vn/thoi-cua-tien-ky-thuat-so699063.htm.

Antikainen, M., Uusitalo, T., & Kivikytö-Reponen, P. (2018). Digitalisation as an enabler of circular economy. *Procedia CIRP*, 73: 45–49.

Antonopoulou, H., Halkiopoulos, C., Barlou, O., & Beligiannis, G. N (2019). Transition from educational leadership to e-leadership: A data analysis report from TEI of western Greece. *International Journal of Learning, Teaching and Educational Research*, 18(9): 238–255.

Berghaus, S., & Back, A. (2016, September). Stages in digital business transformation: Results of an empirical maturity study. *MCIS 2016 Proceedings*. 22. https://aisel.aisnet.org/mcis2016/22.

Bilgeri, D., Wortmann, F., & Fleisch, E. (2017). How digital transformation affects large manufacturing companies' organization. *ICIS 2017 Proceedings*, 1–9.

Bond, M., Marín, V. I., Dolch, C., Bedenlier, S., & Zawacki-Richter, O. (2018). Digital transformation in German higher education: Student and teacher perceptions and usage of digital media. *International Journal of Educational Technology in Higher Education*, 15(1): 48.

Boulton, C. (2020). What Is Digital Transformation? A Necessary Disruption. https://www.cio.com/article/3211428/what-is-digital-transformation-a-necessary-disruption.html.

Carbó-Valverde, S. (2017). The impact on digitalization on banking and financial stability. *Journal of Financial Management, Markets and Institutions*, (1): 133–140.

Catlin, T., Lorenz, J.T., Sternfels, B., & Willmott, P. (2017). A Roadmap for a Digital Transformation. McKinsey & Company. Available at https://www.mckinsey.com/industries/financial-services/our-insights/a-roadmap-for-a-digital-transformation.

Chircu, A. M., Sultanow, E., & Sözer, L. D. (2017). A reference architecture for digitalization in the pharmaceutical industry. *INFORMATIK 2017.* Gesellschaft fürInformatik, pp. 2043–2057.

Denicolo, P., Long, T., & Bradley-Cole, K (2016). *Constructivist Approaches and Research Methods: a Practical Guide to Exploring Personal Meanings.* SAGE Publications.

Eurofound (2018). *Automation, Digitalisation and Platforms: Implications for Work and Employment,* Publications Office of the European Union.

Gbadegeshin, S. A. (2019). The effect of digitalization on the commercialization process of HighTechnology companies in the life sciences industry. *Technology Innovation Management Review,* 9(1): 49–63.

Hartl, E., & Hess, T. (2017). The role of cultural values for digital transformation: Insights from a Delphi study. *AMCIS 2017 Proceedings.* 8. https://aisel.aisnet. org/amcis2017/Global/Presentations/8.

Heavin, C., & Power, D. J. (2018). Challenges for digital transformation–towards a conceptual decision support guide for managers. *Journal of Decision Systems,* 27(sup1): 38–45.

Hess, T., Matt, C., Benlian, A., & Wiesböck, F (2020). Options for formulating a digital transformation strategy. In B. D. Galliers, D. E. Leidner, & B. Simeonova (eds.), *Strategic Information Management* (pp. 151–173). Routledge.

Imran, M., Hameed, W. U., & Haque, A. U (2018). Influence of industry 4.0 on the production and service sectors in Pakistan: Evidence from textile and logistics industries. *Social Sciences,* 7(12): 246.

Karimi, J., & Walter, Z (2015). The role of dynamic capabilities in responding to digital disruption: A factor-based study of the newspaper industry. *Journal of Management Information Systems,* 32(1): 39–81.

Kärner, E (2017). The future of agriculture is digital: Showcasting e-Estonia. *Frontiers in Veterinary Science,* 4: 151.

Kockmann, N., Bittorf, L., Krieger, W., Reichmann, F., Schmalenberg, M., & Soboll, S (2018). Smart equipment–A perspective paper. *Chemie Ingenieur Technik,* 90(11): 1806–1822.

Kozarkiewicz, A (2020). General and specific: The impact of digital transformation on project processes and management methods. *Foundations of Management,* 12(1): 237–248.

Larsson, A., & Teigland, R (2019). *Digital Transformation and Public Services: Societal Impacts in Sweden and Beyond.* Routledge.

Latos, B.A., Harlacher, M., Burgert, F., Nitsch, V., Przybysz, P., & Niewohner, S.M (2018). Complexity diversion digitalized work systems: Implications for cooperative forms of work. *Advances in Science, Technology and Engineering Systems Journal,* 3(5): 171–185.

Luong, J. (2020). Salesforce series Part 1: Digital Transformation? Magenest. Available online: https://magenest.com/vi/chuyen-doiso-digital-transformation-la-gi/-

Matt, C., Hess, T., & Benlian, A. (2015). Digital transformation strategies. *Business & Information Systems Engineering,* 57(5): 339–343.

Metallo, C., Ferrara, M., Lazazzara, A., & Za, S. (Eds.) (2020). *Digital Transformation and Human Behavior: Innovation for People and Organisations.* Springer.

Neubert, M (2018). The impact of digitalization on the speed of internationalization of lean global startups. *Technology Innovation Management Review*, 8(5): 44–54.

New Digital Economy. (2011). Introduction. In M. Peitz & J. Waldfogel (eds.), *The Oxford Handbook of the Digital Economy*, Oxford Handbooks (2012; online edn., Oxford Academic, 21 November 2012). Accessed 28 July 2023. https://doi.org/10.1093/oxfordhb/9780195397840.002.0007.

Nham, N. (2020). Digital Currency: Trends and Management Policies. CafeF. Retrieved 30 December 2022, from https://cafef.vn/dong-tien-ky-thuat-so-xu-huong-va-chinh-sach-quan-ly-2020102807541385.chn

OECD Digital Economy Papers. (2019). http://www.oecd-ilibrary.org/science-and-technology/oecddigital-economy-papers_20716826

Osmundsen, K., Iden, J., & Bygstad, B. (2018). Digital transformation: Drivers, success factors, and implications. *MCIS 2018 Proceedings*. 37. https://aisel.aisnet.org/mcis2018/37.

Ozdogan, B., Gacar, A., & Aktas, H (2017). Digital agriculture practices in the context of agriculture 4.0. *Journal of Economics, Finance and Account*, 4(2): 186–193.

Paritala, P. K., Manchikatla, S., & Yarlagadda, P. K (2017). Digital manufacturing-applications past, current, and future trends. *Procedia Engineering*, 174: 982–991.

Priyono, A., Moin, A., & Putri, V. N (2020). Identifying digital transformation paths in the business model of SMEs during the COVID-19 pandemic. *Journal of Open Innovation: Technology, Market, and Complexity*, 6(4): 104.

Shahbaz, M. S., Sohu, S., Khaskhelly, F. Z., Bano, A., & Soomro, M. A. (2019). A novel classification of supply chain risks. *Engineering, Technology & Applied Science Research*, 9(3): 4301–4305.

Siebel, T. M. (2019). *Digital Transformation: Survive and Thrive in an Era of Mass Extinction.* RosettaBooks.

Srai, J. S., & Lorentz, H (2019). Developing design principles for the digitalisation of purchasing and supply management. *Journal of Purchasing and Supply Management*, 25(1): 78–98.

Stolterman, E., & Fors, A. C. (2004). Information technology and the good life. In B. Kaplan, D. P. Truex, D. Wastell, A. Trevor Wood-Harper, & J. I. DeGross (eds.), *Information Systems Research* (pp. 687–692). Springer.

StudyCorgi. (2022, November 7). Digital Transformation: Social Effects. Retrieved from https://studycorgi.com/digital-transformation-social-effects/

Taşaltin, N (2019). Digitalization of solar energy: A perspective. *Journal of Scientific Perspectives*, 3(1): 41–46.

The Impacts That Digital Transformation Has on Society - IEEE Digital Reality. (2022). Retrieved 30 December 2022, from https://digitalreality.ieee.org/publications/impacts-of-digital-transformation#:~:text=Digital%20transformation%20has%20a%20profound,use%20are%20the%20new%20currency.

Thuong, H, Hop, T.K., & Trong, T.D. (2019). Digital Development Perspectives in Vietnam. ICT Vietnam. Available at http://ictvietnam.vn/nhung-vien-canh-phat-trien-ky-thuat-so-tai-viet-nam-9642.htm.

Ting, D. S. W., Carin, L., Dzau, V., & Wong, T. Y. (2020). Digital technology and COVID-19. *Nature Medicine*, 26(4): 459–461.

Warner, K. S., & Wäger, M (2019). Building dynamic capabilities for digital transformation: An ongoing process of strategic renewal. *Long Range Planning*, 52(3): 326–349.

Westerman, G., Bonnet, D., & McAfee, A. (2014). *Leading Digital: Turning Technology into Business Transformation*. Harvard Business Press.

White, H. C. (2008). *Identity and Control: How Social Formations Emerge*. Princeton university press.

Yoo, Y., Boland, R. J. Jr, Lyytinen, K., & Majchrzak, A. (2012). Organizing for innovation in the digitized world. *Organization Science*, 23(5): 1398–1408.

Chapter 5

The Role of AI and the Impact of the Metaverse in Football Management and Marketing: Marketing Tactics and Strategies Used by Brands to Promote Themselves through Football Tournaments

---

Harshita Kallem, Kaushik Gurram, and Prasad Moligari
Woxsen University
Hyderabad, India

Anil Audumbar Pise
University of the Witwatersrand
Johannesburg, South Africa

5.1 Introduction

An organization's marketing strategy is a comprehensive plan to meet its long-term objectives by anticipating its customers' wants and requirements and meeting them in a way that gives it a significant and lasting edge in the marketplace. It includes deciding who those consumers are and how to

DOI: 10.4324/b23404-5

contact them (Ferrell et al., 2022). A marketing plan lays out the foundation for a business's advertising and promotion efforts, product development, strategic alliances, and market positioning. Every company needs a solid marketing strategy to grow and thrive.

5.2 Market Demand for Football

A little less than half of the people in the globe are interested in football (also known as soccer), and around one-fifth of those individuals actively play the game. Smart businesses are aware that ardent fans outperform the typical individual in terms of media consumption and planned purchases. As a result, these brands take advantage of football tournaments in order to expand and maintain their brands. Football is the most popular sport in the world and brings together millions of supporters from different countries to celebrate their favorite club teams, national teams, and the game of football itself (Morgan et al., 2019).

The sport has a special place in the hearts of billions of people, but in order for football to arrive on their televisions, in their homes, and in their stadiums, there is a team of professionals from all over the world who are skilled in a variety of areas and who work together to accommodate the enjoyment of football everywhere in the world.

5.3 The Football Marketing Strategy Based on the Four "Ps"

When it comes to sports organizations and the administration of sports, the marketing mix is of the utmost importance. In sports management instruction and online sports business education, we will learn that the "marketing mix" comprises what is often referred to as the "four Ps." Product, pricing, placement, and promotion are known as the "four Ps. Each sports company is going to use a unique blend of these four Ps in order to achieve its goals. To appeal to any specific subset of the population, each of them will provide a "differentiated product, a different price, a different location, and various promotional activities." This is true not just for local organizations but also for sports on a worldwide scale. If you are able to market your product or service to a certain demographic or audience, customers will interact with your brand more often.

The football market strategy incorporates a total of four different marketing strategies.

5.3.1 Product

The match that was broadcast to the public serves as the brand for professional clubs and the football industry. The most recent edition of the FIFA World Cup was played in 2022 and received an incredible reaction from the spectators. Thirty-two teams from five different provinces took part in the competition. As the winner of the bid, the State of Qatar was put in charge of organizing the tournament.

5.3.2 Price

The price takes into account all of the costs associated with the matches, including prize money, money for bidding, money for cooperation, transportation and lodging, costs associated with cultural activities, and everything else that has been engaged for the conduct of the match. As of the year 2021, Qatar has a plan for the investment of the International Federation of Association Football (FIFA) for the 2022 FIFA World Cup Qatar. Figure 5.1 shows the investment budget for it. For the purpose of investing in operating expenditures, a total of USD$322 million was made available. Over USD$1.7 billion will be spent on investments related to the "2022 FIFA World Cup," which will be held in Russia.

5.3.3 Place

The country of Qatar will play host to the 2022 FIFA World Cup. The matches are slated to take place in a total of eight different venues in the city of Doha, as well as the cities of Lusail, Al Khor, Al Rayyan, and Al Wakrah, which are located in the surrounding area.

5.3.4 Promotion

Promotional efforts for the world are often carried out in the form of games, contests, discount coupons, celebrity endorsements, brand collaborations, cultural events, internet platforms, or television partners. Viacom 18 served as the official television broadcaster for the FIFA World Cup 2022, and some of the celebrity guests included Sharukh Khan, Deepika Padukone, Elon Musk, and Paul Pogba (Vrontis et al., 2014). Disney and Hotstar worked together to broadcast live matches on their respective over-the-top (OTT)

1:51 ◌ ☂ Ⓐ Ⓕ •   ⏰ ⓌⓁ ⓞ ◢ 4G ◢ ▯

✕ 🔒 **2022 FIFA World Cup Qat…**   ⋘ 🔖 ⋮
       statista.com

The graph depicts the investment budget of the International Federation of Association Football (FIFA) for the 2022 FIFA World Cup Qatar by segment as of 2021. In total, 322 million U.S. dollars were allocated for investment in operational expenses. The total investment budget for the 2022 FIFA World Cup Russia amounts to over 1.7 billion U.S. dollars.

Investment budget for the 2022 FIFA World Cup Qatar, by segment

(in million U.S. dollars)

Characteristic	Budget in million U.S. dollars
Prize money	440
Operational expenses	322
TV operations	247
Club benefits programme	209
Workforce management	207
Team services	117
Other FIFA World Cup items	72
ICT	49
Marketing rights delivery	33

Showing entries 1 to 9 (9 entries in total)

© Statista 2023 ⚑

Figure 5.1 Marketing investment budget.

platforms during the tournament. Coca-Cola, Vivo, Byju, and Hyundai, among other brands, were among the promotional partners for the event. In addition, they promoted the FIFA World Cup 2022 with discount coupons, meal delivery services, and other types of promotional campaigns.

5.4 The Importance of Developing a Marketing Strategy for a Sport Such as Football

As marketers, we are always looking for new methods to increase the allure of our goods and services to potential customers. When we carry out a plan well, we know that we have created marketing juju. Brands like Starbucks, Google, Apple, eBay and Whole Foods Market all have loads of marketing juju. (Marketing Juju means mastering the art of marketing or having special powers in marketing skills.)

The firms in question do more than just catch customers' attention. They are really enthralled with them as a whole. Each of these businesses generates positive marketing karma by

1. supporting, rather than commanding the utilisation of its goods
2. building community
3. aiding customers in accomplishing their goals and dreams

(Manoli, 2022)

Putting together a marketing plan might be of assistance to you in achieving this goal. Because you want your material to be appealing and pertinent to the intended audience you are searching to engage, you may wish to assign a marcomms officer (marketing communication) to your committee so that they can assist you (Obaid, 2022).

5.5 Football Marketing Strategy

Benedek et al. (2022) said there is a plethora of free or cheap website builders out there. You don't need to be a web design expert or a developer to use many of these builders since they are built on pre-made, user-friendly templates.

On the official website of the Sydenham Football League (Wessex), for instance, you may find information about forthcoming matches, the current results, and even tweets from your favorite clubs. Providing valuable content like this will attract readers and win you the support. As a side hustle, you can utilize the club's website to sell club-related products.

5.5.1 Hosting

A football festival to honor your team and its supporters. Have some fun as a family by organizing a youth game wherein kids may sign up in pairs and play for rewards. For example, the Canton Rangers Football Club has a summer festival at a local park with games, face painting, food, drinks, and young teams from all over the United Kingdom.

As a way to remember the event, you could also hold a football festival in honor of club members who have made important contributions or who have passed away. Make the celebration even more special by designing a one-of-a-kind jersey or other mementoes that showcase your club's logo as well as the honoree's name and the reason for the celebration.

5.5.2 Community/Word-of-Mouth Marketing

It also includes providing educational opportunities at no cost. If you want to get kids in your community involved, you might host a week of free exercises or training sessions and open them up to the public. They'll bond with other members of your squad while they practice together and have a good time (Aichner, 2019). An event button badge may be personalized and given to attendees as a memento to help them remember the experience.

5.5.3 Increase Club Funding

Holding weekly drawings or lottery-style gifts or making creative use of personalized sports pins as well as badges are ways through which we can raise funds for the clubs. The best form of promotion is the yearly pin drive, in which club members and parents work together to design a unique trade pin that can be sold online, at games and festivals, and in stores all year long. Choose a different design each season so your supporters may build a collection as marketers raise money.

Include branded team uniforms and training gear as well as cheaper items like keychains and pin badges. For instance, Leicester City Football Club sells a wide variety of merchandise, including jigsaw puzzles, scarves, and even pet supplies. Individuals may add their names to LCF presents if they so choose.

5.6 Role of Artificial Intelligence in Football Marketing and Management

It has great potential for recording and forecasting such instances. Information about a fan's favorite club or player is what really gets them excited. Serving out these insights at scale and at the correct moment is the difficulty. Sportsmen, marketers, and broadcasters all benefit from AI's improved world of real-time information, having a major effect on game plans both before and during play.

The use of AI will significantly raise the bar for athletic competition. To improve its forecasts of competition outcomes, it needs improved sensors and algorithms.

The various AI tools used in football marketing include the following.

5.6.1 AI Scout

An artificial intelligence (AI) platform called Ai SCOUT is used by professional football teams and organizations to scout players using video recognition software. The mechanical, physical, and cognitive, including psychometric talents of players, as well as their overall performance, are all analyzed and evaluated by the system.

5.6.2 AI Predictive Analysis

This method powered by artificial intelligence can estimate both the total number of spectators anticipated to attend the game as well as the time they are likely to do so. This data is also useful for enhancing security and rearranging supplies in response to the volume of customers.

5.6.3 Artificially Intelligent Referees

This tool may help keep tempers down amongst coaches, players, and spectators by making fair and impartial decisions during sporting events. As an example, AI computer vision may help referees in a variety of sports determine if a penalty should be called, thereby lowering the number of controversial calls and the resulting blunders.

5.6.4 Food Visor

Each player's food plan may be tailored to their specific requirements and busy schedule. For athletes, AI may provide tailored nutrition advice depending on whether they have an upcoming match or are in recovery. Food Visor is a well-liked example of an AI-assisted diet app. Through object identification, it is able to determine the nature of meals and provide a full analysis of their nutritional value.

5.7 Impact of the Metaverse on Football Marketing and Management

The metaverse is more like the 3D model of the internet, which allows humans to experience life in a way that is physically not possible. It is completely changing the way individuals live and lead a better life. The metaverse allows one to create avatars of themselves and interact with other avatars in the virtual world. The best examples of this are games such as *Fortnite* and *Second Life*, which allows people to talk, fight, and work together on the game.

Similarly, the metaverse is also creating a huge impact in the corporate world. Especially in the marketing department, famous brands have already started making use of metaverse to create a unique identity for themselves in the customer's eye.

For instance, Hyundai and Roblox collaborated to develop the Hyundai Mobility Adventure, which enables young users to engage with other avatars and learn about Hyundai's goods and services. In 2021, Warner Bros. also held a virtual party to advertise a film, allowing viewers to partake in the celebration from the comfort of their homes.

There are various ways through which metaverse can be incorporated into the marketing of the products and services that a firm is offering.

- **Virtual events:** One form of metaverse marketing is through virtual events (as mentioned in the above example). Brands can promote, launch their products, and keep their customers engaged by conducting virtual events through which customers can interact with the brand and with each other and give back instant feedback on the new offering.
- **Networking events:** Another form of metaverse marketing is by organizing an event where individuals create an avatar of themselves in the virtual world and interact with the brand, and its executives and the brand could create an avatar wearing clothing that carries the company's logo.

There are various other retail outlets as well that allows the user to experience and be a part of their virtual retail outlet.

However, for firms to take up and make technology such as the metaverse, their business objectives and long-term goals have to be very specific and futuristic in nature.

There are various challenges that come with integrating metaverse into the business:

■ **Lack of awareness of AR/VR**: There are only a few brands, and firms that are ready to invest in VR and AR, mainly because not everyone believes their customers are ready for that kind of technology and because the investment that goes into it is huge.
■ **Privacy concerns:** There is still a lot of stigma and risk in the virtual world where data privacy becomes an issue and hence more work needs to be done in that segment to give more assurance to the customer.

5.8 Performance Marketing for Marketing Football Club

Performance marketing keeps track of many things, like when people click on display ads, sign up for emails, or buy football jerseys online. Since the advertiser only has to pay when a sale is made, they can be sure that their money was well spent on marketing.

Digital advertising platforms like Facebook Ads and Google Ads often use cost-per-click pricing as a form of performance marketing. Cost per click (CPC) is a mechanism in which advertisers only pay if and when their ad is clicked. It is essential to remember that some pricing models, such as "cost-per-sale (CPS)" and "cost-per-acquisition (CPA)," may vary significantly depending on the online channel they use (Benedek & Pedersen, 2022).

In theory, performance marketing could help (almost) any company that sells sports gear reach more people. But at the beginning, it's important to create a whole digital marketing plan instead of just focusing on one part of performance marketing (Balliauw et al., 2020).

Also, keep in mind that if you want the best results from performance marketing, your marketing efforts need to be optimized all the time. This may be a time-consuming and expensive procedure if you don't have the help of a performing marketing agency.

Methods for performance marketing:

■ **Google ads search engine advertising (SEA):** Lets you market your goods and services to keyword-searching visitors. When consumers search for "Real Madrid shirt" on google.com or bing.com, they obtain results on a search engine results page (SERP). A keyword-targeted paid text ad may appear. SEO and SEA are sometimes confused. They're unique ways that function together.

■ **Advertisements:** Display advertising on third-party websites and applications lets football teams contact prospective clients. Display advertising includes a URL to your website and pictures, videos, music, or animations displayed on desktop PCs, tablets, smartphones, or digital billboards on subways, airports, and public spaces.

A person who meets your criteria clicks on your ad, visits your website, and buys. Google Advertising, YouTube Ads, and other free web platforms may also insert display and video ads.

5.9 Engaging Fans in the Marketing Game

5.9.1 Match Reports

These are an excellent method to explain how the game has gone so that supporters who were unable to attend may still experience it. You may upload match reports (if they're not too lengthy) to your social media profiles or broadcast them on your site and offer links to them. Football enthusiasts like receiving live updates from their favorite clubs and players. Consider how much interaction football teams receive when they post anything on social media immediately after a game. Live updates maintain their followers' interest and return to your website for more.

5.9.2 Promoting Match Highlights

Fans are usually situated far from the action, thus publishing images or videos filmed on ground level near to the action allows them to appreciate the players' speed and energy. Close-up images and videos of a famous moment during the game are also terrific methods to build debate and interest within your fan community.

5.9.3 Social Media Engagement

When fans interact with professional athletes and teams' social media profiles, they become one of the millions of voices. One of the benefits of having a small football team might be the chance to connect with fans on a more personal level through social media. This entails carefully reading and responding to each comment on your page. A great way to handle football social media is to use your fans' content and share it on their accounts (with their permission, of course).

5.9.4 Behind-the-Scenes Videos/Footage

What do your guys do while they're not on the field? Some behind-the-scenes material is an excellent opportunity to highlight your players' personalities while also providing fans with a sneak peek at things like practice sessions or glimpses of a player's personal life (Henderson, 2014). Fans like having special access to their favorite athletes and becoming acquainted with them.

5.9.5 Content Marketing for Football

Clubs are realizing that the value of their "SMMS content," instead of the quantity of posts published on each platform, is the most important factor in the success of their SMMS implementation.

5.9.6 Content Calendar

All teams use a content calendar to plan posts both during the season and in the offseason (Lardo et al., 2017). This ensures timely delivery across resource-constrained platforms and consistency with other channels' information, such as the website. They normally base it off of important dates and events, such as kit releases, in the schedule.

After that, they plan each month's content, making changes as needed based on game results, league standings, and cup standings. Important dates in the club calendar. Figure 5.2 is an example of a football club promoting through Twitter. There are also important anniversaries and player birthdays to consider. It's a resource both the media and commercial teams may use. It undergoes constant revision and updating.

5.9.7 Feedback Marketing

The ability to monitor the reactions of our supporters gives us valuable insight into the efficacy of the efforts and points to areas where they may improve in the future. Many nightclubs have found that if they let people

Figure 5.2   Customer engagement.

talk and give feedback, they can get a lot more people to come. This kind of communication is important for maintaining a sense of community and unity even as the site gets read by more and more people from all over the world.

5.10 Social Media Marketing

During the 2018 World Cup in Russia, more than 7.5 billion were spent on FIFA's official digital platforms. This made it the most active World Cup in history. The best teams have tens of millions of fans and need agencies to handle their finances and client relationships. In the world of football, it is very important for social media marketing campaigns to build brand awareness and fan loyalty (Ong and Leng, 2022). The impact of fans on their favorite teams' on- and off-field results is undeniable. Organic material like matchday reporting, fan Q&As, and behind-the-scenes video in addition to paid content like friendly matches, promotions, and marketing are few forms of social media marketing.

5.10.1 Social Media (SMM)

These posts can be about different things, depending on what the clubs think their target demographics on each channel would like. They are aware that many of their fans follow them on more than one platform, each of which provides a unique experience. Facebook's algorithm favors and promotes long-form posts, but many sports teams will only use Twitter as a news feed and direct fans to their official website (refer to Figure 5.3 to know how). Because most Instagram users are young, clubs have adapted their brand's content to fit the platform. Funny and personal posts do especially well.

5.10.2 YouTube Marketing

Social media marketing includes multiple ways and multiple platforms to reach an audience. Football critics on YouTube bring more engagement

Figure 5.3   Brand awareness—Twitter.

to the match. The YouTubers make their video explaining any particular move or provide reviews on the player's performance of the live match. This brings engagement to the target audience. Marketers/football clubs can collaborate with YouTubers and reach their target audience.

5.11 Brand Campaigns for FIFA World Cup 2022

- FIFA partner Hisense partnered with Terrell Owens and Chad Ochocinco for a smart TV giveaway. A Hisense intern unintentionally picks the incorrect football players for the World Cup. The commercial featured USMNT starter, Walker Zimmerman.
- The company has also promoted World Cup travel prizes on social media. Fans may compete to win Hisense TVs, Amazon gift cards, and an all-expenses-paid trip to Qatar for the World Cup final.
- McDonald's largest ad ever, "Wanna Go to McDonald's?," is a FIFA partner. Figure 5.4 show has several famous actors. Their beating the hunger campaign was also a huge success.

Figure 5.4   Hunger campaign—McDonald.

Figure 5.5   Adidas marketing campaign.

■ Adidas, one of the most famous World Cup partners, announced their global campaign "When Football is Everything, Impossible is Nothing." In Qatar, Adidas will organize a huge fan zone. "Fans will be able to view every live game, test their talents on the specially constructed field, meet their favourite football heroes and record a variety of material using augmented reality" (Figure 5.5).

5.12 Brand Sponsorships

Here are the names of the companies that are supporting the 2022 FIFA World Cup in football.

5.12.1 Byju's

It is the biggest ed-tech firm in India, and its products are making waves in the corporate world. In 2011, its co-founders, Byju Raveendran and Divya Gokulnath, established the company. There are more than 115 million people who have downloaded the app with the intention of using it as a learning tool. Byju has made headlines for becoming the inaugural Indian official partner of The FIFA World Cup 2022. A sponsorship deal with FIFA cost Byju's between $30 and $40 million.

5.12.2 Budweiser

Budweiser is a popular beer that also has its own line of alcoholic drinks and swag. It's up there among the world's best-known beer brands in terms of recognition and consumption. In 1876, while the company was young, it launched its first product. It's the best-selling brew in the USA. Budweiser has served as the official sponsor of the FIFA World Cup for almost 25 years, and the 2022 tournament will be no different.

5.12.3 Hisense

The well-known, global Chinese multinational technology corporation Hisense specializes in consumer electronics. Since its inception in 1969 by Zhou Houjian, the firm has been providing its goods to customers all over the globe. Qingdao, China, is home to the company's main office. The FIFA World Cup has Hisense as its official sponsor.

5.12.4 McDonald's

Richard McDonald and his brother, Maurice, started the fast-food empire McDonald's in 1940, and it quickly became the world leader in the burger and French fry categories. McDonald's is a popular spot for breakfast and snacks since it is available in over 119 countries. A large portion of the population now considers the company's products to be must-haves. Due to its immense popularity, it has also signed on as the official partner of the FIFA World Cup 2022.

5.12.5 Crypto.com

An example of a cryptocurrency trade app is Crypto.com. This Singapore-based business was established in 2016 by Bobby Bao, Rafael Melo, Gary Or, and Kris Marszalek. It claims to be the most rapidly expanding bitcoin platform, and it now employs more than 4,000 people in over 100 countries. Among the sponsorship rights of the 2022 FIFA World Cup is crypto exchange crypto.com.

5.12.6 Radio Advertising

The other platforms, like new channels, radios can be used for sharing the live scores and the match highlights with the audience who could not make it to the grounds.

5.13 Conclusion

Football is the most competitive league in the world, and as a result, it draws together millions of fans from a variety of nations to celebrate their preferred club clubs, national teams, and the sport of football itself. Content marketing and social media marketing are two key tools for engaging the target audience. The most recent FIFA World Cup was the finest example of how to promote events using digital media. The popularity of football is only growing, and football clubs are able to generate cash via competitions and games centered around matches. These games and contests allow fans to practically compete alongside their favorite players.

Meanwhile, AI is going to change the future of football marketing. It will provide real-time information as well as help improve investment opportunities. AI tools are now the most used form of analytics to better understand the audience, analyze and create match reports and use it to gain better traffic in the public. It will be a learning curve for companies and technology to keep up with new media as the metaverse audiences continue to expand.

For those firms/companies who are eager to try new things, there are amazing possibilities to try and test them out. Although it might seem risky because of the investment that goes into it, it is the future of tomorrow and is more in line with millennials' thoughts and actions.

References

Aichner, T. (2019). Football clubs' social media use and user engagement. *Marketing Intelligence & Planning, 37*(3), 242–257.

Balliauw, M., Onghena, E., & Mulkens, S. (2020). Identifying factors affecting the value of advertisements on football clubs' and players' social media: A discrete choice analysis. *International Journal of Sports Marketing and Sponsorship, 22*(4), 652–676.

Benedek, J. J., & Pedersen, P. M. (2022). Challenges in the marketing of intercollegiate athletics: Perspectives of college football marketing directors. In R. M. Crabtree & J. J. Zhang (eds), *Sport Marketing in a Global Environment* (pp. 51–69). Routledge.

Benedek, J. J., Ratts, T., & Pedersen, P. M. (2022). Marketing areas of oversight and organizational elements: A qualitative examination of the marketing of a sport within intercollegiate athletics. International Journal of Sport Management, 23(2).

Henderson, J. C. (2014). Hosting the 2022 FIFA World Cup: Opportunities and challenges for Qatar. *Journal of Sport & Tourism, 19*(3-4), 281–298.

Lardo, A., Dumay, J., Trequattrini, R., & Russo, G. (2017). Social media networks as drivers for intellectual capital disclosure: Evidence from professional football clubs. *Journal of Intellectual Capital, 18*(1), 63–80.

Manoli, A. E. (2022). *Integrated Marketing Communications in Football.* Routledge.

Morgan, N. A., Whitler, K. A., Feng, H., & Chari, S. (2019). Research in marketing strategy. *Journal of the Academy of Marketing Science, 47*(1), 4–29.

Ong, W. H., & Leng, H. K (2022). Social media marketing strategies of football clubs: Limitations of social influence. *International Journal of Technology and Human Interaction (IJTHI), 18*(1), 1–10.

Vrontis, D., Thrassou, A., Kartakoullis, N. L., & Kriemadis, T (2014). Strategic marketing planning for football clubs: A value-based analysis. *Journal for Global Business Advancement, 7*(4), 355–374.

Chapter 6

Brand Management in the Metaverse

Kritika Kulkarni, V. Vikram Adithya, and Krishna Hitesh
Woxsen University
Hyderabad, India

Neelam Kumari
Dublin Business School
Dublin, Ireland

6.1 Introduction

The process of developing, maintaining, and enhancing a company's brand or brands is known as brand management. It involves a number of different strategies and tactics that are made to make a brand's identity, build brand equity, and make its target audience more aware of and loyal to the brand. Brand management is to establish an identifiable brand that interacts with users and also promotes loyalty and trust in the customers [1, 2].

Positioning, messaging, identity development, brand differentiation, communication, and brand monitoring are all components of brand management. With the help of strong brand management, it will help a business stand out from rivals, raise its profile, and boost sales and revenue. It entails comprehending the target audience, evaluating the brands of rivals, and putting together marketing initiatives and campaigns to promote the brand [3, 4].

A company can create a strong, recognizable brand that resonates with its customers and helps it stand out in a crowded market with effective brand management. It can likewise increment client devotion, drive deals, and work on an organization's general standing and monetary execution. In summary, brand management is vital to creating a brand image, brand equity, and customer loyalty, raising product awareness, and it will also promote brand advocacy among customers [5].

6.2 Brand Management in Metaverse

Brand management entails developing an engaging, immersive brand presence that is in line with the brand's values and messaging [6]. This can incorporate creating virtual conditions that address the brand's items or administrations, making marked symbols and advanced resources, and drawing in with clients through virtual occasions and encounters [2].

Companies can use the metaverse to connect with new audiences, raise brand awareness, encourage engagement, and increase sales. It requires a profound comprehension of computer-generated reality innovations, client conduct and inclinations, and the capacity to make convincing and vivid encounters that reverberate with clients.

6.3 How Can Brands Enter the Metaverse?

Businesses can utilize AR and VR to practice duties they have to perform within the company while also experiencing the metaverse within it and we can save money and customers will also be satisfied. Using gaming to its full potential, which now delivers fully realized immersive experiences that few others can match, is one of the simplest ways for companies to get started in the metaverse. The metaverse is a rapidly growing space for companies to engage with consumers and build new types of experiences for customers [5].

Brands and users can communicate with one another and with virtual items in the immersive and interconnected metaverse. Brands are starting to investigate methods so that they can interact with consumers in the metaverse as more people spend time there [7].

These are some ways that brands can enter the metaverse:

1. Identify the virtual world in the metaverse: The first step is to recognize the metaverse, its potential, and the ways in which it might be applied to interact with customers. and there are many platforms like Second Life, Roblox, and many more virtual worlds that should be studied by brands with proper research.

2. Create a metaverse plan: Brands or businesses must come up with a clear plan for their participation in the virtual world, including the goals they want to achieve, and also they must focus on their consumers so that they can achieve the goal.
3. Choose the platform: After having a clear knowledge of their metaverse goals, companies can select the appropriate platform to suit their requirements.
4. Establish a virtual presence: Brands or businesses can establish a presence in the metaverse by developing their own virtual world or by setting up a virtual shop or showroom on one of the many platforms already in use. This enables customers to engage in a distinctive and immersive way with the company and its products.
5. Create branded content: Businesses can also make entertainment that is intended to be experienced in the metaverse, such as video games, virtual experiences, and even films. As a result, the brand can interact with customers and create content for them.
6. Build an interactive experience: Businesses must provide interactive experiences that draw customers in and give them the chance to engage with their brand in novel ways. Virtual product presentations, branded games, or virtual events may fall under this category.
7. Metaverse influencers: The metaverse has influencers with a lot of influence, just like the real world, so many businesses or companies will work together with these influencers so that they may promote their brands and increase their sales.
8. Support events and experiences: Companies can also support metaverse-based events and activities like virtual concerts and gaming competitions. This enables the company to interact with customers in a unique and enjoyable way while also reaching a larger audience.

By these means, brands can successfully enter and engage customers in the metaverse by developing immersive experiences and assessing the effectiveness of their strategy.

6.4 Brand Experience in the Metaverse

Brand experience is viewed as a personal, internal reaction of the customer that encompasses feelings, information, and behavioral reactions brought on by brand-related stimuli. The design, brand identity, packaging, messaging, and settings can all include these incentives. Brakus et al.'s four-dimensional model of brand experiences includes [1]:

1. Sensory brand experience.
2. Affective brand experience.
3. Intellectual brand experience.
4. Behavioral brand experience.

The sensory dimension is based on the five human senses: touch, sight, smell, feel, and hear. The metaverse is a world where this sense can be inculcated to give a high-quality brand experience. This experience allows the users to get immersed into the brand experience that a brand wants to showcase.

Customers want more engaging encounters with brands, thanks to the increased use of video, live broadcasts, augmented reality (AR), and virtual reality (VR) in marketing efforts during the last two years [8, 9]. The pandemic's issues have prompted companies to propose novel solutions, but the immersive consumer experience offered by the metaverse seeks to give today's consumers the chance to interact digitally with companies in ways they have never had the chance to do so before.

Brands can initially take several important steps to improve their metaverse experience, including:

Set objectives,
Study and analyze the competition,
Search for opportunities and applications,
Plan the product or service entrance,
Prepare for rewards and risks.

A brand manager must think out of the box in order for them to provide creativity and storytelling objectives. Brands should create experience, starting from the customers' life cycle to purchase and after-sales services. These stages can be given a whole new experience in the metaverse.

6.5 How Can We Build a Brand in the Metaverse?

A brand is an identity for a product or service to be recognized by customers. Building a brand is not easy. Companies take years to make and build a brand. In today's world, it will not take years for anyone to build a brand. As technology and connectivity increase, it becomes easier to connect with your audience. The experience and value the brand gives to an individual make it stand out. With better customer experience, brand loyalty will also increase. Building a brand involves building an image in your customers' minds about your brand. When a brand name is heard, the customer's mind starts to associate it with what you are building.

Some steps that can be followed to build a brand in the metaverse are listed below.

1. Decide on your vision and mission.

   Your vision and mission statements are what your company values and stands for. The company will follow strategic steps to reach these goals. Every step you take will be associated with your vision and mission statements. The customers will start recognizing you by the actions you take to reach these goals. Creating a vision of what the company believes in is possible in the metaverse. The company can create a whole world about their brand and position itself clearly to the customers.

2. Target the audience.

   Understand your customers. The company must anticipate its customers' needs, wants, and desires. Your product must find the right fit for the audience [10].

   The metaverse is still gaining popularity and finding the right audience can be daunting. But, by analyzing your customers, the company can find their target audience.

3. Read your competitors.

   A company must know their competitors. Customers have the choice to choose between many players who may offer the same types of products or services. It is necessary to understand where you and your competitors are in the market. You must conduct an analysis to see the positions you stand with the competitors. Some analyses that can be used are SWOT analysis and perpetual maps [11, 12]. The SWOT analysis gives a view of the external factors that affect the company. If the customers are not satisfied with your brand, they will choose to move to your competitor. Most of the time, if the competitor offers something that you lag in or something that you are not providing, the customers tend to switch to the competitor's product or services. In the metaverse, the companies are competing for providing the brand experience. They are leveraging the gamified experience and are inculcating their brand experience in the metaverse [13].

Brands are recognized by brand assets such as logos, jingles, color combinations, brand ambassadors, mascots, etc. In a virtual world, protecting your brand assets is of the utmost importance as it holds the greatest value of a brand that is recognized.

6.6 Trademarks in the Metaverse

By deterring copycats, trademarks safeguard a company's identity and the repute of its brand(s), especially in the metaverse. The trademark registration safeguards the owner's rights and establishes the business's legal standing. Therefore, the registered trademark owner will have the only right to use it and will have access to crucial legal resources to stop unauthorized use of the trademark by other parties. The following are some benefits of trademark use in the metaverse:

1. Makes finding things easy and affordable for customers.
2. Lowers marketing costs.
3. Strengthens brand identity.

Here are the advantages of trademark registration.

Each business wanting exclusive rights to a mark in a country must register its trademark. The law secures the trademark against any violation in the physical world and the metaverse. Hence, trademark owners may file a lawsuit against infringement in virtual environments in the same way as they may do so to stop the sale of fake goods on online marketplaces. However, it is crucial to remember that a trademark for clothing does not cover virtual clothing. Thus, the mark's owner should register the mark for digital products and services. Following trademark registration, different classes of goods and services are eligible for legal protection. If a third party abuses the mark's unique qualities or reputation, the trademark owner may also stop using the mark for unrelated goods and services [14].

6.7 Trademark Problems in the Metaverse

Mixed and augmented realities have offered brand owners access to a new market and client, but they have also created issues for the owners and users of trademarks, primarily in the gaming sector. Due to the growth of user-generated material in recent years and online "virtual world" games, there are several issues with using third-party trademarks in virtual worlds. For instance, players may create virtual worlds, create and market intellectual property, and even sell branded goods for profit in a popular multiplayer role-playing game with an online economy. Users of *Second Life* may even set up an online store to sell their goods in the real world. For instance, avatars can exchange virtual goods with third-party trademarks on the market. Trademark owners must be mindful of the hazards of using their brands within those virtual environments, even though the legislation governing the use of trademarks online is continually developing [15].

6.8 Examples of Metaverse Brands

Businesses are finding various new use cases for virtual environments as interest in the developing metaverse landscape grows. Some well-known companies have developed their metaverse strategies in recent years to engage consumers better, teach staff members through immersive training, and foster cooperation.

6.8.1 Luxury Brands

Luxury companies with a long history include Louis Vuitton, Gucci, Hermes, Rolex, Prada, Chanel, Dior, Burberry, Cartier, and Tiffany & Co. They have all created powerful, identifiable brands linked to exclusivity, luxury, and excellence. These companies are now searching for strategies to increase their visibility in this new digital space as the metaverse spreads. Each of these businesses has a different strategy for developing their brand in the metaverse, but they all want to engage customers in fresh and creative ways [16, 17].

Louis Vuitton uses the metaverse to create virtual experiences that are true to the brand's heritage. The brand has launched a VR experience called "Louis Vuitton X" that allows customers to explore the brand's history and craftsmanship. The experience is designed to be immersive and engaging, giving customers a deeper understanding of the brand.

Prada is creating a more engaging and customized purchasing experience, by utilizing the metaverse. Customers may now explore the company's product lines and collections in a virtual setting thanks to the brand's "Prada Virtual" virtual pop-up store. A virtual personal shopping service inside the store allows consumers to speak with Prada specialists one on one.

6.8.2 Automobiles

The automobile industry has started using the metaverse in its platforms from design to dealerships and it would also reduce costs for the industry through virtual advertising of the products without the requirement of traditional advertising; virtual test-drives, and by this we can make sure customers understand the features of different models; and virtual showrooms where we can showcase all our cars without the requirement of showrooms, and we can also virtually customize our cars according to our imagination [18].

6.8.2.1 BMW

BMW has invested millions of dollars in CAD drawings and also in the real-time world for cars for designing cars, data-driven insights, 3D CAD designs, tracking engine performance, and many more.

6.8.2.2 Volvo

Recently, Volvo launched its new model Volvo xc40 electric recharge in the metaverse and launched the brand called Volvo verse in the metaverse for the first time in the automobile industry.

So many companies have launched their metaverse experiences in the Auto Expo 2023, like Tata, Mahindra, MG, KIA, and many more.

6.8.3 Sports Brands

The metaverse area in sports enables teams and athletes from various environments to interact with fans in a fresh, more interesting setting.

6.8.3.1 Nike

Nike is one of the most well-known athletic apparel and footwear brands. It started engaging in metaverse activities in 2021. They created and introduced Nike land, a virtual environment in the metaverse. Nike land has a lot of sporting events and keeps a sports theme throughout. A well-known site for immersive technologies, Roblox, features Nike land. Users may purchase clothing and sporting goods from Nike land using Bitcoins and use them to outfit their avatars in the metaverse. Many avatars may interact in realistic ways, and in Nike land, players can exchange their clothing and equipment after matches, exactly like players do in real life.

6.8.3.2 *Ferrari*

Ferrari and Fortnite worked together to introduce the 296GTB, a new generation of sports vehicles, in 2021. There is not a real version of this automobile model yet. Nevertheless, the metaverse version is accessible to, and used by, *Fortnite* players.

6.8.4 *Fashion Brand*

The metaverse has assisted luxury fashion firms by growing their sales and decreasing unnecessary branding costs in the metaverse. Large profit margins are also available, enabling firms to revive vintage—or old—designs and profit from them. Here are some of them.

6.8.4.1 *Tommy Hilfiger*

Thomas Jacob Hilfiger launched the upscale brand Tommy Hilfiger. It sells designer items and produces footwear, accessories, fragrances, clothing, and furniture for the house. Now, it operates over 2,000 physical stores in over 100 countries worldwide. Tommy Hilfiger has succeeded in making a reputation for itself and, like most businesses of its level, continues to be receptive to innovations and technology. By collaborating with Nintendo's 2020 social simulation game *Animal Crossing New Horizons*, it made its first foray into the metaverse. Eventually, the company collaborated with the well-known gaming platform Roblox to launch its virtual apparel line for user avatars, following the lead of illustrious companies like Louis Vuitton and Balenciaga. They are offered in 3D and 2D, demonstrating the company's dedication to providing customers with immersive digital experiences. Users may easily get 30 virtual fashion pieces from the assortment.

6.8.4.2 *Burberry*

Founded in 1970, Burberry is a renowned British fashion brand. Due to its recognizable check pattern, which gives it a strong sense of identity, it is particularly recognizable. Burberry's popularity may be because most people who wear its clothing are seen as fashionable and elegant. This premier company joins others like Louis Vuitton, Nike, and Gucci in investigating the metaverse, or the future of the internet, as most major tech entrepreneurs refer to it. They noticed that most upscale residences we studied employ online gaming as their primary metaverse entrance point. The first non-fungible token Burberry and Mythical Games created was Blanks Block Party. As a result, it produced a virtual universe known as Blanks, or vinyl toys, for any game collector who enjoys the metaverse.

6.8.5 Food Brands

Metaverse-made food firms adapt and provide a brand experience that combines their online and offline brands for consumers to enjoy, in addition to their products, in order for them to be meaningful in the virtual space [19]. Here are some of the examples.

6.8.5.1 McDonald's

For its name, logo, NFT services, food and drinks, and virtual restaurants, McDonald's submitted a trademark application. Customers of the virtual restaurant can accumulate points or Bitcoins with the metaverse, which they can utilize to purchase meals in the physical world. In February, McDonald's and creative director Humbert Leon collaborated to develop a horoscope line in the metaverse for a brief period. Fans may use VR platforms during that time to examine the zodiac collections, receive horoscope readings, and launch lanterns into the sky.

6.8.5.2 Wendy's

By its name, goods, and services, along with its cyber restaurants, Wendy's has submitted trademark applications. After seeing that Burger King kept its beef in freezers, the brand decided to enter the metaverse by sending an avatar of its brand mark into *Fortnite* to destroy every freezer in the game's "food battle mode." The company used the chance to promote its fresh, non-frozen beef in the virtual reality (VR) game, seizing the opportunity to build its brand in the metaverse.

6.8.6 Real Estate

The term "real estate" in the context of the virtual world relates to digitally created environments where customers from every corner of the world can view, use, and interact with virtual properties and real estate [1].

Real estate in VR can be purchased, bought, traded, sold, rented, and developed in the metaverse, exactly like real estate does in the actual world, but it is just not real [20]. Virtual property or land can be used to construct virtual houses, companies, buildings, offices, entertainment venues, commercial spaces, and even complete virtual towns or cities. It will have a variety of sizes, places, and characteristics. By this, you can have 100% ownership of the platform (Saengchote, 2022).

In India, a company called "proptech" has started using metaverse for real estate by showing customers 3D diagrams of the land or building and also explaining the maps nearby with multiple data layers.

6.8.7 Gaming

Gaming is the main activity that takes place in the metaverse. The metaverse is where online video games are headed. Gamers can interact with one another as well as the game world in real time in this immersive virtual setting and it will have a game environment [11, 21]. By this, we can say that players can play mini-games, online casinos, and new trial games with people around the world, without even leaving their own room. To offer customers a more comfortable simulation, the metaverse made use of MR and AR (mixed reality and augmented reality). In the future, the metaverse market will reach $1.6 trillion by 2030, from $100 billion.

For this, we can clearly say that *Fortnite* is the best example in this category. It has a massive VR world, with the largest open games concept in the world. *Fortnite* has around 250 million users per month. In this, the players are seamlessly connected to people around the world. Due to the broad appeal of its various gaming variants, and bright and colorful virtual settings, *Fortnite* has had a significant influence on the mainstream culture. *Fortnite* is now worth almost $28 billion.

6.8.8 Movies/TV Shows

Movies and TV shows can be turned into active experiences in the metaverse through virtual cinemas, virtual premieres, fan communities, and interactive experiences so that they will replicate the experience without the requirements of big screens. The fans could also attend VR with the cast or crew of the movie/TV shows and, for some fans, conduct Q&A with the cast or crew without the requirement of a physical place. By this, the producers can reduce the costs of promotions and reach more fans. It would be a more interactive activity for fans and for the cast and crew.

Zee Company, which is famous for movies and TV shows, started using the metaverse for advertising its upcoming films by bringing a set of NFTs. It has launched an innovation center in Bengaluru. The metaverse of Zee Company has already started using a combination of physical reality and VR in its app to increase customer retention. They hired more than 700 people and many new teams for this to succeed. Now their primary focus is to launch the metaverse in its app for customer satisfaction.

6.8.9 Education

There are ways that education can be turned into a metaverse because it has the capacity to reach and change the way we learn and teach. Offering innovative and engaging learning experiences outside of the traditional classroom will have the potential to change today's traditional education. Education in the metaverse will have virtual classrooms, new stimulations, and new experiences, and will be able to give worldwide experience. Teachers and students can conduct VR experiments like a virtual chemistry lab or real-time physics lab or a real environment, and many more [22, 23]. By these, children can learn more things because it would look like a cartoon show and children would be more interested in it. This would help kids understand the importance of teams, teaching, and studying and also improve their communication skills. It would make the learning experience more memorable. Education in the virtual world could alter how we teach and learn by introducing fresh possibilities for contact, connection, engagement, participation, and customization according to the world today. The virtual world will provide a strong tool for education, allowing children a fresh and innovative way to study. The metaverse is a very powerful tool for education and will play a major role in the future [24].

6.9 Impact of the Metaverse on Branding

The metaverse has been able to successfully design its own environment for brands. A more realistic experience than traditional advertising is provided by the metaverse. It can provide marketers with a fresh immersive platform to engage with consumers in new ways. It is anticipated to emerge as the new digital marketing for branding. Businesses can use 3D virtual worlds to give customers an immersive and interesting experience. As technology is evolving, we can see that it will have a significant impact on branding.

There are many ways that the metaverse could impact branding:

1. Customer experience: For any start-up or business, the customer experience is the key point. We must provide an engaging or an interactive experience for customers. This would help brands enhance the customer experience and build a strong relationship for the future [10, 25].

2. New business opportunities: The metaverse provides a unique opportunity for brands to create immersive experiences that can engage users in new and exciting ways. Brands have a special chance to develop immersive experiences that can captivate users in novel and interesting ways, thanks to the metaverse. This will provide a completely different universe in which they can have new worlds, new laws, and many more.

3. Virtual world placement: The metaverse is a way to place items in virtual worlds, such as in-game ads or product endorsements in virtual worlds. It offers businesses a new method to connect with customers [26].

4. Concerns about brand safety: It will exist in the metaverse, as with any digital platform, due to factors including the possibility of improper or counterfeit goods. The businesses may fear the metaverse because it is still in trial and we do not know what will happen in the future.

5. Brand differentiation: By providing distinctive experiences that cannot be duplicated in the real world, the metaverse gives brands the chance to stand out from their rivals. Also, it would be different from all the remaining brands. This would be a better idea for brands and businesses to have new customers.

6. New revenue streams: The metaverse might offer new ways for businesses to make money, including offering virtual items or a new type of experience inside virtual worlds. Businesses can make money by using cryptocurrencies in the VR world.

Ultimately, the metaverse really does have the potential to have a big impact on branding by introducing new opportunities for engagement and also new revenue generation. And it entirely depends on brands and the customers to properly explore how they use the metaverse to develop the brands as well as technology advances by engaging customers in fresh ways.

6.10 The Future of Brands in the Metaverse

Brand marketing in the metaverse is the production of virtual brand experiences, such as branded virtual locations or experiences that allow people to interact with a brand's products or services in a more immersive way. Brands may also need to think about how they may develop virtual versions of themselves that are congruent with their real-world brand identities. This would help brands reduce costs by a lot and brands know that the metaverse is the future.

Managing user-generated content that could not reflect a brand's values or dealing with virtual influencers are just two of the additional issues that the metaverse will have to overcome. Brands will need to be proactive in setting policies and procedures for their participation in virtual worlds and monitoring their brand reputation in these areas.

The metaverse's growing virtual surroundings, as well as the shifting preferences and expectations of users who spend time there, will probably influence how brands are managed in the future.

6.11 Benefits of Brands Entering the Metaverse

There is a potentially vast global audience that can be accessed through the metaverse. This platform can be used by brands to reach new audiences that might not be reached through traditional marketing channels and we can interact with them.

Brands can create immersive experiences that can be tailored to their target audience's interests and preferences. These experiences have the potential to be interactive, engrossing, and memorable, which can assist in fostering brand advocacy and loyalty [3].

This may result in increased customer engagement, which may ultimately result in an increase in revenue and sales. Brands can use virtual goods and services to generate revenue in new ways, thanks to the metaverse.

Brands can, for instance, sell virtual goods, provide virtual services, or even establish their very own virtual economies. The metaverse offers a wealth of customer behavior data and insights that can be used to enhance marketing strategies, personalize user experiences, and make data-driven business decisions.

6.12 Disadvantages That Brands Face

The metaverse is yet to be adopted by most of the population. Therefore, the audience or market of people is less compared to the real world.

Socioeconomic problems are one of the biggest issues. Not everyone can afford the gadgets to enter the metaverse. The older population may find it difficult to adapt to the new concept and technological concepts of the metaverse [27].

Not everyone in the younger generation is willing to enter the metaverse. An early 2022 poll taken by news site Axios and AI platform maker Momentive found that most respondents were ambivalent about the metaverse, with 60% indicating they were unfamiliar with the idea of the metaverse. Although far more respondents were "scared" than "excited" about the metaverse, 58% said they were neither scared nor excited about the coming immersive digital world (Pratt, 2022).

6.12.1 Privacy and Security for the Customers

Many customers are skeptical about their privacy and are uncomfortable with sharing their information with the metaverse or the brands they love [28]. There are many unanswered questions about how the data will be handled and what data will be collected [29].

6.13 Conclusion

Companies are motivated to connect with their customers. Connecting with their customers increases loyalty and competitive advantage. Brands are finding it difficult to give their customers their brand experiences or they are looking for a way to give a completely new branding experience to their customers. The metaverse is the key to creating a new branding experience. The customers are immersed in the brand experience that companies have provided in the metaverse. The metaverse gives companies a new market to explore and expand. The metaverse is allowing customers to connect with the brands better and open a whole new world of opportunities. The metaverse is opening opportunities, but it has barriers that need to be solved. The issues that are being faced by the brands need to be resolved and legal protection must be increased. The acceptance of the metaverse is coming soon, but until then, brands need to find ways to connect with their audience better in the metaverse.

References

1. Spajić, J., Mitrović, K., Lalić, D., Milić, B., & Bošković, D. (2022, September). Personalized brand experience in metaverse. In *10th International Conference on Mass Customization and Personalization–Community of Europe (MCP-CE 2022)* (pp. 21–23).
2. Helal, A. E., & de Marco Costa, T. Branding in the Metaverse. School of Economics and Management, Lund University. https://lup.lub.lu.se/luur/download?func=downloadFile&recordOId=9096606&fileOId=9096607.
3. Shtovba, S., Shtovba, O., & Filatova, L. (2020). The current state of brand management research: An overview of leaders and trends in branding research over the past 20 years. *The Bottom Line, 33*(1), 1–11.
4. Bushell, C. (2022). The impact of metaverse on branding and marketing. Available at *SSRN 4144628*.
5. Jeong, H., Yi, Y., & Kim, D. (2022). An innovative e-commerce platform incorporating metaverse to live commerce. *International Journal of Innovative Computing, Information and Control, 18*(1), 221–229.
6. Nalbant, K. G., & Aydin, S. (2023). Development and transformation in digital marketing and branding with artificial intelligence and digital technologies dynamics in the metaverse universe. *Journal of Metaverse, 3*(1), 9–18.
7. Dwivedi, Y. K., Hughes, L., Wang, Y., Alalwan, A. A., Ahn, S. J., Balakrishnan, J., … & Barta, S. (2022). Metaverse marketing: How the metaverse will shape the future of consumer research and practice. *Psychology & Marketing,* 40(4), 750–776.
8. Lee, L. H., Lin, Z., Hu, R., Gong, Z., Kumar, A., Li, T., & Hui, P. (2021). When creators meet the metaverse: A survey on computational arts. *arXiv preprint arXiv:2111.13486*.
9. Hirsh-Pasek, K., Zosh, J., Hadani, H. S., Golinkoff, R. M., Clark, K., Donohue, C., & Wartella, E. (2022). A whole new world: Education meets the metaverse. *Policy.*
10. Wongkitrungrueng, A., & Suprawan, L. (2023). Metaverse meets branding: Examining consumer responses to immersive brand experiences. *International Journal of Human–Computer Interaction,* 1, 1–20.

11. Demir, G., Argan, M., & Halime, D. İ. N. Ç. (2023). The age beyond sports: User experience in the world of metaverse. *Journal of Metaverse, 3*(1), 19–27.
12. Lee, J., Im, E., Yeo, I., & Gim, G. (2022, July). A study on the strategy of SWOT extraction in the metaverse platform review data: Using NLP techniques. In *Software Engineering, Artificial Intelligence, Networking and Parallel/Distributed Computing* (pp. 173–188). Springer International Publishing.
13. Czepiel, J. A., & Kerin, R. A. (2012). Competitor analysis. In *Handbook of Marketing Strategy*. Edward Elgar Publishing.
14. Park, K. (2022). Trademarks in the metaverse. *WIPO MAGAZINE,* (1), 30–33.
15. Vig, S. (2022). Intellectual property rights and the metaverse: An Indian perspective. *The Journal of World Intellectual Property, 25*(3), 753–766.
16. Joy, A., Zhu, Y., Peña, C., & Brouard, M. (2022). Digital future of luxury brands: Metaverse, digital fashion, and non-fungible tokens. *Strategic Change, 31*(3), 337–343.
17. Liu, J. (2022, December). Metaverse and brand: A study of luxury brand digital marketing strategy-taking Gucci as an example. In *2022 4th International Conference on Economic Management and Cultural Industry (ICEMCI 2022)* (pp. 1907–1913). Atlantis Press.
18. Gonzales Sepulveda, M. (2022). What is the metaverse and how is it shaping the future of marketing; the role of cultural codes in virtual experiences: A cross cultural case study.
19. CHA, S. S. (2022). Metaverse and the evolution of food and retail industry. *The Korean Journal of Food & Health Convergence, 8*(2), 1–6.
20. Azmi, A., Ibrahim, R., Ghafar, M. A., & Rashidi, A. (2023). Metaverse for real estate marketing: The impact of virtual reality on satisfaction, perceived enjoyment and purchase intention.
21. Kshetri, N (2022). Web 3.0 and the metaverse shaping organizations' brand and product strategies. *IT Professional, 24*(02), 11–15.
22. Teng, Z., Cai, Y., Gao, Y., Zhang, X., & Li, X. (2022). Factors affecting Learners' adoption of an educational metaverse platform: An empirical study based on an extended UTAUT model. *Mobile Information Systems, 1*, 1–15.
23. Hyun, J. J (2021). A study on education utilizing metaverse for effective communication in a convergence subject. *International Journal of Internet, Broadcasting and Communication, 13*(4), 129–134.
24. Zhang, X., Chen, Y., Hu, L., & Wang, Y. (2022). The metaverse in education: Definition, framework, features, potential applications, challenges, and future research topics. *Frontiers in Psychology, 13*, 1–18.
25. Ali, S. A., & Khan, R (2023). Metaverse marketing vs digital marketing. *Inter-National Journal of Innovative Science and Research Technology, 8*(1), 385–388.
26. Ning, H., Wang, H., Lin, Y., Wang, W., Dhelim, S., Farha, F., & Daneshmand, M. (2021). A survey on metaverse: The state-of-the-art, technologies, applications, and challenges. *arXiv preprint arXiv:2111.09673*.

27. Smaili, N., & de Rancourt-Raymond, A. (2022). Metaverse: Welcome to the new fraud marketplace. *Journal of Financial Crime, (Ahead-of-Print), 1,* 1–13.
28. Wang, Y., Su, Z., Zhang, N., Xing, R., Liu, D., Luan, T. H., & Shen, X. (2022). A survey on metaverse: Fundamentals, security, and privacy. *IEEE Communications Surveys & Tutorials.*
29. Zhao, R., Zhang, Y., Zhu, Y., Lan, R., & Hua, Z. (2022). Metaverse: Security and privacy concerns. *arXiv preprint arXiv:2203.03854.*

Chapter 7

Operations Management in the Indian Premier League

Rekulakunta Greeshma, Boggarapu Sudeep Gupta,
and Kalluri Poorvaj

Woxsen University
Hyderabad, India

Chinna Swamy Dudekula

Northumbria University
Newcastle, UK

7.1 Introduction

A professional Twenty20 cricket league in India is called the Indian Premier League (IPL). It is regarded as one of the most well-liked and successful cricket leagues in the world and was established in 2008 by the Board of Control for Cricket in India (BCCI). The league features eight teams representing different cities in India, with each team playing a total of 14 matches during the league stage of the tournament. The top four teams advance to the playoffs, with the winner of the tournament being crowned the IPL champion.

The IPL uses a player auction process to determine which players will play for each team in the league. Each team is given a certain amount of money to spend on players during the auction, and the team that makes the highest bid for a player is awarded that player. The league also features several international players, which helps to attract a global audience. The IPL is known for its high-energy matches, star-studded teams, and innovative

DOI: 10.4324/b23404-7

use of technology and social media to engage fans. The league has also been successful in developing a strong brand and generating significant revenue through sponsorships, merchandise sales, and media rights (Indian Premier League: How It All Started, 2013).

Operations management is the process of planning, organizing, and overseeing the day-to-day operations of a business or organization. In the context of the IPL, operations management includes managing everything from the scheduling and planning of matches to the logistics of transporting teams and equipment to venues, to the marketing and promotion of the league. Another important aspect of operations management in the IPL is the league's ability to effectively market and promote itself. One of the most well-known and widely watched cricket leagues in the world, the IPL is renowned for its creative and eye-catching marketing initiatives.

7.2 Planning Process

The planning for the IPL typically includes the following steps:

7.2.1 Scheduling of Matches

The BCCI announces the schedule for the league, including the dates and venues for all matches. The schedule is typically released a few months before the start of the league.

7.2.2 Player Draft and Auction

The teams participate in an auction to acquire players for their teams. Players are divided into different categories, such as Indian players, overseas players, and uncapped players. The teams have a set budget for the auction and can bid on the players they want to acquire.

7.2.3 Logistics and Facilities

The BCCI coordinates with the venues to ensure that they have the necessary facilities and infrastructure to host the matches. This includes setting up the grounds, providing accommodation and transportation for the teams and officials, and arranging for security and crowd management.

7.2.4 Promotion and Marketing

The BCCI promotes the league through various media channels, such as TV, radio, and social media. The teams also have their marketing and promotion strategies to attract fans and sponsors.

7.2.5 Coordination with Other Cricket Boards

The BCCI coordinates with other cricket boards to ensure that the league does not clash with any international fixtures and also to ensure the availability of overseas players in the league.

7.2.6 Player Management and Injury Management

Individual teams have their medical staff and support staff to take care of the players' fitness and well-being during the league (Chetty, 2011).

7.3 Designing Process

Designing the IPL involves several steps.

- Forming a governing council or board of directors to oversee the league and make important decisions.
- Setting the format for the league, including the number of teams, the length of the season, and the schedule for games.
- Securing a broadcast deal with a television network or streaming service to ensure that the league is widely available to viewers.
- Creating a revenue-sharing model for teams, which takes into account factors such as ticket sales, sponsorship deals, and broadcasting rights.
- Recruiting and signing high-profile players to participate in the league, to attract fans and generate interest.
- Developing a marketing strategy to promote the league and generate excitement among fans.
- Building and maintaining strong relationships with the teams, players, and other stakeholders involved in the league to ensure its long-term success.

7.4 Scheduling Process

Scheduling is an important aspect of the IPL, as it plays a critical role in determining the overall success and popularity of the tournament. The scheduling of matches is a complex task that involves balancing various competing factors, such as player availability, stadium availability, weather conditions, and broadcast schedules.

The IPL usually starts in the last week of March or the first week of April, and it runs for around 2 months. The tournament involves 8 teams playing 60 matches in total, with each team playing 14 games. Each team faces every other team twice during the round-robin format of the games—once at home and once away. After the round-robin stage, the winning team is determined by where they place on the table.

One of the key challenges of scheduling matches in the IPL is ensuring that the tournament does not clash with other major sporting events. Additionally, it also requires taking into account the player's availability, particularly for international players who may have other commitments with their respective national teams.

Another important aspect of scheduling in the IPL is ensuring that matches are played in suitable weather conditions. India's weather conditions vary greatly during the tournament period, and the scheduling of matches must take into account factors such as temperature, humidity, and the likelihood of rain (R. Saxena, 2019).

7.5 Budgeting Process

Taking into account any exceptional expenditures, such as the establishment of novel stadiums or enhancements to existing facilities.

7.5.1 Estimation of Income

Anticipating the projected earnings originating from diverse channels, including ticket sales, broadcasting rights, and sponsorships.

7.5.2 Management of Operating Costs

Evaluating the expenditures linked to the day-to-day operations of the league, encompassing player salaries, stadium rentals, and staffing outlays.

7.5.3 Capital Investments

Taking into account any exceptional expenditures, such as the establishment of novel stadiums or enhancements to existing facilities.

7.5.4 Contingency Strategy

Assigning resources to address unforeseen costs or insufficiencies in revenue.

7.5.5 Balance of Profits and Losses

Forecasting the financial performance of the league over a designated timeframe and adapting the financial plan as required.

7.5.6 Allocation of Financial Resources

Determining the distribution of the league's financial resources across different expenditures, including player remuneration, marketing endeavors, and enhancements to infrastructure.

7.5.7 Financial Oversight

Consistently supervising the financial performance of the league to guarantee adherence to the budget and implementing necessary adjustments as recommended (Malhotra, 2022).

7.6 Facilities Management

Facilities management is a critical aspect of the IPL, as it helps to ensure that the tournament runs smoothly and provides a high-quality experience for players, fans, and other stakeholders.

One of the key components of facilities management in the IPL is the maintenance and upkeep of the stadiums where matches are held. This includes ensuring that the playing surfaces are of a high standard, the stadium is well-maintained and clean, and that it has all the necessary facilities for players and fans such as seating, lighting, restrooms, food and beverage, and parking facilities, etc. These things are important to create a safe and comfortable environment for players, support staff, and fans alike.

Another important aspect of facilities management in the IPL is managing the logistics of transporting teams and equipment to venues. This includes arranging transportation, accommodation, and other travel-related needs for teams and support staff. Additionally, it also includes ensuring that all equipment, such as cricketing gear, is transported to the venues on time and in good condition.

In addition to logistics and stadium management, facilities management also includes ensuring the tournament's compliance with various regulations and laws. This includes ensuring that the tournament complies with health and safety regulations, environmental regulations, and any other relevant laws or regulations. This is to ensure that the event is safe and complies with the legal framework.

7.7 Quality Management

Quality management plays a crucial role in the IPL, ensuring that the tournament maintains the elevated standards anticipated by players, fans, and stakeholders.

A pivotal aspect of IPL's quality management revolves around the maintenance and upkeep of the stadiums where matches take place. This encompasses ensuring that the playing surfaces meet stringent safety and performance standards, guaranteeing the players' well-being. Moreover, it involves meticulous maintenance of the stadiums, providing fans with a comfortable and enjoyable experience during the matches.

Another important aspect of quality management in the IPL is the league's ability to attract and retain high-quality players. This requires a commitment to providing competitive compensation and benefits, as well as investing in player development and training programs. Additionally, it requires IPL to have a strong team and support staff who can perform their role efficiently (Shanshan Ma, 2010).

The umpiring and match refereeing also play a crucial role in maintaining the quality of the tournament. The teams of umpires and match referees are chosen with great care, and they are trained to ensure that they can make accurate and fair decisions during the matches.

7.8 Implementation Process

Implementing the IPL involves several steps, including the following.

7.8.1 Forming a Governing Council or Board of Directors

This includes appointing key members to lead the league and make important decisions.

7.8.2 Setting the Format and Schedule

This includes determining the number of teams, the length of the season, and the schedule for games.

7.8.3 Securing a Broadcast Deal

This includes partnering with a television network or streaming service to ensure the league is widely available to viewers.

7.8.4 Creating a Revenue-Sharing Model

This includes determining how to distribute revenue among teams, taking into account factors such as ticket sales, sponsorship deals, and broadcasting rights.

7.8.5 Recruiting and Signing Players

This includes identifying and signing high-profile players to participate in the league and attract fans.

7.8.6 Developing a Marketing Strategy

This includes creating promotional campaigns and events to generate excitement and interest among fans.

7.8.7 Building and Maintaining Relationships

This includes working closely with teams, players, and other stakeholders to ensure the league's long-term success.

7.8.8 Venue and Facilities

The IPL needs a proper infrastructure to conduct the league, which includes arranging the venues, facilities, and all the necessary arrangements.

7.8.9 Legality and Compliance

This includes ensuring that the league is operating in compliance with all relevant laws and regulations.

7.8.10 Auditing and Monitoring

This includes regularly monitoring the league's financial performance and making adjustments as needed (Maurya, 2009).

7.9 Roles and Responsibilities

The main roles and responsibilities of the IPL include the following.

7.9.1 Organization and Management of the League

The IPL is responsible for organizing and running the league, including scheduling matches, setting rules and regulations, and overseeing the teams and players.

7.9.2 Players' Auction

The IPL conducts an annual auction to allow teams to buy players for their squads. The league sets a salary cap for each team and sets rules for the auction process.

7.9.3 Player Regulations

The IPL is responsible for overseeing the regulations related to the players. It monitors the teams' compliance with these regulations, including rules related to player retention, salary caps, and player behavior.

7.9.4 Venue Management

The IPL is responsible for managing the venues where the matches are played, including arranging ground preparation, ticketing, and other logistical arrangements.

7.9.5 Broadcasting and Media Rights

The IPL manages the broadcasting and media rights for the league, including negotiating deals with broadcasters and streaming platforms to ensure the matches are widely available to viewers.

7.9.6 Sponsorship and Advertising

The IPL is responsible for securing sponsorships and advertising deals for the league. This helps to generate revenue for the league and the teams.

7.9.7 Anti-corruption

The IPL has an Anti-Corruption Unit that oversees the league's operations to ensure that there is no corruption or match-fixing (Rajesh. J, 2020).

7.10 Value Chain

The IPL value chain refers to the various activities that contribute to the production and delivery of the league's product (live cricket matches) to consumers. These activities can be broadly categorized into primary and support activities.

7.10.1 Inbound Logistics

This includes activities such as acquiring and storing raw materials, acquiring and maintaining equipment and facilities, and arranging transportation for players and teams.

7.10.2 Operations

This includes activities such as creating schedules, organizing and promoting matches, and maintaining the league's website and social media channels.

7.10.3 Outbound Logistics

This includes activities such as arranging transportation for fans to attend matches, and managing the distribution of merchandise and other products.

7.10.4 Marketing and Sales

This includes activities such as creating and executing marketing campaigns, promoting the league and its teams, and selling tickets and merchandise to fans.

7.10.5 Service

This includes activities such as customer service, fan engagement, and maintaining relationships with partners and sponsors.

7.10.6 Procurement

This includes activities such as acquiring and maintaining equipment and facilities, and arranging transportation for players and teams. The support activities support primary activities include the following.

7.10.6.1 Human Resource Management

This includes activities such as recruiting, training, and managing league personnel.

7.10.6.2 Technology Development

This includes activities such as developing and maintaining the league's website and other digital platforms, and developing and implementing new technologies to enhance the fan experience.

7.10.6.3 Infrastructure

This includes activities such as acquiring and maintaining equipment and facilities, and arranging transportation for players and teams.

The value chain of the IPL is a complex process with many different activities that work together to create and deliver a high-quality product to fans. The league's success depends on the efficient and effective management of these activities, as well as the ability to continuously improve and innovate to meet the changing needs of fans (Sonali Gupta, 2018).

7.11 Supply Chain

The league consists of eight teams representing various cities in India. The IPL has a complex supply chain that involves several stakeholders, including the BCCI, franchises, broadcasters, sponsors, and vendors.

The BCCI is responsible for overseeing the overall operations of the league, including scheduling, player acquisitions, and revenue generation. The franchises, which are owned by individual or corporate entities, are responsible for building and managing their teams, as well as for generating their revenues through ticket sales, sponsorships, and merchandise sales.

Broadcasters play a key role in the IPL supply chain by acquiring the rights to broadcast the league's matches and making them available to viewers on television and digital platforms. Sponsors also play an important role by providing financial support to the league and teams in exchange for advertising opportunities (Mathews, 2021).

Vendors provide a variety of goods and services to support the league, including equipment, uniforms, hospitality, transportation, and more. Additionally, the cricket players themselves, who come from different countries and have to travel to India for the tournament, also form part of IPL supply chain.

7.12 Push and Pull View

In the context of the IPL, push and pull operations refer to the strategies used to manage the flow of players and teams in the league.

Push operations involve "pushing" players and teams into the league through a variety of methods. This can include the player auction process, where teams bid on players to add to their rosters, as well as the process of team expansion and new team creation, where new teams are added to the league.

Pull operations, on the other hand, involve "pulling" players and teams out of the league through a variety of methods. This can include the process of team contraction, where teams are removed from the league, as well as the process of player releases, where teams release players from their rosters.

The IPL uses a combination of push and pulls operations to manage the flow of players and teams in the league. The league uses the player auction process as a push operation to bring new talent into the league, while also using the process of player releases as a pull operation to remove underperforming players from the league (Bagchi, 2020).

In addition, the IPL also uses the process of team expansion and contraction to manage the number of teams in the league. The league uses team expansion as a push operation to bring new teams into the league, while also using team contraction as a pull operation to remove underperforming teams from the league.

7.13 Responsiveness and Efficiency

Responsiveness and efficiency are two important factors that play a key role in the success of the IPL.

Responsiveness refers to the ability of the league and its teams to quickly adapt to changing circumstances and customer needs. This can include things like quickly addressing issues that arise during matches, such as weather delays or player injuries, or quickly responding to fan feedback and complaints.

Efficiency, on the other hand, refers to the ability of the league and its teams to effectively use resources to produce and deliver the league's product (live cricket matches) to customers. This can include things like effectively managing the league's finances, effectively scheduling and promoting matches, and effectively managing logistics such as transportation and ticket sales.

The IPL has been successful in achieving both responsiveness and efficiency in its operations. The league has a well-structured system in place to address any issues that arise during matches, such as weather delays or player injuries. IPL also has a dedicated customer service team to attend to the fan's queries and feedback. Additionally, the league has implemented technology such as digital platforms and social media to improve communication and fan engagement.

In terms of efficiency, the IPL has been successful in effectively managing its finances and resources, and in effectively scheduling and promoting matches. The league has also been successful in effectively managing logistics such as transportation and ticket sales, which has helped to increase attendance at matches.

7.14 Marketing Strategies Used

The IPL uses a variety of marketing strategies to promote the league and generate excitement among fans. Some of the strategies used in conjunction with the operations team include the following.

7.14.1 Digital Marketing

The IPL uses social media platforms like Twitter, Facebook, Instagram, and YouTube to connect with fans and promote the league. This includes live streaming of matches, behind-the-scenes footage, player interviews, and fan polls.

7.14.2 Sponsorship and Brand Partnerships

The IPL partners with a variety of brands to promote the league and generate revenue. This includes partnerships with companies such as Vivo, Dream11, and Coca-Cola.

7.14.3 Merchandising and Licensing

The IPL sells a wide range of merchandise, including team jerseys, caps, and other accessories, as well as licensing its logo and branding to other companies.

7.14.4 Event Marketing

The IPL organizes a variety of events, such as opening ceremonies, closing ceremonies, and fan events to promote the league and engage fans.

7.14.5 Publicity and Media Relations

The IPL works closely with the media to generate coverage of the league and create buzz around the matches.

7.14.6 Ambush Marketing

The IPL also uses ambush marketing strategies to reach out to the audiences, where it creates an event or a campaign that is similar to the main event or campaign, to capture the attention of the audience and divert it to the main event (Rajaram, 2021).

7.15 The Operational Approach in the Valuation of Players

The IPL uses a variety of operational approaches to determine the value of players, including the following.

7.15.1 *Performance Metrics*

Teams use a range of performance metrics, such as batting average, bowling average, and fielding percentage, to evaluate the performance of players. These metrics are used to determine the value of a player based on their past performance.

7.15.2 *Player Scouting*

Teams use a combination of scouting and analysis to identify and evaluate potential players. This includes watching live matches, reviewing footage, and gathering data on players' performance.

7.15.3 *Market Trends*

Teams take into account market trends and the demand for certain types of players when determining player value. For example, if there is a high demand for fast bowlers, the value of fast bowlers may be higher than other types of bowlers.

7.15.4 *Player Potential*

Teams consider a player's potential and future performance when determining their value. This includes factors such as age, experience, and physical fitness.

7.15.5 *Injury History*

Teams take into account a player's injury history when determining their value, as injuries can greatly impact a player's performance and ability to play.

7.15.6 *Experience and Reputation*

Teams take into account the experience of the player and reputation of the player. A player with more experience and a good reputation may attract more value than a new player.

7.15.7 *Salary Cap*

Teams also consider the salary cap when valuing players. The IPL has a salary cap for each team and teams have to make sure that they don't exceed the cap while buying players.

7.15.8 Auction

The IPL uses an auction to buy and sell players. This includes the process of bidding for players and determining the final price for each player (Navyaashali Chauhan, 2018).

7.16 Controlling Process

The IPL has a complex organizational structure, with multiple stakeholders involved in controlling the various processes of the league. Some of the key controlling processes in the IPL include the following.

7.16.1 Governance

The BCCI is the governing body for cricket in India, and it is responsible for the overall organization, management, and control of the IPL. The BCCI has a governing council that is responsible for making decisions about the league, such as setting the rules and regulations, approving teams, and determining the schedule and venues for matches.

7.16.2 Player Acquisition

The teams in the IPL acquire players through a player auction or by trading with other teams. The BCCI sets the rules and regulations for the player acquisition process, and the teams are controlled by their owners and management.

7.16.3 Match Operations

The BCCI is responsible for organizing and controlling the operations of the matches, such as scheduling, venues, umpires, and security. The league also has an Anti-Corruption Unit in place to monitor and control any potential corruption or illegal activities.

7.16.4 Financial Management

The IPL has a complex financial structure, with revenues generated from various sources such as broadcasting rights, sponsorship, and ticket sales.

The BCCI is responsible for managing and controlling the league's finances and for distributing the revenue among the teams and other stakeholders.

7.16.5 Branding and Promotion

The BCCI is responsible for promoting and branding the league, through marketing campaigns, partnerships, and sponsorships, among other things.

7.16.6 Doping Control

The IPL also has an Anti-Doping Unit that is responsible for monitoring and controlling the use of performance-enhancing drugs (PEDs) among players. The unit conducts regular testing of the players and takes action against those who are found to have violated the rules.

7.17 Statistical Methods Used

In the IPL, various statistical methods are used to analyze the performance of teams, players, and matches. Some examples of statistical methods used in the IPL include the following.

7.17.1 Descriptive Statistics

This is used to summarize and describe the data, such as mean, median, mode, and standard deviation. This helps to understand the performance of teams and players in terms of runs, wickets, and other statistics.

7.17.2 Inferential Statistics

This is used to make predictions about population parameters based on sample data. Teams use inferential statistics to make predictions about the outcome of matches and the performance of players.

7.17.3 Time-series Analysis

This is used to identify trends and patterns in the data over time. This helps teams to identify trends in the performance of players and teams across the seasons.

7.17.4 Probability Distributions

This is used to model the likelihood of different outcomes. This helps teams to understand the probability of a player scoring a certain number of runs or taking a certain number of wickets in a match.

7.17.5 Hypothesis Testing

This is used to test assumptions about population parameters. Teams use this method to test assumptions about the performance of players and teams.

7.17.6 Correlation and Regression

This is used to understand the relationship between two variables. Teams use this method to understand the relationship between various performance metrics and the outcome of matches.

7.17.7 Machine Learning

This is used to analyze large data sets and make predictions. Teams use this method to analyze the performance of players and teams and to make predictions about the outcome of matches (Mantri, 2021).

7.18 How Statistical Methods Are Used

Statistical methods are widely used in the IPL to analyze performance data, predict outcomes, and make strategic decisions. Some examples of how statistical methods are used in the IPL include the following.

7.18.1 Player Analysis

Teams use statistical methods to analyze player performance data, such as batting averages, bowling averages, and fielding percentages. This data is used to identify strengths and weaknesses, make roster decisions, and set player performance goals.

7.18.2 Game Analysis

Teams use statistical methods to analyze match data, such as team scores, run rates, and wicket-taking patterns. This data is used to identify trends and make tactical decisions, such as team selection and field placement.

7.18.3 Predictive Modeling

Teams and broadcasters use statistical methods to make predictions about the outcome of matches and the performance of players. This can include predicting the probability of a team winning a match, or the likelihood of a player scoring a certain number of runs.

7.18.4 Audience Analysis

Broadcasters use statistical methods to analyze audience data, such as viewership numbers, to understand which matches and players are most popular among viewers. This information can be used to make scheduling decisions and adjust advertising rates.

7.18.5 Business Analysis

IPL management uses statistical methods to analyze various business-related data, such as ticket sales, merchandise sales, and digital engagement, to understand the financial performance of the league and make strategic decisions to maximize revenue.

References

Bagchi, A. (2020). *Academia*. Retrieved from https://www.academia.edu/44721915/IPL_as_a_Catalyst_for_Sports_Tourism_in_India_a_Learning_Curve_for_Other_Indian_Leagues

Chetty, P. (2011, September 18). *Project Guru*. Retrieved from https://www.projectguru.in/marketing-strategies-of-ipl/

Indian Premier League: How It All Started. (2013, April 2013).

Malhotra, G. (2022). A comprehensive approach to predict auction prices and economic value creation of cricketers in the Indian Premier League (IPL). *Journal of Sports Analytics, 8*(3), 149–170.

Mantri, Y. (2021). A statistical analysis of the Indian premiere league. *International Journal of Statistics and Applied Mathematics 2021, 6*(4), 16–22.

Mathews, S. (2021, June 9). 5 supply chain lessons from Indian premier league.

Maurya, A. (2009). IPL: Birth of cricketainment: A case study on sports marketing by board of control for cricket in India.

Navyaashali Chauhan, P. J. (2018). A study of the application of operations research in the valuation of players in IPL.

Rajaram, B. (2021, April 6). *The Strategy Story*. Retrieved from https://thestrategystory. com/2021/04/06/ipl-marketing-strategy/

Rajesh. J, R. M. (2020). A critical study on Indian Premier League (IPL) and Its marketing implication to overcome the challenges of controversy, clutter and significance beyond cricket.

Saxena, R. K. (2019). Sports analytics: Indian premier league scheduling problem.

Shanshan Ma, C. L. (2010). Evaluating the metadata quality of the IPL.

Sonali Gupta, A. R. (2018). *EMBA Pro*. Retrieved from https://embapro.com/ frontpage/portervaluechainanalysis/20929-ipl-league

Chapter 8

Impact of Metaverse in the Supply Chain, Logistics, and Manufacturing Sector

Guda Vineeth Reddy, Dr. Hemachandran K.,
and Hitesh Kumar Devaki
Woxsen University
Hyderabad, Telangana, India

Zita Zoltay Paprika
Corvinus University
Budapest, Hungary

8.1 Introduction

The concept of the "metaverse" refers to a shared virtual world in which users may communicate and interact with one another as well as with digital objects. By merging virtual reality (VR), augmented reality (AR), and other digital technologies, consumers are provided with a smooth and immersive experience. The metaverse's function in production, logistics, and supply chains: The metaverse may have an impact on the industrial, logistics, and supply chain industries. The integration of VR and AR technologies in the metaverse may provide new opportunities for businesses to improve their operations, increase efficiency, and save money.

The purpose of the chapter is to provide a comprehensive overview of how the metaverse may affect the manufacturing, logistics, and supply chain industries. It intends to investigate how businesses may enhance

DOI: 10.4324/b23404-8

quality assurance, decrease waste, and optimize manufacturing processes by utilizing VR and AR technology inside the metaverse. It will also go over how the metaverse might open up new doors for cooperation, communication, and innovation in the manufacturing, logistics, and supply chain industries.

8.2 Literature Review

The metaverse concept has recently gotten a lot of interest due to the advancement of virtual and augmented reality technologies. The metaverse is a completely immersive, interconnected virtual environment that allows users to interact with one another and their surroundings in a way similar to that experienced in real life. This technology has the potential to transform several industries, including business.

Companies are already investigating the metaverse's potential for developing cutting-edge new goods and services. Businesses in the entertainment industry, for example, employ the metaverse to give clients with immersive experiences. *Fortnite*, a popular video game, has created its own metaverse, allowing users to engage in virtual activities and communicate with one another in a virtual setting.

The retail sector offers a lot of promise for the metaverse. Businesses may utilize the technology to build virtual stores that enable people to browse and buy goods in a fully realistic setting. This may result in a brand-new kind of purchasing experience that is more involved and engaging than standard internet shopping.

New options for corporate training and education might be made possible via the metaverse. Through the use of immersive training programs that imitate real-world situations, businesses may provide staff members the chance to practice their skills in a secure setting. This might be especially helpful in fields like health care or manufacturing, where practical training is necessary but can be challenging to offer.

Virtual conferences and meetings are yet another possible commercial use for the metaverse. The prevalence of remote work and the COVID-19 epidemic have both increased the frequency of virtual meetings. By building completely immersive settings that give participants the impression that they are truly in the same physical area, the metaverse has the potential to advance virtual meetings. This may make online meetings more interesting and effective.

The Metaverse has advantages, but it also has significant barriers to its usage in business. One of the most significant barriers is the cost of developing and implementing the technology. A completely immersive virtual world necessitates a significant investment in both technology and content creation. There are also concerns regarding data security and privacy, as well as accessibility and diversity issues.

The metaverse has the potential to revolutionize many aspects of society, including business. Its immersive and networked qualities may offer up new avenues for growth and innovation. Businesses must carefully consider these risks before investing in the technology because there are significant barriers to its adoption.

8.3 The Role of Virtual Reality (VR) and Augmented Reality (AR) in the Metaverse

How the metaverse makes use of VR and AR technologies is an important component of the metaverse. Users may engage with virtual settings as if they were in the real world, thanks to VR. AR, on the other hand, superimposes digital data over the user's perception of the outside environment. Users of the metaverse can have a more engaged and interesting experience by utilizing both VR and AR technology [1]. The supply chain, logistics, and industrial industries may all profit from the employment of VR and AR in the metaverse. By offering a shared virtual space where they may collaborate in real time, for instance, VR and AR can be used to enhance cooperation and communication among suppliers, manufacturers, and distributors. Furthermore, the utilization of VR and AR may be made to provide a more engaging and dynamic consumer experience, which may boost sales and customer loyalty. VR and AR may be utilized in logistics to streamline routes, lower the possibility of delays or accidents, and enhance employee training. VR and AR may be utilized in manufacturing to increase quality control, streamline production, and cut down on waste. Manufacturers may acquire real-time insights into their operations and make data-driven choices by building digital twins of their physical assets [2]. Workers may be trained via VR and AR, which enables them to gain new skills and enhance their performance, increasing productivity and reducing costs. In the end, the employment of VR and AR in the metaverse can provide companies in the manufacturing, logistics, and supply chain sectors new chances for cooperation, communication, and innovation, resulting in increased effectiveness and cost savings.

8.4 Supply Chain Management in the Metaverse

Supplier, manufacturer, and distributor virtual cooperation and communication: The metaverse can facilitate supplier, manufacturer, and distributor virtual collaboration and communication. Businesses are able to exchange real-time information and take quicker choices by offering a shared virtual environment. For instance, suppliers may exhibit their goods using VR and AR in a more dynamic and engaging way, giving manufacturers a chance to see how the items will fit into their workflows [3]. Faster product development and increased supply chain effectiveness may result from this. Additionally, virtual conferences and meetings may be held in the metaverse, enabling distributors, producers, and suppliers to connect and work together in real time, regardless of where they are physically located.

8.4.1 Improved Customer Experience with VR and AR

Additionally, the metaverse can deliver a more engaging and participatory user experience. Customers may use VR and AR, for instance, to picture how things will work in their homes or how a car would operate on the road. Sales and customer loyalty may rise as a result, increasing consumer involvement and satisfaction. Customers may also virtually visit businesses and showrooms using VR and AR [3], which enables them to engage with things in a more engaging way even when they are unable to physically visit the store. Additionally, it could result in more sales and devoted clients.

8.4.2 Potential Impact on Sales and Customer Loyalty

Sales and client retention can be greatly affected by the metaverse. Businesses may boost customer happiness and engagement, which will result in more sales, by offering a more immersive and engaging customer experience. Additionally, by enabling customers to picture how things will fit into their lives, firms may boost customer loyalty since clients are more inclined to select their goods over those of rivals [3] while doing so.

The metaverse can also contribute to the improvement of the supply chain's efficiency, which can result in cheaper costs and more sales, by facilitating virtual cooperation and communication among suppliers, manufacturers, and distributors.

The supply chain, logistics, and manufacturing industries may all benefit from the metaverse by making use of the increased opportunities for cooperation, communication, and innovation it offers. Businesses may optimize manufacturing processes, boost quality assurance, and cut waste to increase efficiency and lower costs by utilizing VR and AR in the metaverse. The metaverse may also boost client engagement and happiness by offering a more immersive and engaging customer experience, resulting in greater sales and customer loyalty.

8.5 Logistics and Transportation in the Metaverse

8.5.1 Use of Digital Twins for Logistics Management

Virtual versions of actual assets including trucks, storage facilities, and cargo are known as digital twins [4]. In order to optimize their routes and lower the possibility of delays or accidents, they may give logistics businesses real-time information about the whereabouts and condition of their assets. For instance, digital twins of automobiles can offer details on the location, speed, fuel usage, and maintenance status of the vehicle, which can be used to optimize routes and cut down on fuel usage. Additionally, by providing details on the location and state of inventory, digital twins of warehouses may help logistics businesses improve their inventory control.

8.5.2 VR and AR for Logistics Worker Training and Simulations

Training and simulations for logistics workers may also be done using VR and AR. For instance, using VR to replicate various driving circumstances enables drivers to hone their abilities in a secure and controlled setting. In order to help drivers make better judgments, AR may also be utilized to give them real-time information on the weather, traffic, and other elements that may impact their travels. Additionally, personnel may be trained in other logistics-related duties including freight loading and unloading, inventory control, and warehouse operations using VR and AR [4].

8.5.3 *Potential Impact on Efficiency and Cost Savings*

Efficiency gains and cost reductions may be substantial when using VR/AR and digital twins for worker training and logistical management. Digital twins can help logistics organizations optimize their routes and use less fuel, which lowers costs by giving real-time information about the location and condition of assets. Additionally, VR and AR may help workers develop their abilities and lower their risk of accidents by giving them immersive and interactive training, which will enhance productivity and cut costs. Additionally, the deployment of digital twins can lower the risk of stockouts and overstocking by enabling logistics organizations to optimize their inventory management, which results in extra cost savings.

By presenting fresh options for cooperation, communication, and invention, the metaverse has the potential to revolutionize the logistics and transportation industry. Logistics businesses may optimize their routes and lower the possibility of delays or accidents by using digital twins [5] in logistics management to offer real-time information on the location and state of assets. Additionally, the use of VR and AR in training and simulations for logistics workers can assist by enhancing worker abilities and lower the chance of accidents, which will increase efficiency and save costs. To ensure the secure and moral use of these technologies, as with any new technology, there are issues about data privacy and security that must be resolved.

8.6 Manufacturing in the Metaverse

Digital twins are virtual versions of actual assets including machinery, equipment, and production lines that are used for production optimization. They may give manufacturers instantaneous insights into their processes, enabling them to enhance quality assurance and decrease waste [6]. Digital twins of machines, for instance, can offer details on the performance of the machine, such as its speed, temperature, and vibration, enabling producers to see and fix issues before they arise. Manufacturers may improve their inventory management by using digital twins of manufacturing lines to offer details on the location and state of their goods.

8.6.1 *VR and AR for Worker Training and Skill Development*

VR and AR may also be used for worker skill development and training. Workers can practice their skills in a safe environment using VR, for example, to simulate different manufacturing situations. AR can also be used to provide workers with real-time data on machine performance, including as temperature, speed, and vibration, to assist them make better decisions. Workers may also receive training utilizing VR and AR for other manufacturing-related professions including quality control, inventory management, and equipment maintenance [6].

8.6.2 *Potential Impact on Productivity and Cost Savings*

The use of digital twins and VR/AR in production has the potential to greatly boost productivity and reduce costs. Digital twins [5] could aid firms in streamlining their processes, improving quality assurance, and reducing waste, which would increase output and lower costs. By providing in-the-moment information on the production process, they do this. By providing workers with immersive and interactive training, VR and AR may also help them improve their skills and reduce the chance of accidents, which can increase productivity and reduce expenses. Additionally, by helping manufacturers to optimize their inventory management and achieve additional cost savings, the use of digital twins can reduce the risk of stockouts and overstocking.

8.7 Conclusion

A shared virtual environment that enables people to connect with one another and digital goods, the metaverse has the potential to alter a number of industries, including the supply chain, logistics, and industrial sectors. VR and AR technology integration in the metaverse can open up new possibilities for organizations to enhance operations, boost efficiency, and make cost savings.

The supply chain's virtual cooperation and communication between suppliers, manufacturers, and distributors can be facilitated by the metaverse, allowing these parties to share real-time information and make speedier decisions. Because VR and AR allow users to see objects and comprehend how they fit into their lives, customers may also enjoy a more immersive and engaging experience. This might lead to more sales and more devoted customers.

Digital twins, which are virtual representations of tangible assets like trucks, warehouses, and freight, may be used in logistics, thanks to the metaverse. By giving logistics organizations access to real-time data on the whereabouts and condition of their assets, they can optimize their routes and lower the likelihood of delays or accidents. Additionally, the usage of VR and AR may offer training and simulations to logistics professionals to enhance their abilities, making them more productive and lowering the chance of accidents.

Digital twins can be used in the industrial industry to streamline operations, boost quality assurance, and cut down on waste. Additionally, the utilization of VR and AR may provide staff members realistic, interactive training that will help them pick up new skills and perform better. Increased productivity and cost savings may result from this.

Future study directions: The metaverse is still a young area, and more effort is needed to fully realize its promise. One potential future study field is examining the implications of the metaverse on various enterprises such as health care, education, and entertainment.

■ Analyzing the moral and sociological ramifications of the metaverse, including data security and privacy, the effect on jobs, and the possibility of a digital divide.
■ Creating new technologies and algorithms that can enhance user experience and open the door to new metaverse use cases.
■ Analyzing the metaverse's economic effects and how they may open up new commercial and entrepreneurial prospects.

Implications for businesses and policymakers: Its growth and possible effects should be monitored by companies and politicians. The metaverse can offer new chances for cooperation, communication, and creativity for organizations, which can increase productivity and save costs. As a result, companies should investigate how VR and AR are used in the metaverse and think about how to integrate them into their daily operations.

The metaverse can have a big impact on the economy and different industries for policymakers. Therefore, legislators should take into account the metaverse's potential effects on various businesses as well as its sociological and ethical consequences. Additionally, they ought to think about how to encourage the metaverse's growth and guarantee that it is utilized in a morally and safe manner. This can contain rules and policies for data security and privacy as well as recommendations to promote the creation of novel technology and applications. Additionally, they should think about the possible effects on employment and the danger of the digital divide and take the appropriate steps to lessen such negative effects.

References

1. Weinberger M. What Is Metaverse?—A Definition Based on Qualitative Meta-Synthesis. Future Internet. 2022; 14(11):310. https://doi.org/10.3390/fi14110310.
2. McKinsey & Company (2020). Digital twin: What it is and why it matters. mckinsey.com/business-functions/digital-mckinsey/our-insights/digital-twin-what-it-is-and-why-it-matters.
3. Akbari, M., Ha, N. and Kok, S. (2022), "A systematic review of AR/VR in operations and supply chain management: maturity, current trends and future directions", Journal of Global Operations and Strategic Sourcing, Vol. 15 No. 4, pp. 534–565. https://doi.org/10.1108/JGOSS-09-2021-0078.
4. Szymon Machała, Norbert Chamier-Gliszczyński, Tomasz Królikowski, "Application of AR/VR Technology in Industry 4.0.", Procedia Computer Science, Volume 207, 2022, Pages 2990–2998, https://doi.org/10.1016/j.procs.2022.09.357.
5. Kinsner, W. (2021). Digital twins for personalized education and lifelong learning, 2021 IEEE Canadian Conference on Electrical and Computer Engineering (CCECE), pp. 1–6. doi: 10.1109/CCECE53047.2021.9569178
6. F. Pires, A. Cachada, J. Barbosa, A. P. Moreira and P. Leitão, "Digital Twin in Industry 4.0: Technologies, Applications and Challenges," 2019 IEEE 17th International Conference on Industrial Informatics (INDIN), Helsinki, Finland, 2019, pp. 721–726, doi: https://doi.org/10.1109/INDIN41052.2019.8972134.

Chapter 9

Influence of Artificial Intelligence in Consumer Decision-Making Process

Divya Gutti, Goda Vardhini Yadav, and Harshitha Kaja
Woxsen University
Hyderabad, Telangana, India

Objectives

To study the influence of artificial intelligence on the consumer decision-making process.

To study the impact of search engine optimization on the consumer buying decision.

To study the impact of AI on buying habits of the consumer.

To study the impact of the automation of AI in the consumer buying decision process.

9.1 Introduction

Consumer decision making: The concept of decision making can be defined as a rational process of selecting the alternatives that are expected to result in the most preferred outcome. It can also be defined as "finding and listening to the alternatives, rating their consequences, and comparing the correctness and efficiency of each of these outcomes." This approach

DOI: 10.4324/b23404-9

is gaining traction in the marketing sector. It assists businesses in better knowing their customers (Stankevich, 2017).

According to Solomon, Russell-Bennett, and Previte (2015), there are three types of decision making based on the elements that influence a customer's purchase decision, such as external, sociocultural influences or a lack of information about the desired or necessary items.

Habitual: This kind of choice is so ubiquitous that it is referred to as "routine" decision making. This happens when people do not seek information when they encounter a problem. The decision is straightforward because of what people generally do (Solomon, Russell-Bennett, & Previte, 2015); when more than one person makes a choice, it is referred to as a collective decision. This means that other people help determine how to solve the problem. In accordance with Solomon et al.'s research in 2015, when numerous individuals collectively determine a product or service for the needs of multiple individuals, they engage in the decision-making process.

Cognitive: This is the most common way of making decisions, and it is seen to be the best way to understand how consumers act. Customers react cautiously in this situation, acquiring as much information as possible and carefully assessing all of their options (Solomon, Russell-Bennett, & Previte, 2015).

Purchases are made by consumers. The study of how people, organizations, and companies choose, acquire, use, and discard ideas, commodities, and services to meet their wants and preferences is known as consumer behavior. Marketers must pay closer attention to how people buy in order to understand what they want.

When a product is selected or bought by the end user, the consumer buying process begins. It is a complicated process that involves recognizing a need, gathering information, evaluating possibilities, making a buying decision, and determining what to do with the goods once acquired. It also defines the processes that an individual or organization will follow to make a purchase decision. Each case has many stages:

Consumer buying process (individual buyers):

- **Need recognition:** Consider this variable to represent the consumer's starting point for decision making. When a "problem," "need," or "want" is recognized by the client, something happens. When a client feels that a new product will solve an existing need, this "problem" or "need" is noted. There are two methods for assessing what someone needs. The first kind arises when a consumer discovers a fault when the product stops working and requires a replacement. The second kind is when a consumer wants a new product, even if he or she does not require it (Panwar, Anand, Ali, & Singal, 2019).

■ **Information search:** When a consumer establishes what he or she needs, he or she starts looking for ways to meet that need. The term "information search" refers to the act of gathering information about a product that meets your needs. Customers get information not just about commodities and goods, but also from other people via recommendations and prior experiences. To make an educated selection, the consumer must develop a list of benefits and negatives (Panwar, Anand, Ali, & Singal, 2019).

■ **Evaluate alternatives:** At this moment, the consumer has acquired all of the essential information, identified his best possibilities, and finally decided on what he needs. At this point, the customer will start looking for the best deal, which might be based on price, quality, or any other criterion that is important to the buyer (Stankevich, 2017).

■ **Product choice:** The consumer has made a buying decision based on all of the information gathered. At this point, the customer is certain of what he wants to acquire and why (Stankevich, 2017).

■ **Post-purchase evaluation:** This is considered the most important stage for both the organization and the customer. If the customer realizes that the product fulfills or exceeds the promises made and his own expectations, he may be able to persuade others to buy it.

Cognitive dissonance: It is a stage in which the customer is dissatisfied with his or her purchasing choice.

Consumer buying process (organizational buyers): Before buying a product, consumers recognize a need, obtain information, evaluate it, decide on a purchase, and take action. Business and institutional markets make purchase decisions following a transparent process involving many participants. Understanding the numerous processes of buying might help industrial marketers sell more.

Organizational buyers make a multi-step choice. The product you seek determines the relevance of each step. Industrial marketers must understand purchasing decision processes and purchase situations to offer products and services. Robinson, Faris, and Wind invented "buy-phases" in 1967. The procedure for making company purchase decisions involves eight distinct steps, such as.

1. Recognition of a problem
2. Description of the need
3. Product specification
4. Supplier search
5. Proposal solicitation
6. Supplier selection
7. Order routine specification
8. Performance review

Artificial intelligence role in decision-making process: Machines can now accomplish everything a human can do, including making judgments. AIs imitate human intelligence. We can safely declare that artificial intelligence is smart enough to be deployed for practical purposes after almost a decade of note-taking. AI will transform many sectors. AI should impact people's daily lives beyond business. Because consumers and companies who interact throughout the buyer's journey generate more ideas, most individuals believe AI will impact manufacturing more than any other manufacturing industry. Recent study has shown that AI has far-reaching user implications. AI also alters purchasing behavior. Many programs may analyze browser history to reveal a person's decision-making process. Watching these programs on a mobile device may make you want the offered goods. Companies are utilizing AI to influence customers' opinions of their products.

Patterns of decision-making processes with AI involved: We analyze its outcomes using the dynamic decision-making theory, which involves considering all possibilities before choosing one. Option assessment involves gathering facts, assessing options, and planning before making a decision. Executing a decision is termed "execution" when someone buys something. At the decision's feedback stage, we evaluate the outcomes to determine whether they were good, matched customer requirements, and functioned properly. All comments and ideas may be utilized in the future allocated phases to make another purchase option or a modified one. AI makes these three decision-making processes unnecessary (assessment, execution, feedback). This study presents seven AI selection models. These recurring themes show how humans and AI work together to evaluate possibilities, choose a path, and interpret the outcomes. Patterns include evaluator, evaluator with hindsight, completely automated, informed

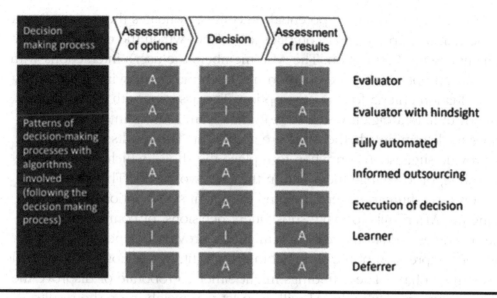

Decision making process	Assessment of options	Decision	Assessment of results	
Patterns of decision-making processes with algorithms involved (following the decision making process)	A	I	I	Evaluator
	A	I	A	Evaluator with hindsight
	A	A	A	Fully automated
	A	A	I	Informed outsourcing
	I	A	I	Execution of decision
	I	I	A	Learner
	I	A	A	Deferrer

Figure 9.1 Overview of patterns of decision-making process with AI involved. (Leyer, Oberlaender, Dootson, & Kowalkiewicz, 2020.)

outsourcing, executioner, learner, and deferrer (Figure 9.1). When AI makes all choices, each pattern is entirely automated, but a human may augment it at any time by handing over automatic execution to AI. Each pattern is discussed and presented with examples of goods and services to demonstrate how abstract they are.

Evaluator: In this strategy, AI provides people with a selection of alternatives that have been scored according to one or more criteria that they first provide (the decision maker). AI first looked for solutions that meet these requirements, ranked them, and then looked for more. In a world where decisions can be made automatically, all a person must do is choose the best option. In this case, the results are not assessed. A flight-booking website that provides the best options based on the travel time, cost, and number of stops for the specified dates and destinations is an example of the evaluator pattern. When a human uses AI to help them decide, they either give the AI a list of options to choose from or they use the AI's results as a jumping-off point for further investigation. In this scenario, a human would look at the data and try to find other options for flying that the AI hadn't thought about. This process may be repeated when a human feeds the AI new information to improve its decision making. Having gained wisdom via prior encounters, in this strategy, AI presents people with a set of options that have already been prioritized according to a set of criteria. The human then makes a choice, and the AI evaluates the outcome. The AI looks for potential outcomes, evaluates them according to predetermined criteria, and compiles a list from which the decision maker can choose the best option. The AI remembers the user's interactions with the chosen option after the decision has been made, allowing it to modify its evaluation criteria for the next option. The assessor with a hindsight pattern utilizes a digital watch to read data from sensors in the runner's shoes to determine whether they are a good fit. The results may be used to provide suggestions on when to replace the shoes, which shoe to buy next time, or to change them within the first two weeks. The improved version has a human either providing the initial set of options to an AI, using the AI's results to make subsequent decisions, or commenting on the outcomes. Additional feedback might be provided, depending on the wearer's impression of the shoe's comfort and fit, in addition to the specified assessment phase. These findings might either corroborate or disprove the AI's conclusion. Maybe the AI will even let you weigh in on the results of its assessment. All decision making in this design is performed by AI without any human involvement. The AI considers potential courses of action, ranks them in terms of importance, ultimately settles on one, and then collects data to inform its future decisions. A dishwasher equipped with sensors to predict when the detergent box will need to be refilled represents a fully automated routine. The machine predicts how dirty it will become, how long and how hard the cleaning program can run, and how much detergent has already been used, and then decides when to make more detergent available. After gathering this information, the AI will utilize it to look for detergents for sale on trading platforms, eventually selecting and placing orders based on the efficiency with which the detergent has been used in the past. Consumption efficiency is measured by comparing the amount of detergent used to clean the dishes with the amount of detergent loaded into the dishwasher manually. In the future, this will help the ordering process make better decisions. In the "augmented" version, a human sets the decision criteria in advance, and the AI acts automatically based on those criteria, as was previously mentioned. The same holds true for weighing options and weighing results, since criteria for doing so could be specified. Therefore, there isn't always two-way communication between the AI and human. On the contrary, decision criteria are created once and then examined on a frequent basis. However, the AI may decide on its own if the human is no longer contributing to the ongoing decision-making process. It is possible to set limits on the maximum amount that may be spent or get feedback on how the dishwasher is being used, as well as configure the dishwasher to only wash "eco-friendly" products (e.g., indicating an upcoming holiday in the parameters suggesting increased demand). The AI in this pattern of informed outsourcing looks for options, evaluates them, and then picks one to implement. For AI to improve, humans must provide feedback on whether or not AI judgments were successful. The AI will take such information into account when making decisions in the future. The informed outsourcing strategy is shown by a music streaming service that gives consumers the option to vote against AI-generated song choices for future playlists. After that, it won't play any songs that are too much like others. A human supplies the AI with the information it needs to make decisions in the "augmented" version of this pattern. A person may choose to ignore an AI's selection by looking over the data and coming to a different conclusion the next time. A user of music streaming services may decide to avoid hearing a certain genre of music.

9.2 Review of Literature

The study examined the influence of diverse criteria, specifications, and characteristics on decision making, aiming to identify the variables that impact consumer behavior. The research found that client internet companies should employ sociology to attract consumers (Rani, 2014b).

The study examined how social factors affect clothes purchases. The poll found that the social factors like age, income, and wealth affect consumers' buying behaviors (Bello-Eze, 2016).

These factors can assist individuals in self-expression and make up for any lack of construction skills. AI can serve non-conformists seeking distinct and customized products that align with consumer needs, and this concept also encompasses pricing strategies for goods (Fox, 2016).

Food pricing, employment, traditions, farmers, and food trade are addressed. Some think huge merchants in India would be good. The government should start with institutional tools to help producer firms and farmers as Indian agricultural business structures develop.

The study addresses various factors impacting consumers' booking intentions, including gender differences, perceived pricing, product image, and the direct, indirect, and mediated effects of trust. The research indicates that gender becomes inconsequential when a brand's image and price exert influence over a purchase decision. The surveys conducted shed light on the online hotel booking behavior of Taiwanese customers, although the findings might not be universally applicable. This study was conducted by Lien et al. (2015).

It examines social issues and internet shopping behavior. These samples included 942 publications during 1993–2012. Consumers dispute about how they use the internet strategically, how they utilize online organizations and networks, how they use it across cultures, how they use user-generated content, and cognitive aspects that affect online behavior (Cummins, 2013).

This research has the potential to assist internet companies in forecasting customer behavior, with a focus on non-consumable products. The author highlights ample room for technological advancements, emphasizing their significant influence on the consumer purchasing process (Kachamas, Chandrachi, & Sinthupinyo, 2019).

This research examines how significant advancements in e-commerce technology are being employed to influence customers into purchasing brands and products. The findings of this study indicate that while AI systems enhance e-commerce, there are certain behaviors that aren't well understood, especially in terms of explaining them. Consequently, the study suggests enhancing machine learning models for AI systems that are more transparent and understandable.

Modern technologies help individuals to grasp things more clearly, enabling them greater flexibility to make choices that promote their own well-being. Furthermore, various domains are utilized to explain how consumer decisions vary, including psychology, neurology, philosophy, economics, and marketing. These are all open topics regarding consumer welfare, well-being, and freedom of choice that need to be researched further (Andre et al., 2018).

Intelligent Simulation Model of Online Consumer Behavior (ISMOCB) employs artificial neural networks and the Naive Bayes Classifier. A study conducted on online shopping in Turkey investigates variables such as education, family size, monthly income, age, gender, and marital status. This study demonstrates the system's capability to make informed decisions and establish an "Artificial Database" containing purchasing transactions and demographic information.

Leveraging big data can aid in pinpointing consumer needs. The study sought to understand the contemporary purchasing patterns by asking, "How do customers buy today?" It delved into consumer behavior from 1700 to 2015. However, insights into consumer behavior beyond 2015 remain undisclosed. Surveying consumer intent and marketing trends indicates that AI is projected to become a competitive necessity post 2017.

Whether AI and finance intersect in several sectors, their connection is evident as they delve into various financial matters through the utilization of agent-based computers, expert systems, and data mining. This convergence demonstrates effective strategies for surmounting challenges in the financial domain. The study delves into the realms of data gathering, neural networks, evolutionary computing, and artificial neural network (ANN) techniques, exploring how these techniques can be synergistically applied alongside intelligent systems to achieve remarkable results. AI examines how quantitative and fundamental stock ratings interact. Agent-based computer economics studies financial market models, whereas ANN studies non-linear interactions (Hiloska, 2012).

It covers a diverse, creative academic field. It also suggests a way to create AI as smart as the human brain. Modern AI and its sub-disciplines reveal that it is aware of its surroundings and makes steps to succeed. Brain-like AI underlies artificial general intelligence, AI with bodies, and biology-based AI. Brain sciences and AI may bootstrap new discoveries by interacting differently and create an impact on the consumers using AI for advertising and the marketing field (Velik, 2012b).

It shows an abstract model where emotions and appreciation explain service customization. Marketing and theory managers and future researchers may apply the paper's results. Customers' remarks may or may not include behaviors while assessing actions (Bock et al., 2016).

It examines how advertising and consumer satisfaction impact retail centers in the Jabalpur area. Five sales promotion mixes and structure questionnaire criteria choose 200 mall examples. This study aids shopping center marketers. This aids in client identification and marketing strategy. To assure client satisfaction, other cities and shopping complexes may adopt this (Ubeja, 2013).

The study investigates customer responses through the application of Artificial Neural Networks (ANNs) alongside comprehensive, long-term survey data. Neural networks exhibit superior proficiency in discerning patterns. Training an ANN model gradually is recommended, as optimized network weights can lead to the potential outperformance of ANN algorithms compared to other methods (Badea, 2014b).

It develops a tourist attraction marketing system using knowledge representation, neural networks, and current data processing. An intelligent system may help non-experts overcome marketing challenges, according to experiments. The ANN classifier and real-time inference engine are discussed in Stalidis, Karapistolis, & Vafeiadis, 2015.

AI evaluates liquidity, revenues, client retention, long-term value, market share, and profit margin to optimize customer strategy. Results are given. Experts employ visual prologue programming language to determine customer demands based on the five elements mentioned. This professional approach is difficult since there are so many marketing methods. The organizational structure will be studied in the marketing strategy.

It assesses research and discusses behavioral psychology. This review examines operant and classical conditioning, foraging theories, and matching in practice. This document recommends a study on behavioral strategy replication, external strategy for marketing researchers and consumers, and external strategy replication.

We use categorization to uncover search trends for what, when, and where. Model predictiveness is assessed using the platform's data set. Client search behaviors are crucial and successful. The approach should include e-retailers and partners. Comparing nations using other criteria is also possible.

Anticipating customer behavior by employing data mining and statistical methods is a common practice. While numerous studies indicate that there is ample room for further understanding the prediction of consumer behavior, artificial neural networks (ANNs) stand out as the frequently employed data mining technique in this pursuit. This study uses the Customer Relationship Management (CRM) technique and data sets to suggest further research since prediction tools aren't flawless.

Encouraging collaboration among small and medium-sized enterprises (SMEs) to achieve mutual profitability is a key objective. This was explored through the analysis of managers and proprietors from service sector SMEs in Russia and China using structural equation modeling. This approach sheds light on potential areas of exploration in the future, including the study of environmental, managerial, cultural, marketing communication, and consumer behavior aspects across diverse organizations and countries.

A survey found that AI is changing how consumers engage in customer service. It eliminates physical communication equipment. AI must be used in the market to boost efficiency and revenue, as shown by customer service.

It examines 12-year behavior to find patterns, categorize, and evaluate subjects, and analyze the most-cited publications, subjects, and titles. This study explains why analyzing structure and consumer behavior is crucial and forecasts how this literature will grow. A revolutionary simple and well-organized coding strategy is proposed. Consumer behavior research could need more journals, articles, patents, and books.

It encourages data mining, text mining, machine learning, and AI to estimate consumer satisfaction based on reviews. An internet-based hotel customer satisfaction study collects and analyzes qualitative and quantitative data, examining big data applications to improve service. The results show that the decision support method will help consumers.

The casual map provides a ranking mechanism, Consumer-Managed Relationship Management (CMRM), and combines quantitative and qualitative data to understand customer behavior. It's easy to set up online, and letting customers view the permit process and maximize modification's influence on their goals. The survey's statistical results suggest that CMRM may boost customers' willingness to buy and happiness with their purchases. CMRM should be examined with other service and production processes.

Emotions, psychology, and their evolution and current state in China are addressed. Collaborative and interactive humanoid robot studies rely on sight and sound communication. Artificial emotions and psychology may mature with research.

This report found that 8 out of 10 retail marketers worldwide believed that "AI will redefine the function of the marketer" and make the market more strategic, efficient, and lucrative. AI helps workers to concentrate on "value-generating jobs," according to Salesforce and IDC research. AI is utilized for sales forecasting, up-selling and cross-selling, lead scoring, and email marketing. This indicated that personalization still has a lot of potential for improvement.

The report is based on a poll of individuals in the United States, Germany, and Japan regarding their perspectives on AI and robots and how they influence society. Case studies such as robots that aid with hotel room service, telemedicine, and retail are used to study the present status of robotics and how people perceive them. According to the study, robots dislike how they appear and conduct their tasks. According to the report, AI has introduced new concepts into our daily lives, such as the internet of people or the Internet of Things, as well as the sharing economy. The tourism business is no exception. The usage of distributed agent systems (DASs) and multi-agent systems (MASs) is predicted to continue. As a result of the Information and Communication Technology (ICT) revolution, changes have occurred, and AI-powered chatbots now deliver tailored services. In the future, AI may be utilized to increase tourism (Zsarnoczky, 2017).

This research centers on the perceptions people hold regarding AI and its potential impact on employment, criminal investigations, retail, and healthcare. Numerous significant AI effects are evident within these extensive domains. Recognizing the advantages and disadvantages of AI is deemed crucial for attaining an informed stance and enhancing the ease of customers' lives.

This initiative aims to create an impact on the fields of marketing communication and consumer behavior by addressing challenges encountered by robots. Businesses should focus not just on human consumers but also on robot consumers. With further research, the realm of marketing could evolve to accommodate the marketing principles applicable to robot customers, reshaping the landscape of the r-marketing domain.

In this study, AI was utilized to classify consumers' online learning aims and actions by modal dimension, functional dimension, and structural dimension. In terms of data collecting and analysis, big data is generated from the top down and from left to right. A multilevel and multidimensional model is used to develop a data model. This model is used to determine where, when, and how data should be gathered. In the correlation study of learning effects, the K-means and page rank algorithms are utilized. This technique to learning to make judgments enhances the basis for educators, researchers, and managers.

This study analyzes how AI is applied in marketing and aims to predict how it will be utilized in future marketing jobs. AI supports marketers in recognizing what will and will not benefit them, resulting in inventive and competent marketing. AI has several benefits in marketing, including enhancing sales and simplifying content generation. Therefore, AI has a major influence on marketing. It aids in acquiring an advantage and increasing consumer relationships in order to better marketing tactics.

It discussed current AI breakthroughs and how corporations and organizations must take on greater responsibility to profit on new prospects. A poll is being done on the current status of big data, the threats it brings to customers, and the potential of AI for empowering people. Analytical and normative methodologies are driving the attempt to bring AI to individual consumers and their companies. AI for consumer help was supposed to work as a change-following wheel, allowing initiatives to integrate into the regulatory process.

The article explores how AI may be utilized in customized marketing, such as how consumers find, shop, enhance customer loyalty, and create long-term connections. To create good marketing choices, it is vital to apply analytical approaches such as AI or ML. The most prevalent complaint raised against these approaches is that they are difficult to learn.

The author box promotes the advantages of AI while boosting awareness about the risks of data mining. AI is utilized to handle social media data by assisting marketers and consumers in knowing more about their surroundings. As a result of new technology, AI may get so jumbled with other things that it cannot be isolated.

According to the survey, AI-based solutions are accessible in areas such as transportation, digital marketing that initiates interactions, industrial production processes, logistics, and medications. In the marketing strategy, the author defined strong AI, narrow AI, and hybrid AI. When AI is educated, it learns the relationship between a consumer's profile and the firms they pick. Furthermore, concluded, "Is it realistic to employ AI to solve obstacles in marketing schemes?"

One of the most popular AI fallacies is that it will become self-motivated. AI will be smarter than humans if computers, memory, and brains develop dramatically. And, as computer speed doubles every 18 months, AI will harness computer power to grow wiser and smarter. Myths argue that we must present greater difficulties to our AI and put it through more rigorous testing.

9.3 Identifying Research Gaps for Future Studies

This chapter discusses and removes the gap of all other papers discussed about how AI has an impact on the buying and decision making of the consumer and also shows the impact of the search engine optimization on the consumer buying decision making and discusses how the browsers' search data has an impact on the buying decisions of the consumer as follows:

■ Enumerates the impact of AI on decision making of consumers.
■ Discusses the impact of search engine optimization on consumer buying behavior.
■ Discusses the impact of AI on buying habits of the consumer.
■ Clearly describes about the impact of AI on consumer buying decisions.
■ Discusses the impact of the automation of AI in the consumer buying decision process.
■ Delivers the solutions for the smooth buying cycle of the consumers with the help of AI.
■ Generates automatic reminders using AI software to impact the buying cycle of the consumers.
■ Discusses how AI acts as record book of the consumers' buying cycles.
■ Discusses how it notifies the consumer with offers and changes the buying decision of the consumer.

9.4 Conclusion

People will have a legitimate interest in finding out about the advantages of AI since it will have a direct influence on their life. With the use of platform data, brands will be able to target consumers who have already shown an interest in a certain product. This chapter examines the ways in which AI impacts consumer behavior and how it may influence purchase habits in the future. Many stores also make use of solutions powered by AI in order to monitor and improve consumer behavior and sales. By studying a user's browsing history, many AIs are able to speculate about the user's preferences as well as their behavior. Multiple AIs keep an eye on the deals and discounts available to customers based on their past purchases and activities online. Customers may get regular reminders from these AIs, which can help them decide what products they want to buy. This chapter examines the application of AI in analytics, with the goal of better comprehending the present behavior of customers and the expectations they have. Consumers' tastes, purchases, and other actions will be influenced by AI systems as a greater number of vendors make their data available. According to the results, the data collected by such systems might be utilized to provide customers with improved service.

References

André, Q., Carmon, Z., Wertenbroch, K., Crum, A., Frank, D., Goldstein, W., & Yang, H. (2018). Consumer choice and autonomy in the age of artificial intelligence and big data. *Customer Needs and Solutions, 5*, 28–37.

Badea, L. M. (2014a). Predicting consumer behavior with artificial neural networks. *Procedia Economics and Finance, 15*, 238–246.

Badea, L. M. (2014b). Predicting consumer behavior with artificial neural networks: Critical review literature.

Bello-Eze. (2016). Factors influencing consumers buying behavior within the clothing industry: Critical review literature.

Bock, D. E., et al. (2016). Artificial intelligence: Disrupting what we know about services: Critical review literature.

Cummins, S. (2013). Consumer behavior in the online context: Critical review literature.

Fox, S. (2016). Domesticating artificial intelligence: Expanding human self-expression through applications of artificial intelligence in presumption: Critical review literature.

Hiloska, K. (2012). Application of artificial intelligence and data mining techniques to financial markets: Critical review literature.

Ibukun T. A., et al. (2019). A systematic review of current trends in web content mining: Critical review literature.

Kachamas, P., Chandrachi, A., & Sinthupinyo, S. (2019). Application of artificial intelligent in the prediction of consumer behavior from Facebook posts analysis: Critical review literature.

Leyer, M., Oberlaender, A., Dootson, P., & Kowalkiewicz, M. (2020). Decision-making with artificial intelligence: Towards a novel conceptualization of patterns. In *PACIS* (p. 224).

Lien, C., et al. (2015). Online hotel booking: The effects of brand image, price, trust and value on purchase intentions: Critical review literature.

Lien, C. H., Wen, M. J., Huang, L. C., & Wu, K. L. (2015). Online hotel booking: The effects of brand image, price, trust and value on purchase intentions. Asia Pacific Management Review, 20(4), 210–218.

Panwar, D., Anand, S., Ali, F., & Singal, K. (2019). Consumer decision making process models and their applications to market strategy. *International Management Review, 15*(1), 36–44.

Rani, P. (2014a). Factors influencing consumer behavior. *International Journal of Current Research and Academic Review, 2*(9), 52–61.

Rani, P. (2014b). Explaining the factors influencing consumer behavior: Critical literature review, Google scholar.

Solomon, M., Russell-Bennett, R., & Previte, J. (2015). Consumer behavior: Buying, having, and being. Pearson Educational Limited. Harlow, England.

Stankevich, A. (2017). Explaining the consumer decision-making process: Critical literature review. *Journal of International Business Research and Marketing, 2*(6), 7–14.

Stalidis, G., Karapistolis, D., & Vafeiadis, A. (2015). Marketing decision support using artificial intelligence and knowledge modeling: Application to tourist destination management. *Procedia-Social and Behavioral Sciences, 175*, 106–113.

Ubeja, S. (2013). A study of customer satisfaction of shopping malls in Jabalpur city: Critical review literature.

Varshney, S. (2016). SME internationalization in emerging markets: Symbiotic vs. commensal pathways: Critical review literature.

Velik, R. (2012a). AI reloaded: Objectives, potentials, and challenges of the novel field of brain-like artificial intelligence. *BRAIN. Broad Research in Artificial Intelligence and Neuroscience, 3*(3), 25–54.

Velik, R. (2012b). AI reloaded: Objectives, potentials, and challenges of the novel field of brain-like artificial intelligence: Critical review literature.

Zsarnoczky, M. (2017). How does artificial intelligence affect the tourism industry?. VADYBA, 31(2), 85–90.

Chapter 10

Metaverse: The Pursuit to Keep the Human Element Intact in the Media and Entertainment Industry

Noyonika Sahoo, Diya Gupta, and Dr. Kakoli Sen
Woxsen University
Hyderabad, Telangana, India

10.1 Introduction to the Metaverse and Usage in the Media and Entertainment Industry

The term "metaverse" was first coined in the Neil Steven novel, *Snow Crash*, where it referred to a virtual escape for the characters to explore outside the grim reality (Sonnemaker, 2021). The metaverse has been described as a new iteration of the internet that utilizes virtual reality (VR) headsets, blockchain technology, and avatars within a new integration of the physical and virtual worlds (Lee et al., 2021; The Verge, 2021). It is beyond the real universe, a perpetual and persistent multiuser environment merging physical reality with digital virtuality by enabling seamless embodied user communication in real time and dynamic interactions with digital artifacts (Mystakidis, 2022).

The entertainment industry also aims to transport people into a make-believe world where things are larger than life and fantasies come alive. The metaverse aids in this transportation of users to a different world that

DOI: 10.4324/b23404-10

is disconnected from reality to provide them with a VR experience. The entertainment and media industries now include a significant amount of metaverse technology to give unique experiences to their consumers and audience. The metaverse is growing and improving at a high speed. Meta, Microsoft, and Google are reshaping the metaverse with new features on already-existing products and services. However, the rise of augmented reality (AR) and VR technology has been the key to the growth of the metaverse. The most immersive metaverse experiences can be had using a variety of AR and VR devices, including Microsoft HoloLens and Google Cardboard. Using avatars, which are representations of oneself in the virtual world, social media companies have created novel ways to express their personalities and engage with larger audiences. The makers of the avatars are increasingly using them to represent themselves on social media in their day-to-day lives, which is broadening the boundaries of the multiverse.

The COVID-19 pandemic sped up the adoption of technology, including virtual meetings, conferences, and all communication online. What would have possibly taken 10–15 years, sped up in just 2 years of lockdown. Many advancements have taken up their space in the metaverse, such as Walt Disney building a virtual theme park that can be viewed using VR headsets or on specific metaverse platforms, concerts in VR, and several others. The Ariana Grande and Travis Scott performances are perhaps the most time and cost-efficient examples because millions of devoted fans attended through the metaverse platforms. The gaming sector is perhaps the largest to profit from it by way of offering the players the near real experience of existing in the virtual world and playing the game, and numerous gaming websites like Minecraft and Fortnite have entered the market. The metaverse still has a lot to develop, nevertheless. Most people view it as a glimpse of how people will interact with their environment and how the internet will change over the years (Sen Gupta, 2022).

10.2 Use of Technology in the Media and Entertainment Industry

At the inception, the media and entertainment industry were just a medium of telling a story; however, the industry today includes film, television, music, gaming, theater, theme parks, etc., and has grown manifold since then. From radios to black-and-white television to colored pictures to OTT platforms, the delivery platforms and styles of entertainment have changed exponentially and so have the employment opportunities (Kapoor et al., 2018). It also substantially contributes to the economy and the nation's GDP. The technological developments, the introduction of affordable 4G and 5G networks, and powerful portable gadgets all have altered the industry's landscape and improved the quality of experience through high user experience and thus more effective delivery methods (Ahuja, 2021).

The media and entertainment sector were also pioneers in quick adoption of technologies like big data and AI, which augmented its fast growth. Thanks to the lockdown and forced staying at home, the industry was required to adapt to the public demand that was hungry for trendy entertainment and relevant information (Lippell, 2016). Big data, cloud computing, and artificial intelligence (AI) have not just amplified the effectiveness of the creative businesses but have also supported the research and development aspect of it. Both the first music album of its kind, "Hello World," and the first script for the movie, *Sunspring*, were generated entirely using AI and that has opened up a number of other possibilities to be explored (Amato et al., 2019).

While studies that approach media innovations from media adoption and diffusion perspective focus on new media technologies or services, studies that approach media innovations from a media management perspective primarily address media innovations as new media products, particularly new content offerings, or focus on organizational changes and innovation at the level of the organization. Additionally, methods in media historical studies take a technology-focused approach to media developments, looking at the socioeconomic contexts in which media technology is used and its societal effects (Dogruel, 2014).

The metaverse has the ability to address the basic shortcomings of web-based 2D and 3D in various segments of industries, especially in the media and entertainment industry (M&E) (Mystakidis, 2022). Like the internet, the metaverse is an infinite phenomenon. Even VR experiences that fall under the purview of the metaverse can now be shared via the internet. The internet that started with sending e-mails opened up to music sharing, e-commerce, video content, and live broadcasts as a result of increased adoption and attached technical advances in both the internet's specific case as well as the communication and information technology environment more generally. Traditionally, the laws have struggled to keep up with the rapid technology advancement. Platforms in the metaverse zone are growing rapidly, but it also needs to make sure that safety principles are built into their technology from the start (Desai, 2022). This is further explained through this book chapter, along with the loss of human touch and how to keep it intact within the M&E industry.

10.3 Adoption of the Metaverse by the Media and Entertainment Industry

The word "meta" entered the market when Facebook rebranded and attempted to offer more opportunities, giving rise to the name "metaverse." Following the footsteps of Meta, businesses of all sizes and shapes started to show interest in the realm of possibilities that the metaverse could offer. They began linking their own products and services and modifying them so they could profit from the metaverse. Many businesses also began creating additional software and the metaverse was suddenly the new thing that started catching people's eyes and becoming popular (Lawton, 2022).

During pre-COVID times, people would travel and visit places for new experiences. But as life came to a standstill, people looked to entertainment online to distract, to engage, and to kill time and loneliness. The pandemic fast-tracked the digital innovation and brought people on the metaverse platforms much sooner. People can now watch their favorite band or artists perform live without having to make a long and expensive trip and simply sitting in the comfort of their own homes (Solanki, 2022). Pop artists and celebrities like Ariana Grande, Travis Scott, Lil Nas X, and Zara Larsson were among the early adopters and made the most of it. They collaborated with Fortnite, a metaverse platform for immersive video games, to provide their fans a musical experience unlike any other so far. The fans around the world could watch their favorite pop stars' performances without any hassle and also experience the same vibe. Even though the performance was pre-recorded and available to fans via streaming, it still provided a realistic tour environment and an immersive musical experience to them at a very low cost. For her fans, Ariana Grande also sold a lot of her merchandise through Fortnite's item shop. The shows were streamed by loyal fans almost three to four times in the whole course of this virtual tour and had over a million attendees. Following the success of this virtual musical experience, new opportunities for experimenting with live performances have also arisen

(Copans, 2021). Daler Mehndi, a well-known Punjabi vocalist, became one of the first Indian musicians to join the others when performing at his first concert in the metaverse. He is noted for drawing enormous crowds to his concerts and had used PartyNite, India's first metaverse platform, which was reported to have over 20 million viewers when he performed virtually (Singal, 2022).

The metaverse has presented enormous opportunities to the gaming sector as well. The gaming business transitioned from providing its users with a more fascinating experience with 3D cosmos from a fairly easy way of playing games with a 2D screen, mouse, and keyboard. Due to innovations like AR and VR, gamers can now have real-life experiences while playing. The gaming industry has also maintained the human touch by allowing players to virtually interact with the game as "avatars" and do tasks independently rather than by pressing a few keyboard buttons. This has made gaming more immersive in nature and altered the entire appearance of the sector. Many platforms have already started adopting it, such as Decentraland and Axie Infinity. The same thing has also been introduced in *Fornite* and *Mindcraft*. With the help of Internet of Things (IoT), the metaverse now has the chance to advance things by providing even more realistic experiences and sees a huge market in the gaming industry (CoinDCX-Blog, 2022).

10.4 The Role of Human Touch in the Media and Entertainment Industry

The media and entertainment industry works on communication and connections with people. Almost all stories deal with people, relationships, emotions, etc. Movies have a huge impact on people and they also depict the times that they are made in. Movies are also called the mirrors of society, highlighting the importance of human connection and interaction. People emulate their heroes and stars from such platforms. Their dialogues, dance movements, styles, behavior, and thought process become the rage among people. Humans are social by nature and need to have people around them to be their best self. While the advancements of the metaverse could enhance the experience of watching a game of cricket virtually sitting at home, it still cannot replicate the exhilarating experiencing of watching the same game at a packed stadium with real people where you laugh and cry with real people, and the live noise that comes with it, depicting life and real emotions, raw in their form. While technology makes it available from the comfort of our homes, it also takes away the charm of meeting new people physically and keeps people isolated from others.

In December 2021, Walt Disney invented a system where visitors could interact with the Disney characters in the theme park virtually while physically being present. The technology, called "Virtual World Simulator," allows visitors to see a 3D figure in the real world without the AR equipment. The company aims to connect the physical and digital worlds for "storytelling without boundaries in our own Disney metaverse." Currently, Disney is still in talks on how it will take the idea of this virtual theme park into the metaverse (Sen Gupta, 2022). Even if the idea of these new technical connections with theme parks sounds appealing, the human experience of really being there would be lost. One will miss the excitement of really seeing Disney characters they have grown up watching. While the virtual experience of theme parks will help people not have to wait in long lines to get on their favorite rides, they will also no longer be able to take leisurely strolls through the park, mingle with new people, or visit their favorite eateries, all of which are part of our socialization process.

Nike became one of the first sports and athleisure brands to embrace the metaverse in its full form. To enable their customers to buy, sell, and experience digital products, they offered a variety of distinct categories within their e-commerce platforms and in their products, including AR, blockchain technology, and non-fungible tokens (NFTs) (LAWLER, 2021). Nike bought a company called RTFKT and now has a presence in the metaverse. It allows the customers to not just buy products that have been designed in the digital world using the application, but also keeps them trademarked within the virtual world. Adidas, Louis Vuitton, Gucci, and many other luxury labels also developed a comprehensive line of clothing that was accessible in the virtual world via various applications and stores such as Decentraland, one of the metaverse gaming platforms (Jung, 2022). It is quite likely that consumers will begin shopping more frequently in the virtual world using avatars rather than physically traveling to stores to buy clothing and accessories. Making a digital avatar, or virtual version of yourself in the metaverse, allows anyone of any size to sit at home and shop for clothing that is most suited to their body type. As you will receive exactly what you see and how it would appear on you in the real world, this can help decrease exchanges and returns and improve your satisfaction levels with the companies. At the same time, the pleasure of physically engaging with a fabric or clothing, trying it out, and the engagement with the salesperson or other buyers will be compromised. While businesses will adopt the new technologies to avoid falling behind in the competition, they should not overlook transferring real-world offerings to digital platforms so that customers may combine both experiences, virtual and real.

10.5 How the Metaverse Is Influencing Its Audiences' Preferences

The consumers of the media and entertainment industries are mostly identified as millennials and Gen-Zers. The different kinds of media platforms used by the audiences are video, gaming, sports, podcasts, music, etc. As the media and entertainment industry has these technological advancements in gaming, music, and other social media platforms, the positioning of these channels is to the Gen-Zers and millennials to attract and retain them. This audience is technologically savvy and can swiftly adapt to changes occurring in the metaverse. Initially, every platform was used for the consumer's entertainment and for fun. As the audience has become more used to the augmented experience, companies have started using the platforms very strategically for business growth. The metaverse-based social media platforms engage companies' audiences, create uniquely tailored experiences, and leverage data for personalization tools to explore companies who could use their products and services. By giving businesses the opportunity to engage with their consumers in a deeply immersive setting, the metaverse can allow profitable collaborations that look and feel user-centric and offer higher customer engagement. It also gives additional opportunities to brands to explore fresh approaches and advance their digital marketing strategies. With its platform, the metaverse is giving businesses the power to use digital marketing strategies more effectively and profitably than ever before by providing an immersive environment where users can interact with brand content (Sarkes, 2022; Blockchain Council, 2023).

Previously, consumers could only upload a small amount of information on the channels they used in the media and entertainment sector, such as name, gender, DoB, mail id, etc. as their profile; however, with the introduction of the metaverse through these channels, individuals are able to create new personalized avatars of themselves, add an IP address, and other details. The consumers could share a lot of personal details and may feel the urge to do so in order to fulfill their social needs. The veiled anonymity on the internet could also lead to aggressive and online disinhibition prompting users towards revealing more about themselves for a feel-good factor and have something that is as close as their own personality. It could also create issues like privacy reduction, cybersecurity, identity theft, harassment and online bullying, and antisocial behavior. Personal information and data may be collected and shared without user consent or used for targeted advertising and other purposes. Users may be at risk of hacking, phishing, and other cyber-attacks. Virtual environments may also be vulnerable to malware and other forms of malicious software. Users' avatars and personal information may be stolen and used for fraudulent activities. Users could also get subjected to harassment and bullying in virtual spaces, which could lead to stress and trauma. It could additionally lead to addiction from the user's end, which can negatively impact personal and professional life.

To address these serious concerns, the metaverse must become secure, ensuring that no privacy breaches occur. Looking at the vulnerable age group it attracts, it is critical to have strong security and privacy measures in place, including encryption, authentication, and access controls. It is also important to educate users on how to protect themselves while in the metaverse and promote a positive and safe community.

10.6 Keeping the Human Touch Alive with Technological Changes

One way to keep the human touch intact with technological changes in the metaverse and media and entertainment industries is to prioritize and integrate real human interaction and storytelling. This can be done by utilizing live events, VR, and other immersive technologies to create opportunities for direct engagement and connection between creators and audiences. Additionally, it is important to ensure that the technology is being used as a tool to enhance and augment human experiences, rather than replace them.

People have a range of expectations from the metaverse in the media and entertainment industry. Some may expect to see a fully immersive and interactive virtual world that allows them to explore and experience new stories, characters, and worlds. This may include the ability to interact with other users and collaborate on creative projects. Others may expect to see a more seamless integration of virtual and real-world experiences, such as virtual concerts or movie screenings that allow them to feel as if they are truly in the same space as the performers or characters and also get an opportunity to interact with them. Additionally, people may also expect the metaverse to provide new opportunities for personalization and customization of their own experiences. Going forward, maybe we could expect performances by the singers/actors, etc. virtually through their avatars. The metaverse in the media and entertainment industry is expected to provide an unprecedented level of interactivity, immersion, and personalization that will change the way people consume and interact with content in comparison to traditional forms of media.

10.7 Conclusion

This chapter presented the various technological advancements that have occurred in the media and entertainment sector as well as the effects of the metaverse in this particular business. The metaverse, or VR worlds, has had a significant impact on the media and entertainment industry by providing new opportunities for interactive storytelling and immersive experiences. In the gaming industry, the metaverse has allowed for more realistic and engaging gameplay, as well as the ability for players to interact with each other in virtual worlds. In the entertainment industry, the metaverse is being used to create virtual concert experiences, allowing people to attend live performances from anywhere in the world. The human element will certainly be required to be included in the metaverse too, as people spend more and more time on it especially as the age group is young and impressionable. There are concerns about the potential negative impact of the metaverse on human interactions, as it could lead to a greater disconnection from the physical world and real-life human interactions. It is essential to be aware of the potential consequences and strive for balance and healthy use of the metaverse. As technology continues to advance, the possibilities for the metaverse are emerging and are immense. Some experts believe that the metaverse will eventually become a parallel reality where people can live and work and that it will become an integral part of everyday life. The metaverse may also be used to create new forms of education, commerce, and social interaction, leading to a new paradigm of human interaction. It is inevitable that any new technology will catch the fancy of people who will want to explore more of it and especially when it relates to the ever-growing field of technology, people are learning and exploring at the same time. It is also critical that developers and marketeers keep in mind that human interaction is retained at the core of it to prevent social isolation, leading to mental and emotional issues.

References

Ahuja, V. (2021). Transforming the media and entertainment industry: Cases from the social media marketing world. *Journal of Cases on Information Technology (JCIT), 23*(4), 1–17.

Amato, G., Behrmann, M., Bimbot, F., et al. (2019). AI in the media and creative industries. https://doi.org/10.48550/arXiv.1905.04175.

Dogruel, L. (2014). What is so special about media innovations? A characterization of the field. *The Journal of Media Innovations, 1*(1), 52–69.

Kapoor, K. K., Tamilmani, K., Rana, N. P., Patil, P., Dwivedi, Y. K., & Nerur, S. (2018). Advances in social media research: Past, present and future. *Information Systems Frontiers, 20*, 531–558.

Lee, L.-H., Braud, T., Zhou, P., Wang, L., Xu, D., Lin, Z., & Hui, P. (2021). All one needs to know about metaverse: A complete survey on technological singularity, virtual ecosystem, and research agenda. https://doi.org/10.48550/arXiv.2110.05352

Lippell, H. (2016). Big data in the media and entertainment sectors. In: Cavanillas, J., Curry, E., Wahlster, W. (eds), *New Horizons for a Data-Driven Economy*. Springer, Cham. https://doi.org/10.1007/978-3-319-21569-3_14

Online Resources

Blockchain Council. (2023). "The Future of Social Media in the Metaverse", https://www.blockchain-council.org/metaverse/the-future-of-social-media-in-the-metaverse/, accessed January 17, 2023.

CoinDCX-Blog. (2022). "How Is Metaverse Powering the Gaming Industry – Everything You Need to Know", https://coindcx.com/blog/metaverse/how-is-metaverse-powering-the-gaming-industry/, accessed January 5, 2023.

Copans, V. (2021). Xliveglobal, "Ariana Grande Joins Metaverse through Fortnite Tour", https://www.xliveglobal.com/content/ariana-grande-joins-metaverse-through-fortnite-tour, accessed January 4, 2023.

Desai, N. (2022). "Nishith Desai Associates 2022, Metaverse: A New Universe Legal, Regulatory and Tax Issues", https://www.nishithdesai.com/fileadmin/user_upload/pdfs/Research_Papers/Metaverse_A_New_Universe.pdf, accessed January 5, 2023

Jung. (2022). Ted Talk, "How the Metaverse Will Change the World", https://www.youtube.com/watch?v=ExUovs0n4bA, accessed January 5, 2023.

LAWLER. (2021). The Verge, "Nike Just Bought a Virtual Shoe Company that Makes NFTs and Sneakers 'for the Metaverse'", https://www.theverge.com/22833369/nike-rtfkt-nft-sneaker-shoe-metaverse-company, accessed January 17, 2023.

Lawton, G. (2022). Tech Target, "History of the Metaverse Explained", https://www.techtarget.com/searchcio/tip/History-of-the-metaverse-explained, accessed January 5, 2023.

Mystakidis, S. (2022). Metaverse. *Encyclopedia*, *2*(1), 486–497.

Sarkes, R. (2022). Geek911, "6 Ways the Metaverse Could Change How You Do Business", https://geek911.com/ways-metaverse-change-business/, accessed January 17, 2023.

Sen Gupta, M. (2022). Lifestyle Asia, "Future of Metaverse Entertainment: Concerts, theme Parks and Movies in the Virtual World", https://www.lifestyleasia.com/ind/gear/tech/what-is-the-future-of-metaverse-entertainment/, accessed January 6, 2023.

Singal, N. (2022). Business Today, "How the Metaverse Will Drive Innovation in Entertainment", https://www.businesstoday.in/magazine/technology/story/how-the-metaverse-will-drive-innovation-in-entertainment-343328-2022-08-01, accessed January 4, 2023.

Solanki, A. (2022). Softwebsolutions, "Previous Next 7 Industries that are Impacted by the Metaverse", https://www.softwebsolutions.com/resources/industries-that-transformed-by-the-metaverse.html, accessed January 5, 2023.

Sonnemaker, T. (2021). Business Inside, "The Creator of the Term 'Metaverse' Wants People to Know He Has 'Nothing to Do' with Facebook's Meta Plans", https://www.businessinsider.in/tech/news/the-creator-of-the-term-metaverse-wants-people-to-know-he-he-has-nothing-to-do-with-facebooks-meta-plans/articleshow/87382659.cms, accessed January 6, 2023.

Readings/Bibliography

Adh. (2022). CryptoStars, "Human Behavior and Metaverse", https://blog.cryptostars.is/human-behavior-and-metaverse-cd4cecb43e61, accessed January 6, 2023.

Augenstein, D., & Morschheuser, B. (2022). Understanding Human Factors in the Metaverse–an Autonomous Driving Experiment.

Chatterjee. (2022). TimesofIndia, "Why Metas Crisis Won't Cause a Dent in Metaverse", https://timesofindia.indiatimes.com/world/why-metas-crisis-wont-cause-a-dent-in-metaverse/articleshow/95453959.cms, accessed January 4, 2023.

Dwivedi, Y. K., Hughes, L., Baabdullah, A. M., et al. (2022). Metaverse beyond the hype: Multidisciplinary perspectives on emerging challenges, opportunities, and agenda for research, practice and policy. *International Journal of Information Management*, *66*, 102542.

Emergent Research. (2022). "Metaverse in Media and Entertainment Market",
    https://www.emergenresearch.com/industry-report/metaverse-in-media-and-
    entertainment-market, accessed January 4, 2023.
Hetler. (2022). Techtarget, "Marketing in the Metaverse: What Marketers Need to
    Know", https://www.techtarget.com/whatis/feature/Marketing-in-the-metaverse-
    What-marketers-need-to-know, accessed January 4, 2023.
Mantegna. (2022). TED Talk, "How to Stop the Metaverse from Becoming the
    Internet's Bad Sequel", https://youtu.be/OYv1dIle47U, accessed January 4, 2023.
Nicoară. (2022). Forbes, "To Preserve and Enhance Humanity, We Must Take
    Only the Right Steps Toward the Metaverse", https://www.forbes.com/sites/
    forbestechcouncil/2022/06/06/to-preserve-and-enhance-humanity-we-must-
    take-only-the-right-steps-toward-the-metaverse/?sh=3fe6cc862de2, accessed
    January 6, 2023.
Tozzi. (2022). Itprotoday, "Humans as a Service? How the Metaverse Turns People
    into Cloud Resources", https://www.itprotoday.com/cloud-computing-and-
    edge-computing/humans-service-how-metaverse-turns-people-cloud-resources,
    accessed January 6, 2023.

Chapter 11

The Role of AI and Automation in Virtual Recruitment

Keerthi Boddapati and Charan P.V.
Woxsen University
Hyderabad, Telangana, India

11.1 Introduction

The metaverse enables people to engage with one another and digital material in a virtual environment using immersive technologies such as virtual reality (VR) and augmented reality (AR). This new reality has the potential to transform our work, communication, and business methods. Businesses are investigating the use of the metaverse to grow operations; attract new consumers; and involve workers, stakeholders, and other parties.

According to Chui and Manyika (2018), the metaverse is an immersive and interactive virtual environment where people can engage with each other and digital content. They argue that the metaverse has the potential to transform various aspects of society, including work and communication.

The metaverse has a tremendous influence on the recruitment process. Using the possibilities of the metaverse, virtual recruiting allows companies to discover and interact with talent regardless of their location. Furthermore, AI and automation technologies may improve the recruiting process, enabling

DOI: 10.4324/b23404-11

organizations to save time and money while enhancing the quality of hiring choices.

Nonetheless, the use of AI and automation in virtual recruiting poses significant concerns over how to preserve the human aspect in this new corporate reality. Even though these technologies have the potential to make the recruiting process more efficient, their abuse might lead to prejudice and discrimination.

Advice on achieving a balance between technology and the human element in recruiting is provided by various sources. They argue that while AI and automation can streamline certain aspects of recruiting, it is crucial to maintain human interaction and empathy to ensure a positive candidate experience and establish a strong employer brand.

In addition, an excessive dependence on technology may result in the loss of the human touch in the recruiting process, which is essential for establishing a favorable employer brand and a rapport with applicants.

The purpose of this chapter is to examine the role of AI and automation in virtual recruiting in light of the metaverse. It evaluates the advantages and disadvantages of employing AI and automation in virtual recruiting and offers organizations suggestions on how to achieve a balance between technology and the human element in their recruitment efforts. This chapter will assist organizations in maximizing the potential of AI and automation in virtual recruiting, while ensuring the recruitment process stays fair, inclusive, and human-centered in the contemporary corporate environment.

11.2 Research Methodology

This investigation employs a qualitative technique, namely a case study approach. This chapter addresses the application of artificial intelligence and automation in the recruiting process, with an emphasis on virtual recruitment strategies in a particular sector. This involves identifying key patterns that emerge from the data, which were then used to give insights into how AI and automation are being utilized in virtual recruiting and their influence on the recruitment process. seeks to give an in-depth analysis of the role of AI and automation in virtual recruiting, using a qualitative methodology that prioritizes the experiences and perspectives of HR (human resource) experts in the sector.

11.2.1 Context and Motivations for the Use of AI and Automation in Online Recruitment

AI and automation are being used more and more in virtual recruiting to locate, court, and employ qualified individuals in far-flung locales. The proliferation of online job boards and applicant tracking systems in the early 2000s marked the beginning of this shift.

According to Davarpanah and Qin (2021), the metaverse has the potential to transform various aspects of business, including communication and recruitment.

Adoption of AI and automation in online job searches is being driven by the availability of data and processing capacity, as well as the need to save time and money. Automation of otherwise tedious but necessary activities, such as résumé reviewing and interview scheduling, might help firms save time and money throughout the hiring process. AI-enabled technologies may make it easier to find and hire suitable individuals. Candidates might benefit from virtual recruiting as well, thanks to the simplified and streamlined application process. Online resources have made it possible for job-seekers to submit applications and communicate with employers at their convenience. AI-powered solutions that provide applicants with tailored and fast feedback might encourage them to participate in the recruiting process.

Kumar et al. (2021) review the impact of AI on the recruitment process, and note the potential for AI and automation to enhance the efficiency and quality of hiring decisions.

An increasingly competitive labor market may explain why organizations are turning to AI and automation in their online recruiting efforts.

11.2.2 Advantages of AI and Automation in Online Recruitment

In recent years, the usage of AI and automation methods has skyrocketed in the online recruiting industry (Girma & Fischer, 2020). Many positive outcomes have resulted, both for companies and people seeking employment.

Using AI and automation, online recruiters are able to efficiently sift through a vast number of applications and résumés. Using natural language processing (NLP) and machine learning (ML) approaches, the most qualified applicants for a post may be swiftly discovered. They might forego the laborious process of filtering through applications and instead concentrate on picking the most qualified people.

An additional benefit is that job postings may be more precisely targeted. By analyzing job advertising and criteria using AI and automation, it is possible to develop advertisements that appeal to qualified applicants. This improves the efficiency and efficacy of the recruiting process and reduces the time required to fill an open job.

Utilizing AI and other forms of automation may improve the application process for prospective employees. HR managers have more time to concentrate on the quality of the application process when boring chores such as interview scheduling and email follow-up are automated.

By simplifying the process, boosting productivity, and enhancing the application experience, AI and automation in online recruiting may be highly beneficial for both businesses and job-seekers.

11.3 Impact and Challenges Faced: Navigating the Consequences of Technological Advances

In a number of scenarios, including online job boards, AI and automation have an impact on the recruitment process. By automating processes such as résumé screening and interview scheduling and using data analysis to determine the m:ost qualified individuals, these technologies are assisting businesses in reducing administrative work so that they can concentrate on hiring and retaining the best talent. The use of AI and automation in online recruitment is not, however, without hurdles.

One of the most significant advantages of employing AI and automation in online recruitment is the ability to rapidly and precisely analyze enormous amounts of data. This allows companies to quickly find the most qualified candidates and make informed hiring decisions.

However, the usage of AI and automation presents certain obstacles for virtual recruitment. One potential challenge with the use of AI and automation in online recruitment is the possibility of bias in the selection process due to the biased data used to train these systems. There should be significant concern over the likelihood of bias in the selection process. The outcome will be biased if the data utilized to train AI and automation systems has inherent bias. As a result, qualified members of underrepresented groups may be missed.

The potential for robots and AI to replace human recruiters is a further cause for concern. The increased mechanization of business operations has the potential to undermine the human economy by displacing recruiters.

The inability of AI systems to successfully defend their outcomes and explain their procedures is sometimes noted as a cause for worry. Organizations must know the motivations of AI systems in order to comply with the law.

AI and other forms of automation have far-reaching consequences for the digital job- searching process. Businesses may be able to rapidly and cheaply discover the most qualified applicants. AI and automation have several potential drawbacks, such as the potential for discrimination, the elimination of human labor, and a lack of transparency and explanation.

To reduce their effect, businesses must be aware of these issues and actively work to fix them. To address these concerns, businesses should invest in developing more transparent and explainable AI systems. It is also important to continually monitor the data used to train and evaluate these systems to prevent biased outcomes (Sethi, 2021).

11.3.1 Legal Barriers to Full Implementation of AI and Automation

Online job boards that use AI and other forms of automation are anticipated to be very beneficial to the recruitment process. Nonetheless, a variety of legal barriers and impediments prevent the broad use of these technologies.

Farooq and Javed (2021) argue that the risk of discrimination throughout the recruiting process warrants legal concerns. The outcome will be biased if the data utilized to train AI and automation systems has inherent bias. As a result, qualified members of underrepresented groups may be missed. Businesses may avoid legal concerns by using AI and automation technologies that are transparent, easy to understand, and consistent with all existing laws and regulations, such as those regulating equal employment opportunity (EEO).

If an AI or automation system commits an error or causes harm, this may raise further responsibility concerns. If someone is hurt as a result of a company's system flaws or usage of one of these technologies, the firm may be held liable. This risk may be mitigated, however, if firms test their AI and automation systems thoroughly and implement error-prevention methods.

Another issue is the lack of standards and rules in the field of AI and automation. As there is no currently accepted standard for the design, development, and deployment of AI and automation systems, it may be challenging for organizations to ensure that their systems comply with relevant laws and regulations. Due to the absence of regulation and oversight in the sector, it is difficult for businesses to negotiate the legal and ethical problems associated with the use of these technologies.

Finally, the legal barriers and restrictions related with the use of AI and automation in online recruitment are little understood and underappreciated Fong and Lucey (2021). Numerous companies may be ignorant of the potential legal challenges or lack the means and or knowledge to resolve them.

In conclusion, the application of AI and automation in virtual recruitment is hindered by a number of legal challenges and impediments, including discrimination, liability, and a lack of standardization and regulation. Businesses may overcome these challenges by investing in AI systems that are straightforward to explain, compliant with all relevant regulations, protected by robust safeguards, and up to date with the most recent research in the field. The government should address these concerns by enacting rules and regulations that protect the rights of both job-seekers and businesses.

11.3.2 Comparing AI and Automation in between Developed and Developing Countries

In both industrialized and emerging nations, AI and automation are widely used in the virtual recruiting process. When comparing the use of AI and automation in online job advertisements and recruitment in developed and developing nations, there are noticeable distinctions.

In affluent economies, using AI or some kind of automation to assist with online job searches is becoming commonplace (William V. Silverman, 2021). In these regions, firms have easy access to the most recent AI and automation technology, and many have already incorporated them into their employment procedures. Due to their stronger infrastructures, developed nations are able to spend more resources on AI and automation.

However, in poorer nations, the use of AI and automation in online job boards is only beginning. It is likely that enterprises in these regions lack access to AI and automation technology or the necessary knowledge. Due to their less developed infrastructures, developing nations have a more difficult time adopting and implementing these technologies.

Despite these distinctions, enterprises and job-seekers in both wealthy and developing nations might gain from the use of AI and automation in online recruiting. When it comes to recruiting, AI and automation may assist organizations in the developed world to discover the best candidates more quickly and make better recruitment choices, but in the developing world, they may increase employment possibilities while reducing the time and money necessary to fill them (McKinsey Global Institute, 2017).

In industrialized nations, the use of AI and automation in online job searches is more advanced. Developed nations commit more resources and expertise to AI and automation; therefore, they are further along in its deployment. While developing nations may be able to lower recruiting expenses and expedite the application process, wealthier nations have more sophisticated systems and a larger applicant pool from which to choose. However, both wealthy and developing nations must invest in the necessary infrastructure and knowledge to apply these technologies effectively.

11.3.3 The Emergence of a New Era: AI and Automation in Virtual Recruitment

Recruiting on the internet has reached a new phase in which it is faster, more precise, and more accessible than ever before, owing to the advent of AI and automation. Several human resources operations, such as sifting through applications, scheduling interviews, analyzing data, and selecting the top individuals, are being automated or simplified using machine learning. Possibilities for joblessness in HR may grow as a result of these innovations, which may disrupt the established means by which organizations recruit new employees.

Using AI and robotic process automation in online hiring may save employers time and effort. Using robotic analysis of data such as résumés, interviews, and more, companies may be able to find the most qualified candidates and make more informed hiring decisions. With this method, firms may be able to reduce costs and speed up the hiring process without sacrificing quality Deloitte (2019). Tech Trends 2019 Utilizing automation and AI in virtual recruitment might help expand the number of available positions. It is possible that AI and automation may make it easier for underrepresented groups to join the workforce by making everyday tasks simpler. Moreover, AI and automation may help connect job-seekers with organizations whose requirements align with their skills. Additionally, the expansion of AI and automated procedures may provide new job opportunities. As business procedures become more automated, human recruiters may someday become obsolete. Those with knowledge of data science, machine learning, and the creation of artificial intelligence may discover new opportunities.

The use of AI and automation in online recruitment ushers in a new era in which the search for and hiring of applicants is accelerated, streamlined, and democratized. These technology improvements may lead to a drastic shift in how businesses attract and choose new employees, and hence generating exciting new job opportunities (World Economic Forum, 2020). Companies must invest in these technologies to improve their recruitment processes and preserve their competitiveness, while job-seekers must invest in the necessary skills to capitalize on the new opportunities. Businesses and governments should take precautions to prevent the spread of bigotry and discrimination when implementing such technologies, and they should do so openly and honestly.

11.4 Assessing India's Societal Approach to AI and Automation in Virtual Recruitment

India has made significant advancements in the realm of remote employment and is also a pioneer in the development of AI and robotics (National Artificial Intelligence Portal). However, there is need for improvement in the Indian culture's stance on AI and automation in online recruiting.

The Indian government has endeavored to expand the usage of AI and robotics in the country's economy and labor. One such endeavor is the National Artificial Intelligence Portal, whose stated purpose is to serve as a hub for the development and distribution of AI-based solutions (Chakraborty & Ali, 2021). In addition, the government has developed a number of policies and programs to encourage the growth and widespread use of AI and automation. Despite these efforts, the positive effects of AI and automation on virtual recruiting are not widely acknowledged or valued in Indian culture. It is likely that many firms and job-seekers are either ignorant of these technologies' advantages or lack the means to use them.

It is challenging for firms in India to verify that their AI and automation technologies are compliant due to the absence of standards and regulation in these areas (Agarwal & Ved, 2019). The absence of rules and standards may make it difficult for corporations to address the legal and ethical concerns raised by the broad use of these technologies.

Existing talent shortages in AI and automation-related fields may limit the general use of these technologies in online hiring. Companies may opt to pay for the training and education of their workers to assist them obtain marketable skills, regardless of the expense.

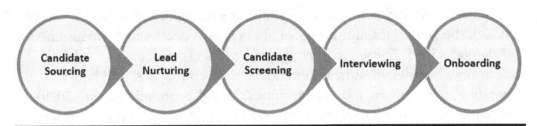

Candidate Sourcing → Lead Nurturing → Candidate Screening → Interviewing → Onboarding

Figure 11.1 Using AI successfully in the recruitment process.

India is making tremendous strides in AI and automation, but the public's view of AI and automation in the context of online job searches needs improvement. Most Indians are ignorant of the advantages and possibilities of virtual recruiting, despite government efforts to promote the use of AI and automation. The expanding use of AI and robotic process automation in online recruiting may be constrained by a lack of rules and laws, as well as a labor scarcity. To realize the full potential of these technologies, a well-trained workforce, a strong public education system, and uniform standards are required.

AI is rapidly replacing human labor in all aspects of the recruitment process. This includes candidate sourcing, screening, and interviewing shown in Figure 11.1. In order to analyze résumés and find people who meet the requirements of a certain post, sourcing systems may make use of AI. The application of AI in automated interviewing software might help sift through résumés and identify which prospects should go on to the next round of review by human recruiters. A candidate's qualifications may be evaluated with the help of AI by analyzing their answers to interview questions. In addition, AI might be used to identify instances of prejudice in the hiring process and give objective criticism. Applying AI here will streamline the hiring process and help find the best applicants faster.

11.5 Shaping the Future: The Evolution of AI and Automation in Virtual Recruitment

It is projected that the use of automated processes and AI, in addition to the proliferation of online bulletin boards for employment opportunities, will continue to increase in this context. These instruments are already very advanced and capable of doing a broad variety of jobs; but, as technology continues to improve, they will only continue to become more effective and adaptable. Because of this, virtual recruiters will be able to more thoroughly screen and filter job applications before focusing on applicants who have the highest level of qualification. This will lead to an increase in the overall efficiency of the recruiting process. Things like virtual interviews, individualized comments, and even job offers are all within reach thanks to the aid of AI and automation. It is likely that the use of AI and process automation (PA) may result in increased levels of productivity and cost-effectiveness in virtual recruiting. AI and automation in online recruitment have an exciting future ahead of them, and it is quite likely that this future will be to the mutual advantage of both companies and job-seekers.

References

Agarwal, I., & Ved, R. (2019). AI in India: Hype or Reality? Brookings India Research Paper.

Chakraborty, R., & Ali, A. (2021). India's National AI Strategy: A Focus on Responsible AI and Skilling? Harvard Business Review.

Chui, M., & Manyika, J. (2018). The technology of the metaverse. Harvard Business Review, 96(6), 92–101.

Davarpanah, M., & Qin, J. (2021). The metaverse and its potential impact on business. Journal of Digital Transformation, 1–12. DOI: 10.1007/s42979-021-00041-9

Deloitte. (2019). Tech Trends 2019: Beyond the Digital Frontier? Deloitte Insights.

Farooq, S., & Javed, F. (2021). Ethical and legal challenges of using artificial intelligence in recruitment. Journal of Open Innovation: Technology, Market, and Complexity, 7(2), 63.

Fong, K., & Lucey, B. P. (2021). Artificial intelligence and employment law: Legal and ethical issues in talent acquisition. Berkeley Journal of Employment and Labor Law, 42(1), 1–45.

Girma, S., & Fischer, M. (2020). Artificial intelligence and the future of recruiting. Human Resource Management Review, 30(1), 100715.

Kumar, A., Vyas, P., & Bansal, M. (2021). The impact of artificial intelligence on recruitment process: A review. International Journal of Management Technology, and Social Sciences (IJMTS), 6(1), 29–35.

McKinsey Global Institute. (2017). Jobs Lost, Jobs Gained: What the Future of Work Will Mean for Jobs, Skills, and Wages? McKinsey & Company.

Sethi, R. (2021). Rise of AI and its impact on recruitment. Human Resource Management Review, 31(1), 101–114.

William V.S. (2021). Artificial intelligence automation in virtual recruiting: Legal challenges and impediments by William V. Silverman. Harvard Journal of Law and Technology, 35(2), 557–578.

World Economic Forum. (2020). The Future of Jobs Report 2020. Geneva: World Economic Forum.

Chapter 12

Interplay of Artificial Intelligence and the Metaverse in HR

Kundu Varshini Naidu, Priyanka Reddy, and Rajesh Kumar K.V.
Woxsen University
Hyderabad, Telangana, India

12.1 Introduction

Today's world is all about data. From consumer behavior to employee engagement, attrition rates, and talent quality, we are surrounded by data. And as we accumulate it, the quantity of data is only increasing exponentially. With vast amounts of data, making logical sense out of it without getting overwhelmed becomes the priority. This is where analytics enters. Analytics has been the savior in this data-driven economy. It has provided quantitative help for analysis of such vast data, resulting in superior decision making and action taking based on trends emerging from the data analysis.

Analytical techniques have an advantage of being predictive, which is objective in nature, in contrast to the reactive aspect, which is subjective (Adel A. 2022 & Xun et.al. 2021). And the result is objective information free from biases and errors, as even qualitative findings are analyzed objectively via analytics. For professionals of the human resources (HR) field, this would mean that advanced analytics has provided a means and opportunity to move on from the traditional functional role to expanding and anchoring the role as an objective, data-driven strategic partner (Bruce et al., 2015).

DOI: 10.4324/b23404-12

Artificial intelligence (AI), on the other hand, can refer to a variety of things, ranging from specific types of AI, such as expert learning systems, to speculative AI that fits requirements for awareness and sensibility. AI-based (AIT) innovations such as machine learning, VR technology, bots, robots, chatbots, process automation, deep structured learning, cognitive dialogue, the IoT, natural-language processor (NLP), analytics, and augmented reality (AR) are changing the approach HR professionals operate. It helps HR executives reduce the strain of recurring operational activities by supporting them in making choices and forecasting employee behavior in the workplace. AIT is primarily utilized in recruiting, learning, employee satisfaction, and holding employees. It saves the budget and energy, making HR responsibilities quicker to do (Pillai & Sivathanu, 2020).

A number of experiments have been painstakingly conducted in the past with varied data sets to understand the correlation between various elements, such as compensation and individual performance (Divandari et al., 2018), extrinsic rewards, and intrinsic motivation (Deci et al., 1999). With a wide range of analytical tools available, and the capacity to perform statistical calculations and execute various mathematical models, it has become effortless to analyze the data of such experiments to gain valuable insights.

AI is a method for creating metaverse assets. The metaverse was indeed envisioned as synthesis of several inventions and developments, including VR technology, mixed reality, dynamic workplace methods, extended reality, and AI, etc., figures, environments, including architecture and feature patterns, are some examples. Utilizing AI, developers can enable automated operating system, empowering participants to produce better, comprehensive resources inside a virtual world using minimal work. Lacking AI, developing a compelling, authentic, and sustainable metaverse encounter would become a challenge.

Looking into the applications of AI in meta and analytics, this chapter delves into the role and impact of AI, the metaverse, and analytics in various domains of HR, such as learning and development, employee performance, compensation, retention, recruitment, talent management, and career development. Finally, AI- and analytics-related challenges and best practice for successful implementation are observed.

12.2 Learning and Training Development

Due to the rapid expansion of technology, the very concept of working is shifting, and firms can no longer regard training and ability development as a premium (Seethalakshmi & Sucharita, 2022). At the moment, modern information such as the network, electronic gadgets, wireless connections, and networks enable an infinite inflow of real-world data created by individuals. This info is referred to as big data. This is critical for enterprises because it can be used to better understand their staff and consumers, allowing them to develop their business appropriately (Gurusinghe et al., 2021). In the view of major changes, re-skilling is labeled "the new pattern in recruitment." In the consequence, businesses are progressively relying on training as well as learning and development (L&D) to bridge talent gap across wide range of different business domains.

The future of employment is changing as technology advances at a rapid pace. Owing to the rise of AI, businesses have begun recognizing the requirements in rehabilitating and training respective employees. Furthermore, learning and progressive services as well are undergoing substantial transformations as a result of contemporary AI applications (Upadhyay & Khandelwal, 2019).

AI assists in assessing training requirements, designing customized material, and delivering training wherever it is convenient for employees (Maity, 2019). AI assists workers by enhancing training procedures and methodologies with contextual, specialization, relevancy, and personalizing. AI has the potential to make learning more targeted, intriguing, interactive, immersive, and quantifiable (Upadhyay & Khandelwal, 2019). During a COVID scenario, one of the major concerns for the HR department is skill building (Gaur et al., 2021). AI has the potential to provide tailored training. When training is appropriate, adaptable, and purposeful, it has a greater impact. AI can accumulate required data about a staff's training ability, talent inclination, and ways on how they deal to complete the job and duties so that it can come up with similar proposed programs that will empower the employee performance and adroitness in the organization.

It allows the employee to go farther by gradually retraining and retesting, while also lowering the total coaching cost. The technology can adapt to individual trainees' learning styles, allowing for more personalization. It categorizes students depending on their talents or capabilities (Upadhyay & Khandelwal, 2019). Furthermore, it also encourages cooperative learning. Individuals from various divisions are habitually required to collaborate in order to gain from each other; here, AI will help organizations to do that. Collaborating with different functions will encourage all-purpose training, improve organizational standards, and create efficient teamwork. The aforementioned types of training are perfect for the present-day workplace, as a majority of routine work is done in groups.

Individuals are required to understand the directions to operate within the meta world. This will expand its span in implementing various L&D programs related to organizational change. By implementing VR in HRM, we should seek reconsidering how personnel will be educated and trained in these new technologies and applications.

The metaverse within HR may use VR to provide engaging as well as realistic training opportunities to workers. Such advanced learning session may increase individual productivity and effectiveness so that businesses might consider teaching and enlightening staff, allowing individuals to practice actual events via the virtual world.

12.3 Recruitment

There is an evident change in how recruitment processes are happening, post-COVID. Companies began to use AI systems to map candidate skill sets to desired employment positions. Implementing the meta will increase the company's capital, but it will also benefit in the long term by decreasing time-consuming tasks.

VR hiring events provide applicants the ability to interact alongside prospective employees while also providing more realistic displays about unique types of organization where candidates may start heading in the future. Candidates expect greater firms to give visual displays so that future employees can acquire some sense about the company atmosphere.

AI technologies have a significant influence in almost every element of recruitment. Conventional recruitment approaches need greater financial, employee, and time investment (Mainka, 2019). AI as an assistant helps the HR department in finding a wide range of suitable candidates (Delecraz et al., 2022). Integrating behavior and cognitive sciences alongside the capability of large information sources and machine learning techniques allows a better understanding of job candidates' talents and the optimum service for fitting them to employment. Using electronic systems in recruiting and selecting processes can assist firms in discovering skilled candidates and hiring those who fit based on person-job fit and person-organization fit (Delecraz et al., 2022).

Organizations may now skip search agencies and their costs by using AI-enabled recruitment techniques to reach out to prospects with accounts on social media sites like Facebook or corporate networking sites like LinkedIn (Black & van Esch, 2021). AI-powered tools also assist in the elimination of redundant information, and negative features of job posts that discourage potential people from registering and would recommend changes that can enhance the advertisement as a whole. They analyze actual data from various sources with similar job specifications to determine what works in the industry in order to attract more suitable individuals.

If a job opportunity is posted online, not only qualified candidates that meet the criteria will apply, but also candidates who don't meet the criteria may apply. It is possible to use analytics to match job information with the behavioral patterns, preferences, and geographical factors of potential candidates. Likewise, although if AI-enabled recruitment tools are excellent at discovering and prioritizing passive job applicants, their application will be determined by both their utility and their efficacy (Black & van Esch, 2021).

Once a company receives large number of applications, it may be difficult to determine which applicant is an ideal fit for the position. AI technologies may analyze candidate credentials, evaluate them depending on the work specification, and then identify the top candidates. If an applicant does not meet the requirements of a specific role, an AI-based analytics tool can assist in recommending a qualified candidate for other positions.

Interviews may be simplified in the near future with the help of AI. AI is capable of reading face gestures and interpreting speech answers. We contend that the battle for ability will be additionally increased by a competition to obtain computer-based intelligence empowered selecting devices (Black & van Esch, 2021). It may assess responses of the candidates that are questioned to applicants at the time of the first interview process. After that, the candidates are given scores and final list is generated according to scores provided by AI by the analytics tool, depending on their response. This method aids in the elimination of prejudices regardless of age, sexuality, region, or color.

Economics, comparative advantage, senior executive backing, HR preparation, competitiveness, and assistance from AI providers all affect the use of AI for recruitment (Pillai & Sivathanu, 2020). HireVue, Mya Systems, Hired Score, Wade & Wendy, and more applications provide AI-based recruiting services for well-known organizations such as Unilever, L'Oreal, Vodafone, and PwC.

12.4 Talent Management

As mentioned by Lewis and Heckman (2006), there are three phases of personnel management in the workforce life cycle, include acquiring, nurturing, and retention of organizational talent. In detail, talent advancement is a subset of talent management that refers to the method of grounding existing talent to improve their present skill set and knowledge so it creates the abilities that they can meet the company's current and prospect needs in order to accomplish organizational progress and build a transition plan for crucial roles (Sivathanu & Pillai, 2019).

AI may help firms maximize their talent management skills by creating an environment that fits employees' requirements and promotes productivity. It aids in personalizing career progression, boosting emergency preparedness, closing skill gaps, and influencing compensation strategy, all of which have the capability to assist the organization. Analytics might provide an opportunity to manage people fairly. For example, Gurusinghe et al. (2021) mentioned analytics may help with talent management choices such as establishing critical roles in firms that impact organization performance, selecting a potential resource to fill such jobs, evaluating performance, and controlling talent turnover.

Successful talent management necessitates concurrent succession pathways so that aspiring expert personnel need not required to give in their true passion in just to advance to positions of leadership or administration (Mayo, 2018). To assist with normal job needs, AI can offer employees with appropriate intelligent coaching or study material suggestions. Employees will acknowledge a transition in an experience that takes into account their specific ambitions and needs as a favorable divergence from the previous multipurpose approach, and administrators will consider investing in employee training and development for more efficiency.

The challenge now is, how can we recognize the needs of employees?

As stated by Saling and Do (2020), a unique database gathering method that identifies both group and person expertise, abilities, and actions will deliver data that will assist management leaders in making the optimal talent management recommendations at the appropriate time. Many aspects of our daily lives are influenced by data analytics, whether streaming suggestions to advertisements that appear in our feeds on digital media. This similar technology has the potential to make a significant contribution in HR functions and talent management by allowing people to sell their talent sets and companies to specify their employment demands (Saling & Do, 2020).

Developing the appropriate judgments in talent management is difficult since decision makers have inadequate data to develop inferences regarding which employee is most suited for a position or function. In a nutshell, many firms base their choices and judgments on personal experience or the organizational ideological systems (Gurusinghe et al., 2021). This is where big data and analytics come into play, assisting top management in making the best judgments possible depending on data analysis. Additionally, big data may be used as a resource to establish successful teams, resulting in significant returns on personnel inputs (Russell & Bennett, 2015).

12.5 Career Development

Today's capabilities are rapidly fading, with some specialists predicting a life span of about 2 to 3 years. A lack of insight into professional growth prospects is a hurdle that many people confront in the workforce. Professionals are also generally uninformed of the sources and linkages available to assist them in achieving their professional objectives (Bennion, 2021). Employees used to stay within respective companies for the duration of employment, rising from beginning-level work to the highest positions of management. In the era of rapid market dynamics, frequent redundancies, and the emergence of new enterprises, employees now have the opportunity for expedited career growth. The influence of Gen-Z workers has ushered in enhancements in the strategies employed by job seekers and employees to achieve professional advancement.

Companies must adopt a deliberate strategy for workforce improvement to retain personnel. The scenarios encompass various stages along the educational journey, spanning from initial enrollment and course progression, through study outcomes, transition into the workforce, and culminating in the enhancement of competencies within a framework of continuous learning (Westman et al., 2021). Workers deserve to know the present-day training and advancement alternatives that help them in their advancement in future careers and carry through to their targets.

Employees may receive personalized advice from AI, such as customized professional development ideas that move with the organization and optimize career possibilities. Professionally crafted material not only supplements management assistance, but also demonstrates to workers that their companies are involved in their careers.

Using data analytics and AI, the acquired observations on each individual's career growth are delivered in a tailored manner. Each individual might know one's working path, and that is combined with the exact training stimulations required for connecting the present and future talent gap. Among all ways that are available, the most potent way is to support the training methods that accommodate workers with information and career advancement trainings they are required to undertake for professional shift.

12.6 Compensation

AI plays a key role in compensation, as it helps deal with equity issues in pay, helps in bench-marking salaries, and ensures that employees get paid for their value and contribution, and not simply tenure or position. The focus has moved from paying for jobs to paying for skills. IBM has been using AI-based compensation, where AI recommends pay increases. While managers are also given the final hold on the decision, very few managers were dissatisfied with the recommendations, in fact less than 5% of them were unhappy (Joanne, 2019). This demonstrates the potential of AI in developing systems and handling them. What then needs focus on is the training data for the AI, because if it is unnoticed, it can cause biases within the algorithm.

The application of HR Analytics to compensation demonstrates a notable interconnection. Based on a study and responses collected for the same, it was conclusive that compensation and benefits assessment significantly improve with the use of analytics in the organization (Nitya et al., 2021).

A highly successful organization in the healthcare industry faced issues of employee productivity and attrition due to variable compensation pay levels. Using analytics to identify compensation thresholds, maximum, and minimum optimum values, this spiked an increase in the productivity levels, engagement levels, and satisfaction rates. An added benefit was a reduced attrition rate and an overall decrease in the compensation expenditures. Similarly, another company, with the effective utilization of predictive behavioral analytics, successfully achieved a reduction in its compensation costs by $20 million in the form of a drop in retention bonuses, and also caused the turnover rate to drop by half of its initial value (Bruce et al., 2015).

Consider the application of analytics in sales. Sales analytics can be used to create an appropriate sales compensation plan. Sales incentives are usually pay for performance based and could depend on number of sales or revenue generated. This can be a tricky combination. So, to ensure fairness in the incentive plan, various factors, including territory is considered, especially for field sales (Chad, 2015).

While there would be resistance to AI-based pay, educating the employees and giving managers the option to use the AI tool rather than a making it a mandate could help lower the resistance and increase the rate of adoption. Its adoption also decreases the load on managers as training an algorithm requires far less effort than training about pay practice changes to all the organization's managers. Also, changes could be started off with one area of compensation, like hiring pay, instead of automating all compensation simultaneously (Dave, 2021).

In meta, the emphasis shifts from simply being an employee to being a meta employee. Employers will be oriented towards cryptocurrency as a form of payment (Tam, 2022). But the key thing to note is the value. What is the value being paid to the employee? The pay could be in different kinds of cryptocurrency. Also, the values keep going up and down. So, not simply managing pay, but making sure the value the employee receives for their work and efforts remains same. That is, the salary mentioned on a document is consistent and provided in liquid cash consistently. A pay hike is provided yearly; this covers the value aspect. In cryptocurrency, the value is ever changing. Hence, maintaining this value is key to a fair work pay system.

Although, with this new work environment, a new set of benefits enter. Now, care and insurance also need to be provided for meta workers based on their work and situations in another realm as well. Finally, for pay equity in this virtual environment, the person behind the avatar needs to be verified and confirmed, so as to avoid an employee interchanging their avatar with another person in the real world.

12.7 Employee Retention

With the evolving role of HR as a strategic partner, HR professionals have been able to assist the leadership and board with one of the unique competitive advantages of any organization: talent. With the analytical techniques, it has become easier to retain talent responsible for great value and contribution in the organization.

The IBM retention strategy for its employee talent is based on an AI system. It helped identify various trends and patterns associated with employee retention in the company and also provided targets of focus for potential investment. With a staggering 95% accuracy, the company has been able to save $300 million. The return on interest (ROI) on this retention program, and the potential benefits associated with retention, have been immense (Pontefract, 2019).

McKinsey uses analytics in a constant journey to develop they own strategy for employee retention. Machine learning algorithms were used to test hundreds of data points and patterns (identifies unobserved patterns in behavior), and make predictions at organizational and individual levels. The approach and techniques led to counter-intuitive insights. Compensation and performance appraisal were the top expected factors for attrition. This was overturned with the analytical insights showing a lack of availability of similar interest groups and people and lack of coaching and mentoring as the topmost reasons for employees leaving the company. After ensuring satisfactory coaching and mentoring, the unwanted attrition rate was down by 20-40% (Bruce et al., 2015).

In most cases, employee engagement directly corresponds to the retention rate of employees in an organization. With meta, not only do employees get the benefit of remote working, but also the added benefit of real life-like social interaction. A study conducted of about 1,500 employees and employers each concluded with a result showing high levels of excitement for an immersive work environment (Lin, 2022). The metaverse provides an opportunity of interacting and participating in a far meaningful way, to the point where employees could design their spaces. It is a way of living. With such excitement and proper flexibility provided in the use of the platform, the engagement levels would turn out to be high, and thus drastically motivating employees to stay.

12.8 Employee Performance

While HR is a unique competitive advantage for any organization, it also represents the output received from those human resources. Performance and productivity drive competitive advantage. With technology, most of the repetitive tasks are handled by AI to enhance productivity. Hence, firms are vying to integrate AI and ML into their processes to boost their businesses by improving performance. After all, there is a high positive correlation and impact of AI on employee performance and employee engagement at work (Wijayati et al., 2022). To gain maximum results, AI and humans must follow a collaborative approach. While uncertainty regarding employment would lurk with new AI, the results achieved and support provided by AI mitigate those concerns to some extent (Chowdhury et al., 2022).

Similarly, analytics used in appraisal systems not only provide useful insights, but they are free of subjectivity bias. This inculcates a feeling of trust and fairness of the appraisal system. Employees perceive the system to be more accurate, and they are highly satisfied and in turn become willing to improve their performance. IBM has been successfully using these systems to provide ongoing feedback to employees instead of a quarterly one. IBM's self-powered analytical tools such as IBM Kenexa and Synergita have been helpful in providing insights to HR professionals to improve performance and manage the organization's talent effectively (Sharma & Sharma, 2017).

The metaverse as a technology has a huge impact on the performance of employees. One of the key reasons is the deep virtual social interactions. Unlike a video, here, people can perform movements, which indulges all the senses. It is no longer a two-dimensional exchange, but a real-life three-dimensional experience. It enables physical expressions, especially non-verbal ones, and the audio is also geographically located, hence giving a more realistic feel (Hennig-Thurau et al., 2022). With this, there is some semblance of a deep social connection with people, thus driving the benefits that come along with social engagement on employee performance.

12.9 Challenges in HR Tech: AI, Analytics, and Meta

AI and analytics have repeatedly proven to be an excellent tool for achieving valuable results with the use of data. Even so, it is not omnipotent. It has several flaws, limitations, and challenges in its utilization for effective output. It can be difficult to catch up the implementation with words of progress and a shift to AI.

1. Complexity of jobs and output expectations in HR
   Understanding and being able to measure what a good employee is in terms of output has become considerably complex. A huge demand has fallen upon the expectations relative to the requirements of ability

structure of employees. And while AI is getting better at handling functions like performance management, issues around its reliability have been floating around. AI lacks in the decision-making ability relative to the emotional experience of humans. While it may be able to match and verify most of the job applicants' required skills for a given job and role and their competency levels, it cannot measure all the human factors like teamwork accurately (Lili & Lei, 2019) because the subjective data fed for analysis and operations might be ripe with biases.

2. Risk of 100% AI decision making

   AI decision making to a huge extent implicitly lies at the mercy of human perception and engineering. The algorithms when engineered and designed can end up attaining and integrating the ingrained biases of humans towards various factors such as gender and background. And this algorithm applied to data and being used to gain insights will only become biased greatly with time if left unchecked and unmonitored (Shrestha et al., 2019).

3. Training data bias

   The insights and patterns gained from data depend upon the quantity and quality of data. Quality would indicate that the data is purely objective and free of any subjective biases from relevant and connected variables. For instance, biases can emerge from any sort of incomplete information and dependence on historical evidence that can be flawed in the present context and no longer applicable to the same extent. These biases could perpetuate further if not monitored and managed carefully.

   Two crucial problems relevant to machine learning include algorithmic bias and overfit. To resolve this, understanding of statistical models and how they can be used to train the algorithms need to be put to practice, although awareness of the problems is the key. With improper training, some necessary data could be excluded or irrelevant data included. Statistical correlations that might be completely irrelevant may occur, causing the problem of overfit (Hamilton & Sodeman, 2019).

4. Prediction of outcomes that are critical, yet infrequent and rare in nature

   Data science deals with vast amounts of data. Lack of data in terms of quantity can affect the reliability and validity of the insights, patterns, and results achieved. Statistically, a greater number of observations yield accurate results as the error factor decreases. So, no matter how efficient the algorithms, lack of data can downgrade the performance output of the machine. Hence, events that rarely occur would need way more data to provide any valuable and meaningful prediction results (Fortuny et al., 2013).

5. Ethical and adversarial issues

   Decisions made around employees must be fair in nature. If not, these AI systems can cause exclusionary feelings, and feel threatening to the one governed by it. Hence, whether an employee is promoted or not, fired, hired, taken action against, who that person is and why that specific person will be a part of this fairness trial becomes consequential to explain what is done, to whom, why, and how with proper justification. Within this framework, decisions can be made procedurally, justly, and ethically. In this respect, perception of fairness is yet another consideration of social and psychological factors that play an important role in defining and shaping this perception of fairness. If the understanding of this perception is unclear or unacceptable, employees can make a subjective assessment to create their own understanding and exploit the system. Human beings are reflective and can monitor and correct their perceptions. But for algorithms it can be especially challenging. "Adversarial machine learning" works as a potential solution that helps to deal with these challenges (Tambe et al., 2019).

Amazon's recruitment analytics failure: Amazon invested in an analytics tool in a bid to acquire the best talent; however, it turned out to be discriminating against women. The algorithm that ran on evidence and past data, preferred men, as historical data showed men as being better performers, and even amongst them, White men. This caused the algorithm to reject résumés that included words such as "women." The algorithm preferred résumés with verb words like *executed, captured*, etc., which are commonly found on male résumés. Amazon tried to fix this by removing the gender aspect from measure, but in instances where it would appear on other parts of résumé, the candidate would be rejected simply based on this word. As an appropriate corrective measure was not found for the algorithm, it was scrapped (Jeffrey, 2018).

The metaverse, being a highly immersive platform, comes with quite a list of challenges.

■ There have been moral and ethical issues surrounding the use of the platform by the people within the metaverse. Hence, this follows the practical challenge of understanding the requirements to create rules around engagement in the virtual world and implementing them at the ground level.

- With meta, there is a chance of the employees being paid in cryptocurrency. Also, the basis on which employees are paid is a question to be resolved.
- The biggest issue is the scope of law. The reach of law usually has been in the real world, which extended to virtual 2D environments. Now, in meta, most of the laws are not applicable. How do you use the laws mandated on real people for doing a crime on someone vs crime done in the meta? After all, where is the physical harm? But it is mental and emotional in nature. How do you assess and judge this nature of crime in a virtual environment? The same goes for the employment protection provided by a nation. Now that workplace is decentralized, how does employment protection law play its role?
- Provided the scale at which companies operate, and the nature of sensitivity of the data involved, it becomes difficult to maintain privacy. The company would want to keep the data private, but it is already exposed to the digital footprint in the meta. Who owns the data, which exact data, to what extent, and how do they ensure the security of this data?
- For small-level companies, the high-tech products and services will be way out of their budget. After all, tech cannot be simply added at the cost of employees. It should augment their experience, not become a burden.
- Finally, looking over the bad aspects of remote work, the challenge lies with mitigating them as they will be carried to the meta environment. This is crucial to avoid employee burnout.

12.10 Best Practices

Most companies have already adopted or are in the process of adopting data technology to revolutionize and transform their businesses. These include analytics, AI, and the most trending metaverse platform. There is no perfect way of adopting and implementing these technologies. It depends on the business and its needs. But there have been companies that have mastered and been successful at institutionalizing some of these technologies. It can be noted how similar and overlapping are a few practices amongst all the technologies. These practices are applicable to the meta environment, where the focus on human is the key. Their experience is the priority.

David Green (2017), in his paper "People and Performance" laid out 16 best practices for high-end people analytics. Amongst them, quite notable is the human factor in the HR being a vital element of focus while making data-driven decisions. At the end, it is about analyzing patterns related to humans involved in businesses. So as objective as it may be, room for exceptions need to be made as necessary. Having a chief human Resource Officer CHRO as the source and mediator for change helps make the transition and adoption easier (Green, 2017). The HR team in people analytics and technology is not the only involved party. The resources needed involve people outside HR, such as a specific analytics team. The expertise of handling the technology and coming up with unique insights is their domain. Patience is required to go through the fundamentals so that errors can be reduced. It might take months to clean data, and to even lay out future processes for the same, but it has to be done. Analytics and the meta go in tandem, as the data from the meta can be analyzed to derive insights and improve the experience further.

Another important factor is communication. At a higher level, making sure that the vision of the organization, the strategy, and expected outcome is communicated to the relevant stakeholders is imperative for alignment of goals and objectives. At a lower level, communication from the analytics team to the relevant team, here, as the HR team plays a role in determining how those insights can be further used to improve performance. This is most effectively done through storytelling, with visualizations to make it compelling evidence for driving action. Communication in the meta environment with all the non-verbal cues the avatar suggests can be a source of effective expression if done properly. So, mastering the avatar expression, or the syncing of both, is important.

It is crucial to monitor the functioning and output of the systems, tools, and meta environment resultant variables and analyze the gap between the actual output from the expected implementation. Also, while collecting data, various biasing factors should be identified and removed.

A culture that promotes decision making based on data, facts, and evidence is essential for the adoption of these technologies. This chiefly depends on the leadership of the organization, as it must be highly data driven in its strategic decision making to attain the best possible output (Steve et al., 2011).

Concerns regarding data collected lurks on the minds of employee. Herein enters the factor of employee trust. With transparency follows trust. To make processes work accurately, the data should be relevant and as accurate as possible. Employee trust is then followed by the provision and availability of relevant and accurate data (Marritt, 2016).

The other aspect would be to have an effective change management process. As new technology keeps developing, assessing them and adopting them for the success of business would be a continuous change at some level. Hence, change management specific to intelligent data-related technology adoption across all levels becomes the key driver to keep up with the competition or surpass them.

12.11 The Metaverse as a Future Scope in HR

The metaverse innovation has enormous promise inside human resources. This might help in generating remote work spaces, allowing people to interact with each other, as well as perform collaboratively virtually. Furthermore, there exists the potential to harness this technology for crafting immersive VR orientation and onboarding experiences, fostering individual development, and facilitating more inclusive and captivating environments. Furthermore, metaverse technologies might also apply to produce VR employment listings, enabling firms to access a larger pool of eligible candidates. Lastly, meta technology might also be utilized to conduct simulated interview processes, giving companies greater understanding about the participant's talents as well as capabilities.

Workplace and collaboration arrangements inside virtual world workplaces are expected to undergo substantial transformation. Over these last two decades, the business workplace has gradually shifted towards a blended management framework, including discussions and cooperation occurring in VR via technological channels.

The metaverse revolutionizes industries by cultivating interconnectedness, communication, and collaboration. It fosters immersive experiences, enabling interactions through remote technologies and avatars rather than conventional electronic devices. Within their allocated group rooms, personnel can bucket their advice together using virtual keyboards, import individual computers along with keyboards within VR via collaboratation, and have communications that are not seen in past working environments.

In addition to its advantages, metaverse implementation comes with some disadvantages if it is not used ethically. In virtual mode, it facilitates more collaborative work, but is associated with high security risks. Thus, companies need to develop new policies that can be applied to the meta world.

12.12 Conclusion

Organizations can and do heavily compete on technology as a consequence of everything being data driven and, in a bid to acquire the best insights to stay ahead of competition and thrive. Several companies employ the use of AI and analytics tools to compete on the data domain to satisfy the customer and sustain businesses. These include companies such as McKinsey, IBM, etc. Even Google uses analytics extensively to manage people, achieve collaboration, and has implemented projects such as Pi-Lab and Project Oxygen (Shrivastava et al., 2018).

AI and analytics tools are reliable when it comes to making sense of vast and complicated data, and delivering actionable insights. But, the tools themselves are not a replacement for engagement with employees. It simply provides data-driven, vision, and goal-specific insights for professionals to make strategic decisions of their human capital. While AI and analytics are mostly used for the core functions of HR, there is a Belgian HR and Well Being Service Provider that utilizes a decision support system with machine learning algorithms embedded in it to enhance the health and well-being at the workplace. This drives in supporting HR decisions, while providing insights into the choice on investments and interventions to apply, all while being cost sensitive (Natalie et al., 2021).

Combining this rich technology with the meta environment only augments the existing business processes to drive exponential growth and sustainability. The swift transition to an accelerated form of remote work means a lot of trial and error. The key aim is making it all real for the workers. Considering major factors such as burnout and engagement are what makes it more human. This would bring a sense of belonging for the employees, causing an uptake in acceptance of meta.

So, consideration of the pros and cons of the tech and virtual world for assessing the fit for the organization, and using best practices for its implementation and adoption, will bring expected results and success to the organizations and businesses.

References

Adel A. (2022). Future of industry 5.0 in society: Human-centric solutions, challenges and prospective research areas. Journal of Cloud Computing, 11. https://doi.org/10.1186/s13677-022-00314-5

Bennion, I. (2021). "The future of work: AI transforms career progression". TalentCulture. Retrieved January 5, 2023 from https://talentculture.com/ai-transforms-career-progression/

Black, J. S., & van Esch, P. (2021). AI-enabled recruiting in the war for talent. Business Horizons, 64(4), 513–524. https://doi.org/10.1016/j.bushor.2021.02.015

Bruce, F. L., Bill, S., & Karen, T. (2015). "Power to the new people analytics". McKinsey Quarterly. https://www.mckinsey.com/capabilities/people-and-organizational-performance/our-insights/power-to-the-new-people-analytics

Chad, A. Z. S. (2015). "Applying analytics to sales incentive plan design". SHRM. Retrieved 3 January, 2023 from https://www.shrm.org/resourcesandtools/hr-topics/compensation/pages/sales-incentiveanalytics.aspx?_ga=2.213266769.439235807.1672753246-2137454974.1672753245

Chowdhury, S., Budhwar, P., Dey, P., Joel-Edgar, S., & Abadie, A. (2022). AI-employee collaboration and business performance: Integrating knowledge-based view, socio-technical systems and organisational socialisation framework. Journal of Business Research, 144, 31–49. https://doi.org/10.1016/j.jbusres.2022.01.069

Dave, Z. (2021). "Using AI in comp decisions? Here's how to build trust". SHRM. Retrieved 3 January, 2023 from https://www.shrm.org/resourcesandtools/hr-topics/technology/pages/using-ai-comp-decisions-how-to-build-trust.aspx

Deci, E. L., Koestner, R., & Ryan, R. M. (1999). A meta-analytic review of experiments examining the effects of extrinsic rewards on intrinsic motivation. Psychological Bulletin, 125(6), 627–668, https://doi.org/10.1037/0033-2909.125.6.627

Delecraz, S., Eltarr, L., Becuwe, M., Bouxin, H., Boutin, N., & Oullier, O. (2022). Responsible artificial intelligence in human resources technology: An innovative inclusive and fair by design matching algorithm for job recruitment purposes. Journal of Responsible Technology, 11, Article 100041. https://doi.org/10.1016/j.jrt.2022.100041

Divandari, A., Nazari, M., Seyed, J. S. R., Haji, K. A., & Rayej, H. (2018). Investigating the effect of compensation on individual performance: A study on the mediating role of internal motivation and the moderating role of self-efficacy and reward expectancy. Journal of Business Management, 10(3), 673–694. https://doi.org/10.22059/jibm.2014.51039

Gaur, B., Bashir, R., & Sanghvi, B. (2021). An AI based training framework for telecommuting employees to combat perennial skill shortages post pandemic. 2nd International Conference on Intelligent Engineering and Management (ICIEM), 171–176. https://doi.org/10.1109/ICIEM51511.2021.9445329

Green, D. (2017). The best practices to excel at people analytics. Journal of Organizational Effectiveness: People and Performance, 4(2), 137–144. https://doi.org/10.1108/JOEPP-03-2017-0027

Gurusinghe, R. N., Arachchige, B. J. H., & Dayarathna, D. (2021). Predictive HR analytics and talent management: A conceptual framework. Journal of Management Analytics, 8(2), 195–221. https://doi.org/10.1080/23270012.2021.1899857

Hamilton, R. H., & Sodeman, W. (2019). The questions we ask: Opportunities and challenges for using big data analytics to strategically manage human capital resources. Business Horizon, 63. https://doi.org/10.1016/j.bushor.2019.10.001

Hennig-Thurau, T., Aliman, D. N., Herting, A. M., Gerrit, P. C., Marc, L., & Raoul, V. K. (2022). Social interactions in the metaverse: Framework, initial evidence, and research roadmap. Journal of the Academy of Marketing Science. https://doi.org/10.1007/s11747-022-00908-0

Jeffrey, D. (2018). "Amazon scraps secret AI recruiting tool that showed bias against women". Reuters. https://www.reuters.com/article/us-amazon-com-jobs-automation-insight-idUSKCN1MK08G

Joanne, S. (2019). "Bringing artificial intelligence into pay decisions". SHRM. Retrieved 3 January, 2023 from https://www.shrm.org/resourcesandtools/hr-topics/compensation/pages/bringing-artificial-intelligence-into-pay-decisions.aspx

Junque de Fortuny, E., Martens, D., & Provost, F. (2013). Predictive modeling with big data: Is bigger really better? Big Data, 1, 215–226. https://doi.org/10.1089/big.2013.0037

Kate, B. (2022). "Metaverse vs employment law: The reality of the virtual workplace". Financial Times. https://www.ft.com/content/9463ed05-c847-425d-9051-482bd3a1e4b1

Lewis, R. E., & Heckman, R. J. (2006). Talent management: A critical review. Human Resource Management Review, 16(2), 139–154. https://doi.org/10.1016/j.hrmr.2006.03.001

Lili, Q., & Lei, Z. (2019). Opportunities and challenges of artificial intelligence to human resource management. Academic Journal of Humanities & Social Sciences, 2(1), 144–153. https://doi.org/10.25236/AJHSS.040036.

Lin, G. P. (2022). "What HR needs to know about the metaverse". SHRM. https://www.shrm.org/resourcesandtools/hr-topics/technology/pages/what-hr-needs-to-know-about-the-metaverse.aspx

Mainka, S. (2019). Algorithm-based recruiting technology in the workplace. Texas A&M Journal of Property Law, 5(3), 801–822. https://doi.org/10.37419/jpl.v5.i3.8

Maity, S. (2019), Identifying opportunities for artificial intelligence in the evolution of training and development practices. Journal of Management Development, 38(8), 651–663. https://doi.org/10.1108/JMD-03-2019-0069

Marritt, A. (2016). "People analytics – what's in it for the employees?". Retrieved 3 January, 2023 from https://www.linkedin.com/pulse/people-analytics-whats-employees-andrew-marritt?trk=mp-reader-card

Mayo, A. (2018). Applying HR analytics to talent management. Strategic HR Review, 17(5), 247–254. https://doi.org/10.1108/shr-08-2018-0072

Natalie, L., George, P., & Marie-Anne, G. (2021). Predicting employee absenteeism for cost effective interventions. Decision Support Systems, 147. https://doi.org/10.1016/j.dss.2021.113539

Nitya, B., Ragini, B., & Subha, K. (2021). A study on the application of HR analytics on talent acquisition, compensation & benefits and employee turnover in the Indian IT industry. Sambodhi UGC Care Journal, 1(14), 44.

Pillai, R., & Sivathanu, B. (2020). Adoption of artificial intelligence (AI) for talent acquisition in IT/ITeS organizations. Benchmarking: An International Journal, 27(9), 2599–2629. https://doi.org/10.1108/bij-04-2020-0186

Pontefract, D. (2019). "IBM's artificial intelligence strategy is fantastic, but AI also Cut 30% of its HR workforce". Forbes. https://www.forbes.com/sites/danpontefract/2019/04/06/ibms-artificial-intelligence-strategy-is-fantastic-but-ai-also-cut-30-of-its-hr-workforce/?sh=73b3be93126a

Ramachandran, K. K., Apsara, S., Shibani, M. A., Asokk, H., Bandi, D., & Pitroda, B., J.R. (2022). Machine learning and role of artificial intelligence in optimizing work performance and employee behavior. Materials Today: Proceedings, 51(8), 2327–2331. https://doi.org/10.1016/j.matpr.2021.11.544

Russell, C., & Bennett, N. (2015). Big data and talent management: Using hard data to make the soft stuff easy. Business Horizons, 58(3), 237–242. https://doi.org/10.1016/j.bushor.2014.08.001

Saling, K. C., & Do, M. D. (2020). Leveraging people analytics for an adaptive complex talent management system. Procedia Computer Science, 168, 105–111. https://doi.org/10.1016/j.procs.2020.02.269

Seethalakshmi, R., & Sucharita, K. (2022). Artificial intelligence in training and development for employees with reference to selected it companies. Journal of Positive School Psychology, 6(9). https://journalppw.com/index.php/jpsp/article/view/12736

Sharma, A., & Sharma, T. (2017). HR analytics and performance appraisal system: A conceptual framework for employee performance improvement. Management Research Review, 40(6). https://doi.org/10.1108/MRR-04-2016-0084

Shrestha, Y. R., Ben-Menahem, S. M., & Von, K. G. (2019). Organizational decision-making structures in the age of artificial intelligence. California Management Review, 61(4), 66–83. https://doi.org/10.1177/0008125619862257

Shrivastava, S., Nagdev, K., & Rajesh, A. (2018). Redefining HR using people analytics: The case of google. Human Resource Management International Digest, 26, 3–6. https://doi.org/10.1108/HRMID-06-2017-0112

Sivathanu, B., & Pillai, R. (2019). Technology and talent analytics for talent management – A game changer for organizational performance. International Journal of Organizational Analysis, 28(2), 457–473. https://doi.org/10.1108/ijoa-01-2019-1634

Steve, L., Eric, L., Rebecca, S., Michael, S. H., & Nina, K. (2011). "Big data, analytics and the path from insights to value. MIT Sloan management review". https://sloanreview.mit.edu/article/big-data-analytics-and-the-path-from-insights-to-value/

Tam, H. (2022, October). "Work in the metaverse: Just imagine the possibilities". SHRM. https://www.shrm.org/hr-today/news/all-things-work/pages/work-in-the-metaverse.aspx

Tambe, P., Cappelli, P., & Yakubovich, V. (2019). Artificial intelligence in human resources management: Challenges and a path forward. California Management Review, 61(4), 15–42. https://doi.org/10.1177/0008125619867910

Upadhyay, A. K., & Khandelwal, K. (2019). Artificial intelligence-based training learning from application. Development and Learning in Organizations: An International Journal, 33(2), 20–23. https://doi.org/10.1108/dlo-05-2018-0058

Westman, S., Kauttonen, J., Klemetti, A., Korhonen, N., Manninen, M., Mononen, A., & Paananen, H. (2021). Artificial intelligence for career guidance – Current requirements and prospects for the future. IAFOR Journal of Education, 9(4), 43–62. https://doi.org/10.22492/ije.9.4.03

Wijayati, D. T., Rahman, Z., Fahrullah, A., Rahman, M. F. W., Arifah, I. D. C., & Kautsar, A. (2022). A study of artificial intelligence on employee performance and work engagement: The moderating role of change leadership. International Journal of Manpower, 43(2), 486–512. https://doi.org/10.1108/IJM-07-2021-0423.

Xun, X., Yuqian, L., Birgit, V. H., & Lihui, W. (2021). Industry 4.0 and industry 5.0-inception, conception and perception. Journal of Manufacturing Systems, 61, 530–535. https://doi.org/10.1016/j.jmsy.2021.10.006

Chapter 13

Artificial Intelligence and Fintech Industry—The Metaverse Adoption

Kondisetti Venkata Bhavana, Hridya Koduri, Ezendu Ariwa, and Vishwa K.D.

Woxsen University
Hyderabad, Telangana, India

13.1 Introduction

In the corporate sector, and especially in the finance industry, artificial intelligence (AI) is the latest trend. It is considered an effective method of encouraging economic expansion through higher productivity and efficiency (Aggarwal, 2022). Public capital markets have seen a clear change over the past 50 years, going from being mostly face-to-face, paper-based, and controlled by banks to being considerably more digital, computerized, and decentralized. *Fintech* is a term that is widely used to describe this phenomenon. The development of Fintech was sparked by developments in technology in the late 1960s. This era may be referred to as "Fintech 1.0." Ever since the 1990s, when the consumer internet started to become more widely used, and from the early 2000s, when machines and social media have grown in popularity, Fintech has developed. Today, Fintech 2.0 allows customers to do all of these things using an app on their smartphone, including opening bank accounts, borrowing money, investing, and making payments. Such apps are rapidly being driven by AI, specifically algorithmic programs created using machine learning (ML) and other statistical approaches, as well as huge quantities of user-provided data. The chances that non-bank, non-financial organizations will provide customer financial services is also rising. The three rules of robotic systems, the replication game, and machines, which were developed in the middle of the 20th century, are often considered as the launch of AI. Globally, it is an essential urge to increase the Fintech sector's competition by putting in place a risk management system that will monitor breakthroughs without limiting its market prospects. Bitcoin, blockchains, data analytics, and AI are some of the technologies that might more effectively fulfill the needs for risk management.

Models based on AI and machine learning are currently being used extensively in the sector of financial services. The biggest hedge fund in the world, Bridgewater Associates, is completing a task to robotic judgment that could save hours and reduce human emotion instability. Two of Goldman Sachs' 600 equity traders remain in one division of the company. It discovered that one computer engineer can replace a few traders. It is anticipated that autonomous software will handle a minimum of 5% of all monetary transactions by 2020.

Through intelligent payments management (IPM), AI might handle payroll processing and gather knowledge regarding consumer behavior. The savings could be significant: AI will assist consumers in monitoring their spending and making daily financial decisions. Personalized advice is created by new personal finance apps that make use of awareness to measure the patterns of spending and their digital footprints.

A well-known AI solution that we can anticipate seeing a lot of is the combination of end-user control and pooled financial data to provide individualized services. Undertaking cross-selling of financial products and mining customer data will be carried out automatically by algorithms, as in JPMorgan, where COIN, an AI-based software elucidates agreements of commercial loans, thereby saving several hours of lawyer time, and rapid automation of cognitive tasks is taking place.

13.2 The Relationship between Artificial Intelligence and Finance

The main reason why Fintech is a disruptor for the long run is that financial intermediation is expensive. This has always been the case historically.

Ashta and Herrmann (2021) present an intriguing study that demonstrates that the average transaction cost has remained stable at approximately 2% of transaction amounts. From 1880 until the present day, this cost has been around this level for an astonishingly long time—more than a century. However, the fact remains that significant rents earned by major players in the financial industry are now within reach of smaller and more agile Fintech companies. This is happening regardless of whether we can fully understand the reasons behind such high costs of financial intermediation, such as a potential lack of competition among suppliers or customers' limited knowledge on the demand side.

Technology frequently acts as a cheaper middleman and a force behind competition. Financial sector employment is seen to be increasing from 5% to as high as 6.5% of the workforce over the past two decades. Fintech has the potential to drastically lower this number.

When it comes to the upcoming major innovation and social transformation, data will be a major factor behind both if we consider capitalism and electrical energy of motion to be the primary drivers of global improvement since the time of great exploration. Data has grown rapidly with the invention of the internet, mobile internet, and the Internet of Things (IoT). As a result, the financial industry has collected a considerable quantity of data through the course of conducting businesses, particularly data on customers, transactions, and assets and liabilities. The relationship between financial services and technology businesses used to have a very clear contractual cooperation. Now, their involvement includes businesses, assets, data, technologies, and infrastructures.

The differences among the technical and economic characteristics of different organizations have been unclear, complicating the legal obligations and connections across organizations. However, financial intelligence's primary function is finances, which only improves and innovates from the ground up. Foremost, comprehensive and in-depth use of AI is in the financial sector. Its users ranging from conventional banks using technology to developing financial structures, financial governing bodies, and technical firms that supply technology-based AI applications to financial firms. The innovative monetization strategies can be split into strategic investments, advising, intellectual service and support, intelligently control hazards, insightful advertisement, etc. depending on the various financial services that use AI technology.

13.3 The Metaverse and the Finance Industry

The metaverse offers several advantages to banks and financial institutions, including improved customer communication, streamlined transactions, reduced costs, and enhanced security. As a result, there is a growing interest in using the metaverse for banking applications. First and foremost, the metaverse makes it simple to store, access, and manage customer account data. This may assist banks in better comprehending the requirements and preferences of their clients, which may result in enhanced services and more individualized offerings. Additionally, banks can easily integrate with other financial systems and applications through the metaverse, thereby lowering costs and increasing productivity. The metaverse is a compelling option for use in the banking industry due to its advantages, which include facilitating cross-border payments, digital identity verification, and account transactions.

We can also buy and sell goods and services to metaverse users, such as virtual meeting or concert passes, non-fungible tokens (NFTs), avatars, and banking services. A digital currency will be the method of payment when so much buying and selling will take place online using digital assets.

Customers can easily access and view their statements online, at any time and from any location, thanks to the use of Web3.0 and metaverse for the delivery of banking statements. Customers who frequently travel or have busy schedules that prevent them from regularly visiting physical branches may find this particularly helpful.

Mortgages are typically provided by banks and other financial institutions. These institutions evaluate the risk of lending to individual borrowers to determine the amount of money they are willing to offer, the interest rates they will charge, and the duration of the loan. However, the metaverse promises to alter everything. This innovative new platform will completely rethink mortgages as we know them today by utilizing blockchain technology. Without having to rely on traditional methods like paperwork or lengthy appointments with bank loan officers, lenders can quickly assess a borrower's creditworthiness using the metaverse, which considers things like their income history, job stability, credit score, and total assets. Additionally, the metaverse's use of smart contracts will help to reduce fraud and the likelihood of loan default while also ensuring that all loan terms are fair and transparent. Because of this, the mortgage on the metaverse will be more secure, faster, easier, and more efficient than ever before, providing individuals with increased access to homeownership at lower overall costs (Dubey et al., 2022).

Metaverse digital identities, cryptocurrencies, and transactions have made it possible for users to conduct digital business in a new and more convenient way. Users can establish their digital identity on the metaverse blockchain network using the secure digital identity system of the metaverse. They can then use this ID to make decentralized transactions involving cryptocurrency or other assets. Since debit or credit cards are no longer required, this makes things easier and safer. The fact that cryptocurrencies are not subject to central bank manipulation like cash or credit card payments is another important advantage. This guarantees that merchant-set prices will not be affected by changes in interest rates.

In addition, compared to conventional methods like wire transfers, which necessitate banks serving as intermediaries between the sender and receiver of funds, cross-border transactions carried out with cryptocurrencies are not only simpler but also less expensive. As a result, the metaverse's cryptocurrency framework and digital identity system give users a more convenient and secure way to transact digitally while overcoming the limitations of credit and debit cards.

Credit card processing is one area where NFTs could be used by banks. Customers would have an easier time managing their financial transactions if banks created branded NFTs that were associated with a specific credit card or line of credit. This could entail things like limiting how much you can spend on particular purchases, setting reminders for when payments are due, or keeping track of how much you spend over time. Utilizing NFTs for mortgages and other types of property loans is yet another option. Customers would be able to track ownership more easily and make any necessary changes as needed if banks issued NFT-based loans tied to specific assets like vehicles or real estate.

13.3.1 Cryptocurrency and Blockchain

Cryptocurrency transactions are set to be recorded into a set of decentralized nodes after their approval and are protected by encryption methods on the blockchain. When a data "miner" begins to process a transaction block with the addition of another number called "the nonce" for a transaction consisting of variable length and then continues to solve a problem of hashing and generate a hash whose length is fixed and is of 256 bits and a specified quantity of zeros which are mandated to be 17 during the time of this writing. This is when a transaction is approved.

The reward for this random guessing, which necessitates electricity and computational power, is a predetermined number of BTC, which at the time of writing is BTC 12.5. The transaction block is validated by a "proof of work" generated by this mining procedure. Every 10 minutes, a block is solved using today's technology. Compared to PayPal's 125 tps and Visa's 4,000 tps, BTC's transaction volumes are currently quite low, hovering around 300,000 per day (about 1.5–2.0 tps). However, the technology is now much more than just a proof of concept; it is widely accepted. It is an essential component of contemporary Fintech.

It was discovered from a study in the paper, "Artificial Intelligence in Fintech: Understanding Stakeholders Perception on Innovation, Disruption, and Transformation in Finance," that the perspectives that its participants had on the Indian financial services industry differed significantly.

Due to its dependence on external factors, some participants were of the opinion that the financial services industry is highly saturated, very competitive, and greatly volatile. Others, on the other hand, claimed that the sector still has some room for expansion, especially in cities categorized under Tier 2, where most financial services are reaching out to rural populations. They came to a conclusion that the monetary help area in the locale is currently at a beginning stage in spite of the good factors that incorporate youthful and taught individuals, rising degrees of pay, and a few monetary education drives driven by legislatures.

More than 40% of the population in India is between the ages of 15 and 29. This is essentially the tech-savvy millennial generation. Additionally, the bank's legacy systems, mindsets, and traditional structures make it harder for it to be on par with Fintech. As a result, it is anticipated that the disruptive technologies will likely be in the heart of almost every possible banking business model in the five succeeding years.

On the basis of these, the millennial customer base may be regarded as offline bank disruptors, while current bank customers may be regarded as sustaining innovators.

13.3.2 Robo Advisory

Fintech competitors consist of several of the most cutting-edge innovations of the modern era, including blockchain and cryptocurrency, AI-powered robo-advisory products, equity crowdsourcing, mentoring (P2P) financing, and smartphone money transfers (Philippon, 2016). Robotic advice facilities are becoming more popular among those who make financial decisions. Virtually everyone in today's highly competitive technological world is moving toward automation, including online payments, online ordering, virtual transportation services, and net-banking platforms (Bredt, 2019).

Robo-advisors are a type of financial assistant that uses virtually no personal communication; thus, a few issues that investors have when using their software and services. Robo-advisory services were first released in the (USA), although according to one research report, just 20% of buyers are conscious of products, and only 3% among them are actually being used. Even while other individual data encourage the usage and acceptance of such apps and services, the implementation of robotic advice services is noticeably low in industrialized countries; nevertheless, the situation is different compared to emerging countries like India (Das, 2019).

The next detailed fundamentally compensate the robo-advisor operational processes: Risk testing is the primary phase, which entails gathering fundamental consumer data via hazard questionnaire, KYC market intelligence, data behavior modification, etc., and performing demand perspectives; asset allocation is the second phase. Utilize conventional quantitative models, ML algorithms, and benefits of the product; in the following phase, process guidance is provided utilizing self-service registration process and one-click capital budgeting; in the fourth, asset management is provided employing economic resource portfolio spread, stockroom modification, and payment and graphical review; and in the fifth and final step, post-investment service is provided using intellectual counselling session and sophisticated advertising of financial products.

13.3.3 Personal Finance

Families are buyers and allocators of capital. They usually borrow money to provide for their consumption and investment on capital asset on the side of consumption. They also make money, save money, and allocate their wealth to different asset classes.

Most recently, the consumption-investment cycle has encountered numerous obstacles for households. First, retirement goals have become more difficult to achieve as a result of extremely low asset returns. Because interest rates that are risk-free have fallen close to zero, thereby causing the risk-free rates of return that are a little decent are no longer accessible to aged investors that depend on income streams, which are safer after their work tenures. Further, risk charges on speculative resources have apparently contracted, however, which contrasts an assessment on normal value hazard charge. Second, clinical improvements made life span risks more extreme. Concerns about elderly people outliving their savings are growing. Third, pursuing yield carries a significant volatility risk. Alternative asset classes carry a significant amount of risk, not only in terms of their secondary returns but also due to the occurrence of excess kurtosis along with negative skewness. Fourth, high-priced financial service providers have maintained their pricing schedules, despite the continuing decline in risk-adjusted returns.

These issues are being addressed by a variety of Fintech initiatives. Now, investors can use technology to place their money in well-diversified asset pools at a much lower cost using robo advising, which also provides solutions to the retirement issue. Using technology, companies like Wealth front and Betterment are eliminating high-priced retirement providers and educating naïve, small investors. On the side of lending, improved credit models have made it possible for businesses to segment customers who were otherwise prevented from obtaining finances due to their FICO scores.

13.3.4 Payment Systems

Both how we move money around and how we view money have changed as a result of digital payments. In recent times, we keep exchanging money on numerous platforms, starting with PayPal, and steer clear of the offline banking system. Venmo, Apple Pay, Google Pay, and Samsung Pay are just a few of the many such services that have emerged since then.

This disintermediation can take many different forms, but it leaves a digital payment trail that worries black markets. It couldn't be any more obvious, for instance, with the new demonetization of the five hundred and thousand rupee notes in India. Millions fell in the hidden store of money, primarily utilized in real estate deals, which hampered cash transactions. However, it also spawned innovative digital payment systems, such as the Paytm platform. Paytm was granted permission in the year 2015 by the Central Bank of India to kickstart a payments bank under the name "Paytm Payments Bank Limited." Almost as high as 250 million wallets and more are currently included in Paytm's stream of transactions as of this writing.

13.4 Risk Concerns and Management

Despite the existence of numerous laws aimed at safeguarding consumers and investors, the rise of lending Fintech platforms leads to "disintermediation," which highlights the necessity for additional measures to ensure consumer and investor protection.

Peer-to-peer lending has two main problems that require to be addressed.

1. P2P platforms are less prepared to manage asymmetric information than traditional banks and have less expertise about their borrowers.
2. P2P lending systems and investors frequently accept the credit risk rather than the platforms.

Both of these factors raise the possibility that P2P lenders' rating systems may not accurately reflect the "true" chance of a loan defaulting.

A modeling credit risk has been proposed in mentoring lending, utilizing connection clustering algorithms. This makes it possible to measure systemic risk, a sort of risk that's very clear in peer-to-peer financing and has lately been applicable to the failure of sovereigns and banks. Additionally, it enables credit risk modeling efficiency to be improved. However, certain risks have not yet been sufficiently assessed and quantified. We consider the following to be the most significant of these: Market risk is the chance that unfavorable changes and volatility in financial markets, whether they are established or emerging (such as cryptocurrency markets), can result in unplanned losses in investors' portfolios. The discrepancy between expected and actual investment risk class is known as compliance risk.

Cybersecurity threat may be rated using a cybersecurity risk metric hazard and prioritize remedies in order to prevent failures and lessen the effect of risk.

13.5 Opportunities

AI is prospering. A number of connected technological and market variables fuel its expansion. First, compared to numerous mainframes that a small number of us utilized 50 years ago, the computational capability of phones and laptops is far more. With its utility computing idea and nearly infinite processing and storage capability, cloud computing has revolutionized the way businesses operate, offering unparalleled scalability, flexibility, and cost-efficiency. This transformative technology empowers organizations to rapidly scale their resources up or down, depending on demand, while minimizing upfront infrastructure costs and maintenance burdens. By leveraging cloud computing, companies can focus on innovation, accelerate development cycles, and drive digital transformation, leading to enhanced productivity and competitiveness in the digital era.

Traders have long utilized a variety of technology to acquire industry knowledge ahead of the competition, and the rapid advancement of technology of global communication has benefited and these are able to pay for it. Real-time analysis is essential for the financial industries. The importance of the information and its evaluation to the business will decrease with every delay. For instance, over the course of nearly 5 years, a major Australian bank reportedly neglected to disclose more than 19.5 million illegal foreign money transfer orders (2019). Data has become widely available, and the financial sector is using an exponential increase in the quantity of "additional information" types to provide investment signals. This is because of the expansion of data on a global scale, which is currently being fueled by smart things and open data economies. Asset managers have a fantastic potential to produce alpha in a distinctive way, thanks to these new data sets, as they enable them to uncover previously unseen patterns, correlations, and insights that can notify more informed investment decisions and outperform the market. By leveraging cutting-edge technologies and advanced analytics, asset managers can gain a competitive edge, optimize their portfolios, and generate superior returns for their clients, ultimately solidifying their position as industry leaders in the ever-evolving financial landscape.

The United States, China, Canada, and the European Union all have a role in shaping global harmony. Because they lack a formal AI policy, other nations like India are not included in the harmonization of AI (Roychoudhury & Alawadh, 2019). However, due of its expansion, a number of nations are actively driving the AI business.

13.5.1 Banks and Financial Service Providers

High-volume data is being mined for personal and personalized banking in order to comprehend contexts and banker's needs. Customers receive personalized offers that are based on their purchasing patterns and unique to each individual. Fraud protection in personal banking involves looking at behavioral factors, purchasing contexts and patterns, utilizing geographic locations, and automating these financial fraud detections to deal with them quickly.

Behemoth firms have been developed as a result of ecosystem development, mergers, and acquisitions. On November 25, 2019, the market capitalization of a prominent financial company, well-known for serving recognized banking institutions, stood at $78 billion. It gained its position as a result of a number of purchases made during the previous three decades. Fiserv acquired First Data, a company that processed credit and debit card payments, in 2019 for $22 billion. All of these big businesses serve little banks; thus, it is in their best interests for banks to continue operating. However, many local banks that use these companies as clients are worried that combined businesses would stifle innovation and put them at a competitive disadvantage with giant banks and nimble Fintech companies (Aggarwal, 2022).

All of these big businesses serve little banks; thus, it is in their best interests for banks to continue operating. However, many of the small banks that these companies serve are worried that merged entities will stifle innovation, giving them an unfair competitive advantage over numerous banks and rapid financial technology companies (Crosman, 2019). This is because of the fact that acquiring techniques make the acquirer's proposal more complicated and uncertain. Smaller, more niche Fintech firms could benefit.

13.5.2 The Investment Sectors

Over the last 50 years, the role that individuals once played in stock trading has significantly diminished. Nowadays, electronically completed deals have replaced floor traders who used to shout in the pits. These electronic transactions are not only faster but also instantly recorded and included in documentation. High-frequency trading can offer significant returns to the quickest investors if a non-discriminating delay is possible across the network. Data-scanning quantitative hedge funds emerged at the turn of the 20th century, with only a quarter of them exclusively managed by professional leaders.

The use of machine learning (ML) is crucial in the field, with many quantified funds, such as Bridgewater and some of BlackRock's funds, employing ML to analyze data. However, human decision making remains essential in selecting investment bets as ML-driven algorithmic investing often recognizes factors that people cannot. Although ML identifies novel explanatory elements, human analysts are still required to comprehend and interpret them. Big data analysis can create correlations between markets and emotions, with emotions now tracked through tweets, social media posts, news articles, and legal documents. As a result of these changes, the stock market has become highly efficient (Hu, 2020).

Robo-markets, which have emerged, significantly impact cost reduction. Passive index funds carry annual fees ranging between 0.03% and 0.09% of assets managed, while demands from active managers typically require 20 times more money.

13.6 Detecting Frauds and Their Prevention

One fascinating attribute of crimes in the field of finance is that most of the time, it allows the criminals to flee the scene. An excellent illustration of this phenomenon is online fraud. Shopping sites now account for a significant portion of credit card fraud, and the traditional practice of copying charge cards using stolen credit card numbers is rapidly becoming obsolete. The three most common methods are account takeovers, the use of fake IDs, and the compromise of business email accounts, all three of which increased in the number of successful attempts and have seen a drastic rise from the years 2013 to 2016.

Record keeping is the first step in managing online financial fraud, and in order to allow for traceback, it is crucial that all online activity be recorded. Additionally, strict authentication is essential. Multifactor authentication, like the well-known two-step verification that is used by many banks and asset management companies, is the foundation of many financial platforms. To stop a man-in-the-middle attack, encryption from beginning to end is necessary. Biometrics, tokens, digital keys, passwords, PIN codes, and other methods of authentication are just a few examples. At least two of the digital passwords that are embedded in many digital wallets today can be used to unlock them, providing a high level of security.

However, if a data breach has resulted in the theft of information, authentication will be useless as the whole system of authentication will duly fail to identify any maliciously used and validly accessed data. It is necessary to conduct activity analysis, and additional data may be utilized. Credit card numbers that are stolen, for instance, provide a digital thief with complete access to any kind of purchasing power; therefore, they ought to be identified by identifying a purchase made that does not adhere to the user's usual behavioral buying patterns. Especially when alternative data are used, this is the area where ML has proven to be extremely useful. Social media can be used to identify unusual behavior, notice various devices, spot patterns that are unexpected in email use, distinguish unusual credit card usage locations from typical ones, and so on are all potential solutions in this area.

The process of identifying credit card fraud, for instance, is burdened with unbalanced groups. This area has a rate of 0.10% of transactions that are fraudulent, or one out of every thousand transactions is fraudulent, meaning that the data has 999 zeros for every one outcome that is binary. In such data environments, precision and recall are extremely difficult to control, and false positives are common.

Oversampling, boosting, deep learning, random forests, and a variety of other machine learning methods are utilized. Authentication, anomaly detection, device monitoring, behavioral modeling, and using ML on big data are all used to address fraud detection in general.

13.7 Fintech, AI, and the Future of Consumer Financial Privacy

Over the past century, there has been a significant evolution in both the notion and the laws governing consumer financial privacy. Consumer financial privacy, also known as the common law duty of bank confidentiality, was initially focused on preserving a customer's trust in their bank and the relationship between them. This was done to safeguard the relationship in and of itself as well as to prevent misuse of financial information, which is of an intimate nature and can reveal much about a person's privacy and data protection, however, grew while bank secrecy wilted (Maiti & Ghosh, 2021). The notion of consumer financial privacy has been greatly broadened under English law as a result of the development of information privacy legislation since the 1970s, notably under the umbrella of data protection regulation. On the other hand, applying AI may help achieve the practical objectives of protecting customer financial privacy. We have encouraged the growth and development of financial innovations, made them sustainable, and reduced any potential negative effects on investors and consumers. The realization of this objective could be achieved through the implementation of efficient risk-reducing strategies; however, the costs associated with their approval might be limited due to digitalization.

Fintech 1.0, or the digitalization and datafication of financial markets, was sparked by technological advancements in computers that started in the late 1960s. The present Fintech period, also known as Fintech 2.0, was ushered in by the commencement of the consumer internet's wider use in the late 1990s and the expansion of mobile computing and social media in the early 2000s. Platforms like PayPal and Google pay were early adopters of Fintech 2.0's electronic payments and mobile money advancements. Following the 2008 global financial crisis, lending by traditional bank lenders shrank, which sparked the emergence of new technology-driven financial start-ups, most notably peer-to-peer lending platforms (Giudici, 2018; Rasiwala & Kohli, 2021). The expanding use of data analytics— particularly employing AI/ML technologies and "alternative data"—to customize and automate consumer financial services is a prominent trend under Fintech 2.0, which is very relevant to the growth and regulation of consumer financial privacy. To start, there are well-known behavioral and cognitive flaws that limit consumers' capacity to "self-manage" their information privacy and the effective exercise of their data protection rights (Hendershott et al., 2021).

The effects of AI-driven finance on the practical objectives of protecting consumer financial privacy are increasingly complex. On the one hand, AI-driven finance has the potential to serve the practical objectives of consumer financial privacy, namely, to safeguard consumers from damage and, in the end, to promote their autonomy (Vutharkar & KV, 2023).

13.8 Conclusion

Our review demonstrates how AI breakthroughs use big data analysis to lower costs, lower risks, and boost personalization, which promotes economic growth by raising overall demand and investment. Our analysis has demonstrated that cost cutting causes significant changes in the financial sector, causing companies to consolidate to develop larger customer platforms. Financial service firms and financial markets have both used this client acquisition method. The more well-known platforms may only benefit in the near term, though, as customers seek to specialist Fintech for their expertise.

New tools for resolving a wide range of financial industry issues have been made available by AI. The development looks very promising; However, AI's application in the financial market and research on AI in finance are still in their infancy in comparison to the rapid technological development of AI. The primary utilizations of AI are in resource valuing, return expectation, and feeling examination. The identification and classification of objects are two common uses for textual analysis. One of the most crucial aspects of AI's application in financial research is its remarkable capacity to capture non-linear relations. In addition to conventional linear regressions, it can offer fresh perspectives. Understanding issues like AI bias, AI fairness, and how humans and AI may interact to enhance human intelligence are also essential for a successful application of AI in finance. Allowing humans to use robo-advising may, for instance, result in a lower return on investments; Specifically, including humans in the AI application loop may be detrimental. The seamless integration of financial services into customers' digital lives poses a technical challenge for financial institutions worldwide and in India. We hypothesize that the key component of online banking and financial technology lies in their integration within the financial system, encompassing market liberalization and centralization. These three distinct features collectively influence participants' preference for partnership.

In particular, these include, among other things, high financial and constant expenses associated with the manufacturing of digital goods like operating systems, software, and apps, reach almost zero costs for transmission and information exchange, high connectivity, and people operating costs. An ecosystem-like collaboration between banks and Fintech may be necessary due to these factors and the need to provide a hassle-free experience for the technologically savvy generation of consumers of a vast spectrum of financial services, frequently supported by AI and big data analytics. By using an open API architecture, banks might promote itself as facilitators of Fintech rather than requiring customers to trade with just offers by each bank. There is likewise trust that a crossover stage will permit monetary organizations not just to give existing clients a superior client-driven insight, but also to target new client categories that are generally underserved by banks. However complementing resources and skills of banking, including their trustworthiness, adaptability, consumer accessibility, and compliance, will be advantageous to fintech.

Hence, it is concluded that the metaverse will have a bright future in the financial sector. We are experiencing the digitization initiative by bankers to transition from the paperwork to a paperless world. Fintech, which does not have a physical presence, is also another trend. Due to the outbreak in 2020, it has set the stage for online banking, and given how quickly technologies is developing, another trend that will be sparked in the next two decades is the migration of financial institutions to the metaverse. It offers various benefits over the conventional financial system and is anticipated to become widely used in the upcoming years. The possibility to promote the digital economy and minimize waste is made possible by moving to the metaverse context. It would completely change how debt works and have a huge positive impact across both clients and businesses. The local public can gain from increased knowledge of the metaverse and its advantages if journalism plays a part in doing so. If the metaverse is generally recognized, it will have a positive effect on the industry by reducing fraud and making cross-border transactions easier, especially starting in 2023, the year in which the metaverse was implemented. We must adopt the metaverse and make the most of it by leading the way in utilizing its advantages and making wise judgments to decrease global loss via R&D facilities and an integrated technology approach.

References

Aggarwal, N. (2022). AI, Fintech, and the Evolving Regulation of Consumer Financial Privacy.

Ashta, A., & Herrmann, H. (2021). Artificial intelligence and fintech: An overview of opportunities and risks for banking, investments, and microfinance. *Strategic Change, 30*(3), 211–222.

Bredt, S. (2019). Artificial intelligence (AI) in the financial sector—Potential and public strategies. *Frontiers in Artificial Intelligence, 2*, 16.

Crosman, K. M., Bostrom, A., & Hayes, A. L. (2019). Efficacy foundations for risk communication: How people think about reducing the risks of climate change. Risk Analysis, 39(10), 2329–2347.

Das, S. R. (2019). The future of Fintech. *Financial Management, 48*(4), 981–1007.

Dubey, V., Mokashi, A., Pradhan, R., Gupta, P., & Walimbe, R. (2022). Metaverse and Banking Industry–2023 The Year of Metaverse Adoption.

Giudici, P. (2018). Fintech risk management: A research challenge for artificial intelligence in finance. *Frontiers in Artificial Intelligence, 1*, 1.

Hendershott, T., Zhang, X., Zhao, J. L., & Zheng, Z. (2021). FinTech as a game changer: Overview of research frontiers. *Information Systems Research, 32*(1), 1–17.

Hu, Z. (2020). Research on fintech methods based on artificial intelligence. *Journal of Physics: Conference Series, 1684*(1), 012034. IOP Publishing.

Maiti, M., & Ghosh, U. (2021). Next generation internet of things in fintech ecosystem. *IEEE Internet of Things Journal*, *10*(3), 2104–2111, doi: 10.1109/JIOT.2021.3063494.

Rasiwala, F. S. & Kohli, B. (2021). Artificial intelligence in fintech: Understanding stakeholders perception on innovation, disruption, and transformation in finance. *International Journal of Business Intelligence Research (IJBIR)*, *12*(1), 48–65.

Roychoudhury, A. & Alawadh, N. (2019). Finance ministry clears NITI Aayog's artificial intelligence proposal. Smart Investor. New Delhi. India.

Vutharkar, S. & KV, R. K. (2023). Fin-cology or tech-nance?: Emergence of FinTech. In *AI-Driven Intelligent Models for Business Excellence* (pp. 124–136). IGI Global.

Chapter 14

The Metaverse Technology in Revolutionizing the Insurance Industry

Krishna Saraf, Swagatika Mohapatro
and Yamasani Keerthi Reddy
Woxsen University
Hyderabad, Telangana, India

Neelam Kumari
Dublin Business School
Dublin, Ireland

14.1 Introduction

The metaverse refers to a theoretical version of the internet that merges virtual reality (VR) and augmented reality (AR) with the physical world, creating an entirely immersive and interactive digital environment. It is described as an embodied virtual space where users can engage with a computer-generated environment and other users in a way similar to the physical world[1]. This concept was first introduced in Neal Stephenson's novel *Snow Crash* in 1992 and has since gained popularity in popular culture, with companies like Facebook (now Meta) planning to develop metaverse technologies. Currently, the metaverse includes various digital experiences like video games, social media platforms, and VR simulations, but its advocates anticipate that it will eventually become a shared, interoperable, 3D virtual space that can be accessed from any device[2].

DOI: 10.4324/b23404-14

The metaverse has the potential to revolutionize how we interact with the digital world, and with technological advancements, further progress in this area is expected.

The metaverse has the potential to be a game-changer in the insurance industry. The "metaverse" is a virtual world where people can interact, create digital objects, and do many things. Although it's mostly a concept, many companies are exploring its potential. The insurance industry can benefit from the metaverse in different ways, such as allowing customers to file claims and interact with agents through a virtual environment, creating virtual environments to simulate different scenarios to better assess risk, and using it for education and training purposes. Metaverse technology has the potential to improve the efficiency of insurance companies and also offer them a chance to increase their revenue by venturing into this growing market. Insurance companies can utilize the metaverse in their regular business operations to enhance the experience of customers and agents, boost operational effectiveness, and lower expenses. While the metaverse is still new, it has the potential to change many aspects of the insurance industry, and companies that adapt will have an advantage in the future.

14.2 Technology and Applications in the Insurance Industry

The *metaverse* is a term used to describe a virtual world where users can interact with each other and digital objects in a fully immersive environment. This concept has gained traction in recent years, with advancements in virtual reality (VR), augmented reality (AR), and mixed reality (MR) technologies. In this answer, we will provide an overview of these technologies and their potential applications in the insurance industry.

14.2.1 Virtual Reality (VR)

VR technology immerses users in a computer-generated environment, simulating a real-world experience. VR headsets like the Oculus Rift or HTC Vive can transport users to virtual worlds where they can interact with digital objects and other users. VR technology has potential applications in the insurance industry, such as virtual inspections of properties for claims processing or virtual training for adjusters. For example, State Farm is using

VR technology to simulate home safety inspections, providing a more efficient and safe way to train their agents.

14.2.2 Augmented Reality (AR)

AR technology overlays digital content onto the real world, enhancing the user's perception of reality. AR can be experienced through smartphones or AR glasses like Google Glass or Microsoft HoloLens. In the insurance industry, AR can be used to provide customers with information about their policies, such as coverage details or claims processing. For example, Nationwide Insurance is using AR technology to create interactive experiences that help customers learn about their insurance policies.

14.2.3 Mixed Reality (MR)

MR technology blends elements of virtual and augmented reality, allowing digital objects to interact with the real world. MR devices like the Microsoft HoloLens can create a fully immersive experience, where digital objects can be placed in the real world and interact with real objects. The insurance industry can use MR technology for virtual inspections, providing adjusters with a better understanding of the damage and the claimant's property. For example, Allstate is using MR technology to train adjusters on how to handle claims in a virtual environment.

In conclusion, metaverse technologies have the ability to revolutionize the insurance industry, providing customers with more interactive experiences and insurers with more efficient claim processing methods. As the technology continues to advance, we can anticipate more uses of metaverse technologies in the insurance industry and beyond.

14.3 Overview of the Metaverse in the Insurance Industry

The insurance industry is a critical component of the global financial system, protecting against various risks faced by individuals, businesses, and governments. This industry encompasses a wide range of insurance products, including life insurance, health insurance, property and casualty insurance, and reinsurance.

14.3.1 Market Size

The global insurance industry is a massive market, with total premiums written exceeding $6 trillion in 2019, according to data from the Swiss Re Institute. Life insurance is the largest segment, accounting for nearly 50% of global premiums, followed by non-life insurance at 33%. The remaining 17% is attributable to health insurance.

The Asia-Pacific region is the largest insurance market in terms of premiums written, accounting for over 40% of global premiums, followed by North America and Europe. However, the highest growth rates in premiums written are in emerging markets, such as China, India, and Latin America.

14.3.2 Business Models

The insurance industry's primary business model involves pooling risk among policyholders and investing the premiums received to generate returns. The amount of risk covered and premiums charged vary based on factors such as age, health status, occupation, and other underwriting criteria[3].

Insurers use various distribution channels to sell their products, including agents, brokers, bancassurance (distribution through banks), and digital channels. Insurtech start-ups are also disrupting the traditional distribution models by using digital platforms and data analytics to personalize policies and streamline the underwriting process.

14.3.3 Challenges

The insurance industry is facing several challenges, including changing customer expectations, regulatory compliance, low-interest rates, and increasing competition from new entrants.

14.3.4 Customer Expectations

Customers' expectations are changing due to advances in technology and the growing popularity of on-demand services. Insurers need to provide more personalized products and services to meet customers' evolving needs and preferences.

14.3.5 Regulatory Compliance

Insurers must comply with complex regulations governing their operations, such as solvency requirements, consumer protection, and anti-money laundering rules. Compliance costs are increasing, and non-compliance can lead to severe financial and reputational consequences.

14.3.6 Low-Interest Rates

Low-interest rates are putting pressure on insurers' investment income, as many insurers invest premiums in fixed-income securities. Insurers are exploring alternative investment strategies to generate higher returns, such as private equity, infrastructure, and real estate.

14.3.7 Increasing Competition

The insurance industry is facing increasing competition from new entrants, such as insurtech start-ups and technology giants like Amazon and Google. These companies are leveraging their technological capabilities and customer data to disrupt traditional insurance models and offer more personalized and cost-effective products.

Overall, the insurance industry is a critical component of the global financial system, protecting against various risks faced by individuals, businesses, and governments. The industry's market size is massive, with premiums written exceeding $6 trillion in 2019. The primary business model involves pooling risk among policyholders and investing the premiums received to generate returns. The industry is facing several challenges, including changing customer expectations, regulatory compliance, low-interest rates, and increasing competition from new entrants. Insurers must adapt to these challenges to remain relevant and competitive in the rapidly evolving insurance landscape.

14.4 Leverage the Metaverse to Provide Better Services to Customers

Life insurance, health insurance, and general insurance are three critical sectors that could benefit significantly from the metaverse. Let's take a closer look at how each industry can leverage the metaverse to provide better services to customers.

14.4.1 Life Insurance

Life insurance companies can use the metaverse to offer personalized policies based on users' behavior in the virtual world. For example, if a user frequently engages in risky activities in the metaverse, such as extreme sports or driving at high speeds, the insurance company can offer a higher premium. On the other hand, if a user leads a healthy and low-risk lifestyle in the metaverse, they can receive lower premiums. This approach can incentivize users to adopt healthy behaviors and reduce risky activities, ultimately leading to a healthier and more risk-averse population[4].

According to a report by Accenture, "the Metaverse can help life insurers develop personalized risk models that go beyond traditional factors, such as age and health status, to include behavior and lifestyle data collected from the Metaverse"[5].

14.4.2 Health Insurance

Health insurance providers can use the metaverse to promote healthy living and offer virtual consultations and treatments. The metaverse can provide users with a gamified approach to fitness, incentivizing them to exercise and stay healthy through virtual challenges and rewards. Additionally, virtual consultations and treatments can provide convenient and cost-effective solutions for users who may have difficulty accessing traditional healthcare[4].

According to a report by Deloitte, "the Metaverse can help health insurers engage with customers in a more personalized and interactive manner, driving greater customer loyalty and improving overall health outcomes"[1].

14.4.3 General Insurance

General insurance companies can use the metaverse to simulate and predict disasters and create insurance policies accordingly. By analyzing data collected from the metaverse, insurers can identify areas with a high likelihood of natural disasters or accidents and create policies that are tailored to those specific risks. This approach can help insurers provide more comprehensive coverage and better manage risks.

According to a report by Ernst & Young, "the Metaverse can help general insurers develop new risk models that use data from virtual environments to better understand and predict real-world risks"[6].

14.5 The Metaverse Helps Insurance Experts and Some Emerging Trends

The metaverse, a virtual space where people can interact with each other and digital objects in real time, has been gaining increasing attention in recent years. One industry that may benefit from the metaverse is the insurance industry. Here are some ways in which the metaverse can help insurance experts and some emerging trends.

14.5.1 Risk Assessment

With the metaverse, insurance experts can simulate real-world scenarios to evaluate risk and determine premiums. For instance, in the gaming industry, players can engage in activities such as driving, flying, and sports, which may pose risks of accidents or injuries. Insurance companies can use data from these simulations to develop risk models and tailor policies to gamers' needs. The use of VR and AR in risk assessment can lead to a 25% reduction in claims costs[7].

14.5.2 Customer Engagement

Insurance companies can use the metaverse to engage with customers in a more immersive and interactive way. For instance, customers can visit virtual offices to purchase policies, file claims, or receive assistance from insurance experts. Companies can also use avatars to provide personalized support to customers, making the experience more engaging and enjoyable. Companies such as Allstate and Nationwide have already started experimenting with virtual agents to assist customers[8].

14.5.3 Fraud Detection

Insurance fraud is a significant challenge for the industry, with an estimated $80 billion lost annually. The metaverse can help combat fraud by enabling insurance experts to detect suspicious behavior in a virtual environment. For example, insurance companies can use AI-powered tools to analyze gaming data and identify patterns that may indicate fraudulent activities. A report by Capgemini suggests that AI and blockchain technologies can reduce insurance fraud by up to 90%[9].

14.5.4 New Business Models

The metaverse is still in its infancy, but it has the potential to create new business models for the insurance industry. For instance, companies can develop policies specifically for virtual assets such as cryptocurrencies, digital artwork, and virtual real estate. Insurance companies can also partner with gaming companies to offer policies that cover risks associated with gaming activities. The metaverse can create a $1 trillion opportunity for insurance companies by 2030.

In conclusion, the metaverse presents significant opportunities for the insurance industry. From risk assessment to fraud detection, and customer engagement to new business models, insurance experts can leverage the metaverse to provide innovative solutions to customers[8]. As the metaverse continues to evolve, it will be interesting to see how insurance companies adapt and innovate to remain relevant in a rapidly changing landscape.

14.6 Advantages of the Metaverse for Insurance

The metaverse, a virtual shared space where users can interact with a computer-generated environment and each other, is increasingly becoming an area of interest for insurance companies. There are several advantages of the metaverse for insurance, which are outlined below with supporting references.

14.6.1 Increased Accessibility for Customers

The metaverse has the potential to provide a higher level of accessibility for insurance customers, especially those who face difficulties in accessing traditional insurance services, such as people living in remote regions or those with mobility or transportation constraints. By utilizing the metaverse, these individuals can access insurance products and services. The metaverse can provide a new opportunity for insurance companies to reach and engage with customers, according to PwC[10].

14.6.2 Improved Customer Engagement

The metaverse's immersive and interactive features present an opportunity for insurance companies to engage with their customers in novel ways, such as by providing virtual agents and customer service representatives to offer personalized support and answer questions. The metaverse could be a valuable platform for insurance companies to cultivate strong customer relationships[11].

14.6.3 More Accurate Risk Assessment

The information gathered in the metaverse can aid insurance companies in enhancing their risk evaluation procedures. By analyzing behavioral data, insurers can recognize trends and determine the probability of specific occurrences. Such insights can help insurers in pricing policies more accurately and reducing the possibility of financial losses.

14.6.4 Faster Claim Processing and Settlements

The metaverse can simplify the claims process, resulting in quicker processing and settlements. Digital submission and processing of claims can be facilitated with the assistance of virtual agents, which can handle mundane tasks. This can allow human agents to concentrate on more intricate matters. Deloitte has pointed out that the metaverse can enhance the efficiency and speed of claims processing, leading to a better experience for policyholders.

14.6.5 Enhanced Fraud Detection

Insurance companies can take advantage of the metaverse's sophisticated analytics and machine learning functionalities to enhance their fraud detection and prevention efforts. Through the analysis of data obtained from virtual environments, insurers can detect atypical or questionable behavioral patterns that may signify fraudulent activity. This can aid insurers in reducing their losses and enhancing the credibility of the insurance system[12].

Moreover, the metaverse offers several advantages for insurance companies, including increased accessibility for customers, improved customer engagement, more accurate risk assessment, faster claim processing and settlements, and enhanced fraud detection. As the metaverse continues to develop, insurance companies will likely find new ways to leverage its capabilities to improve their products and services.

14.7 Application of Insurance in the Metaverse

The metaverse, a virtual world that enables the users to interact with digital objects and other users in a shared online space, has gained significant attention in recent times. Despite being a concept that originated in science fiction, the metaverse is gradually becoming a reality due to advancements in virtual and augmented reality technology. This has opened up numerous possibilities for utilizing the metaverse, including in the insurance sector.

The metaverse can be utilized in the insurance industry for virtual claims handling and assessment. This involves using virtual reality technology to create a more engaging and interactive experience for customers when submitting claims, enhancing their comprehension of the procedures and actions involved[13]. Furthermore, virtual assessments can be conducted, enabling claims adjusters to examine the damage and evaluate the extent of the claim in a virtual environment.

The metaverse has the potential to be employed by insurance companies for risk assessment and mitigation purposes. By creating virtual environments that replicate real-life situations, insurers can detect potential risks and hazards that may have been overlooked before. This approach can aid in the development of more comprehensive risk management techniques and enhance underwriting practices[14].

Another potential application of the metaverse in the insurance industry is for the training and education of insurance agents. By utilizing VR simulations, agents can partake in a more immersive and interactive learning experience, enabling them to practice their skills in a safe environment. This approach has the potential to enhance their expertise and self-assurance in dealing with intricate insurance matters[7].

The metaverse can also serve as a platform for virtual product demonstrations and sales in the insurance sector. By establishing virtual showrooms, insurers can display their offerings more engagingly and interactively, giving customers the ability to interact with them within a virtual environment. This can also be beneficial for targeting customers who may not have access to physical locations or who prefer virtual experiences[15].

14.8 Challenges and Potential Risks

14.8.1 Security Concerns

The insurance industry is facing a significant obstacle related to security, specifically regarding the expanding use of digital technologies and the large amount of data that is being produced and stored. As insurance companies integrate new technologies into their operations, they need to establish adequate measures to protect customer data and prevent unauthorized access. Additionally, insurance companies must remain informed about the latest cybersecurity risks and implement the most effective strategies to secure their systems. The insurance industry faces significant risks due to security concerns, especially as cyber threats continue to become more sophisticated. Insurance companies that do not implement adequate security measures are vulnerable to data breaches that can result in harm to their reputation, financial losses, and legal consequences.

14.8.2 Ethical and Legal Implications

The utilization of data analytics and AI in the insurance industry has the potential to create ethical and legal dilemmas. For instance, there may be apprehensions regarding the fairness of using particular data points to determine insurance premiums, as this may result in discriminatory practices against specific groups. Furthermore, there may be uncertainties regarding the transparency of the algorithms employed in AI systems and the possibility of bias in decision making. Therefore, insurance companies must guarantee that their implementation of AI is conducted ethically and aligns with relevant laws and regulations. The implementation of data analytics and AI in the insurance industry also carries potential ethical and legal hazards. One example is the legal and ethical implications that may arise from the utilization of personal data to determine insurance premiums. Moreover, there may be reservations regarding the transparency of the algorithms utilized in AI systems, as well as the possibility of partiality in decision making.

14.8.3 Integration with Traditional Insurance Processes

Incorporating modern technologies into conventional insurance procedures can present difficulties. Insurance companies must guarantee that these new technologies are harmonious with existing systems and procedures, and do not interfere with the customer experience[16]. Furthermore, implementing new technologies may necessitate changes to the insurance company's organizational structure and culture, which can be challenging to execute. The integration of modern technologies into conventional insurance procedures can also create possible hazards. If new technologies are not installed appropriately, they may result in mistakes, system breakdowns, and customer discontent. Furthermore, the acceptance of new technologies may call for adjustments to the insurance company's organizational structure and culture, which can be hard to handle.

14.9 Using Michael Porter's Framework, Analysis of the Insurance Industry's Potential Challenges and Opportunities in the Emerging Metaverse[17]

14.9.1 *Competitive Rivalry*[17]

Insurance professionals see new market and marketing opportunities in the metaverse.

a. Virtual insurance agencies could be established for conducting sales, as demonstrated by Heungkuk Life Insurance's "virtual counseling window" in Korea.
b. Other market participants are also exploring the use of gamification technology, such as the MetLife Infinity app in Hong Kong, which enables people to manage their legacy and share important documents with loved ones.
c. Technology like Microsoft Mesh could be utilized to create virtual underwriting rooms for collaboration between underwriters and brokers.
d. The Omniverse tool could be leveraged to digitally evaluate insurable assets and provide risk mitigation recommendations, as well as for virtual damage assessment in claims.

14.9.2 *Buyer Power*[17]

In terms of buyer power, there are questions about who the metaverse's consumers of insurance products are and what they will want to insure.

a. The buyers may include present purchasers of existing products in the real world, and catering to this market is unlikely to lead to drastic changes in products or services.
b. Gamification can be used to engage younger customers who use the Metaverse, and specific products have to be developed for metaverse applications.
c. People may want to insure their metaverse lives/assets, such as in-game currencies and metaverse assets, which could require new insurance products.
d. Personal data and identity are identified as primary risks by several insurance professionals consulted in the research, indicating a need for insurance against these risks.

Despite the widespread digitization of businesses, personal identity verification remains a challenge as financial service providers are required to comply with anti-money laundering regulations, which impose significant burdens on consumers. These consumers are required to present official documentation either in person or as notarized physical copies, leading to a need for a secure digital identity that can verify personal information without the need for physical documents. Self-Sovereign Identity (SSI) offers a solution by allowing individuals to control the information they share without storing it in a central database. The insurance sector is still in its early stages of offering cybersecurity safeguards against data or identity fraud. The lack of available products for individual data or identity theft protection may hinder the adoption of metaverse offerings until further clarification on associated obligations, risks, and compensations is provided[17].

14.9.3 Supplier Power[17]

Insurers need to think about the services they might require from their suppliers to leverage the potential of the metaverse. This may involve traditional services like ICT, but it should also include advertisers who need to figure out how to target a new audience in a new medium, and legal services who must consider legal risks and litigation in an environment with ambiguous jurisdictions and regulatory frameworks[17].

14.9.4 Substitution[17]

Insurance contracts have four key features:

a. The insurance buyer must have an insurable interest, meaning if the risk event occurs, they will suffer a financial loss[11].
b. The risk should be present or identifiable at the beginning of the agreement.
c. The insurance contract transfers a portion of the risk from the purchaser to the seller in exchange for a premium.
d. The agreement was entered into with sincere intentions.

14.10 Implications for the Future of Insurance

In the past few years, the insurance sector has experienced significant transformations due to technological advancements and evolving customer demands[18]. These changes are likely to impact the industry in various ways, such as disrupting the conventional insurance business models, intensifying competition and innovation, and creating more individualized insurance products and services to meet customer needs.

The emergence of insurtech start-ups that are utilizing modern technologies like blockchain, AI, and the Internet of Things (IoT) is a potential disruption to conventional insurance business models[8]. These start-ups are often more flexible and adaptable than traditional insurance companies, and they can employ data and analysis to make more accurate pricing and underwriting decisions. Consequently, they might be able to provide cheaper insurance premiums to customers while remaining profitable[1].

The adoption of digital platforms and ecosystems to distribute insurance products is another factor that could disrupt the insurance industry. Companies like Amazon, Google, and Alibaba are among those who use these platforms, which could potentially eliminate the need for traditional insurers by providing customers with a more streamlined and user-friendly insurance purchasing process. Additionally, these platforms are capable of leveraging their vast amount of customer data to gain insight into their customers' insurance requirements and offer personalized and tailored insurance products[19].

As a result of these potential disruptions, there is expected to be a rise in competition and innovation within the insurance industry. Conventional insurance companies will have to adjust to these new market circumstances to maintain their competitive edge. This may entail allocating resources towards new technologies and data analytics abilities, collaborating with insurtech start-ups or digital platforms, and reconsidering their product and business strategies[1].

The creation of more individualized and customized insurance products and services is another crucial trend in the insurance industry. With the aid of advancements in data analytics and machine learning, insurers are now capable of comprehending their customers' risk profiles better and can provide tailored insurance solutions. An instance of this is the use of telematics data obtained from customers' vehicles to offer pay-as-you-go car insurance policies that can provide reduced premiums for safe drivers[19].

To sum up, the insurance sector is experiencing significant transformations due to technological advancements and evolving customer demands. This is expected to disrupt conventional insurance business models, intensify competition and innovation, and result in more individualized and customized insurance products and services[8].

14.11 Insurance Companies Have to Take the Following Measures

i. Acquire knowledge and understanding of the metaverse, visualization, AI, big data, connectivity, and other advancements of the fourth industrial revolution, as well as emerging areas such as NFTs or cryptocurrencies[18].

ii. Build expertise in various aspects of the metaverse by investing in training and hiring professionals who are knowledgeable in visualization, machine learning, connectivity, big data, aesthetics, or psychology.

iii. Form a new partnerships and relationships with non-insurance companies that are engaged in the metaverse. This would allow insurers to leverage the disparate skills provided by other companies, particularly in areas such as claims management or risk assessment processes.

iv. Develop innovative insurance products and services, such as managing risks associated with personal and corporate data, digital assets, and offering specific insurance products for metaverse applications.

v. Consider new funding mechanisms, such as extensions of crowdfunding, to insure particular online assets linked to users' guarantees or gambling markets to build risk management portfolios. This would be particularly suitable for the metaverse, given its potential for scale.

14.12 Conclusion

The metaverse has the potential to revolutionize the insurance industry and bring about significant changes in how insurers interact with customers, assess risks, and handle claims. By utilizing VR, AR, and MR technologies, insurers can create immersive and interactive experiences, improving customer engagement and satisfaction. The metaverse can also aid in risk assessment, fraud detection, and training of insurance agents, leading to more efficient and effective operations. However, the implementation of metaverse technologies comes with challenges and potential risks, such as security concerns, ethical and legal implications, and integration with traditional insurance processes. Despite these challenges, the insurance industry must adapt to the rapidly evolving technology landscape to remain competitive and relevant. The emergence of insurtech start-ups, digital platforms, and personalized insurance products and services is expected to intensify competition and innovation in the industry. As the metaverse and other emerging technologies continue to advance, it will be fascinating to observe how the insurance industry responds and incorporates these technologies into its existing operations. Insurers should take several actions to prepare for the emergence of the metaverse, including familiarizing themselves with emerging technologies such as AI, big data, and NFTs, investing in training and recruiting specialists in these areas, and forming new partnerships with non-insurance firms involved in the metaverse. They should also consider developing new products and services, such as managing risks associated with personal and corporate data in the metaverse, protecting digital assets, and offering risk control and mitigation products. Additionally, insurers may want to explore new funding mechanisms, such as using crowdfunding or gambling markets, to manage risks associated with the metaverse. Insurance companies improve their image by adopting metaverse technologies early and using them to enhance the experiences of their customers, agents, and employees. With numerous possibilities throughout the insurance process, insurers need to pinpoint the appropriate applications to provide a unique experience for everyone involved. Insurers should begin experimenting with these technologies now, while they are still in the early stages of development.

Moreover, the metaverse can bring about a significant transformation in the insurance industry, affecting various aspects ranging from claims management to sales of insurance products. As the technology of VR and AR advances, it will be intriguing to observe how insurance companies respond and incorporate these technologies into their existing processes.

References

1. See You in the Metaverse | Deloitte Legal Blog. (2021). Deloitte. https://www. deloitte.com/global/en/services/legal/blogs/see-you-in-the-metaverse.html
2. Krewell, K. (2022, January 27). Building the Metaverse. Forbes. https://www. forbes.com/sites/tiriasresearch/2022/01/27/building-the-metaverse/
3. Hernandez, R., Kakumani, S., Gupta, A., & Jackson, J. (2023). The Metaverse and Insurance: A New Frontier in User Experience and Risk Coverage. PwC. https://www.pwc.com/us/en/tech-effect/emerging-tech/the-metaverse-and-insurance.html

4. Bhattacharya, S., Varshney, S., & Tripathi, S. (2022). Harnessing public health with "metaverse" technology. Frontiers in Public Health, 10, 4452. https://www.researchgate.net/publication/365929260_Harnessing_public_health_with_metaverse_technology

5. Going Beyond with Extended Reality | Accenture. (n.d.). Going Beyond with Extended Reality | Accenture. https://www.accenture.com/us-en/about/going-beyond-extended-reality

6. The Metaverse: Commerce in Three Dimensions. (2023). The Metaverse: Commerce in Three Dimensions | EY - US. https://www.ey.com/en_us/financial-services/the-metaverse-commerce-in-three-dimensions

7. Insurance Technology Trends 2022 | Tech Vision | Accenture. (n.d.). Insurance Technology Trends | Tech Vision 2022 | Accenture. https://www.accenture.com/us-en/insightsnew/insurance/technology-vision-insurance

8. Why Insurance Business Models are Going to Change. (2023). Why Insurance Business Models Are Going to Change | EY - Global. https://www.ey.com/en_gl/innovation-in-insurance/why-insurance-business-models-are-going-to-change

9. Huynh-The, T., Gadekallu, T. R., Wang, W., Yenduri, G., Ranaweera, P., Pham, Q. V., da Costa, D. B., & Liyanage, M. (2023). Blockchain for the metaverse: A review. Future Generation Computer Systems, 143, 401–419. https://doi.org/10.1016/j.future.2023.02.008

10. PwC. (2022). The Impact of the Metaverse on the Insurance Industry. https://www.pwc.com/jp/en/knowledge/column/metaverse-impact-on-the-insurance-industry.html

11. Milian, S. (2022). What Does the Metaverse Mean for Insurers? Insurance Blog | Accenture. https://insuranceblog.accenture.com/technology-vision-metaverse-insurers

12. Metaverse and Meta Risks | Marsh. (2022). Metaverse and Meta Risks | Marsh. https://www.marsh.com/us/industries/technology/insights/metaverse-meta-risks.html

13. Marom, L. (2022). Council Post: The Metaverse and the Insurance Industry: Three Tips for Managing Technological Changes. Forbes. https://www.forbes.com/sites/forbescoachescouncil/2022/11/15/the-metaverse-and-the-insurance-industry-three-tips-for-managing-technological-changes/

14. Insurance Industry - The Future of Insurance. (n.d.). Insurance Industry - The Future of Insurance | IBM. https://www.ibm.com/industries/insurance

15. Metaverse-Report-2022. (2022). Deloitte India. https://www2.deloitte.com/in/en/pages/technology/articles/metaverse-report-2022.html

16. Embracing Metaverse in Insurance to Enhance Customer Experience. (2022). Embracing Metaverse in Insurance to Enhance Customer Experience. https://www.tcs.com/what-we-do/industries/insurance/blog/metaverse-insurance-enhance-customer-experience

17. Mainelli, M., & Mills, S. (2022). The Metaverse & Insurance-Pixel Perfect? https://www.researchgate.net/publication/358047734_The_Metaverse_Insurance_Pixel_Perfect_T

18. Metaverse: Revolution or Evolution? And Where Does Insurance Come in? | Swiss Re. (2022). Metaverse: Revolution or Evolution? And Where Does Insurance Come in? | Swiss Re. https://www.swissre.com/risk-knowledge/risk-perspectives-blog/metaverse-in-insurance.html
19. Future of Insurance: Unleashing Growth through the New Business Building. (n.d.). McKinsey & Company. https://www.mckinsey.com/industries/financial-services/our-insights/future-of-insurance-unleashing-growth-through-new-business-building

Chapter 15

Education and Metaverse

Sai Kiran Kadari, Shashank Raj Gupta, and D. Prithvi Raj
Woxsen University
Hyderabad, Telangana, India

Gabriel Kabanda
United Nations Office for Project Services
Hyderabad, Telangana, India

15.1 Introduction

> We need technology in every classroom and in every student and teacher's hand, because it is the pen and paper of our time, and it is the lens through which we experience much of our world.
>
> **– David Warlick**

Education is a basic human right and, as mentioned in the quote above, is essentially a tool to prepare for tomorrow. In this chapter, we explore the educational opportunities and potential of the metaverse. It will begin by providing an overview of education as a whole, comparing the traditional means of education opposed to the rise of online education. The chapter will then focus on the significant propellent for online education, the COVID-19 pandemic. As a follow-up, the framework of the metaverse in education, including its potential benefits and challenges will be presented. This chapter will also discuss the technology stack and components needed to implement a metaverse-based learning system. Finally, the chapter will explore how educators, researchers, and policymakers can use the

DOI: 10.4324/b23404-15

metaverse to create transformative, immersive learning experiences for students.

The metaverse, when implemented as an educational platform, offers a range of unique opportunities and benefits. It provides an environment in which students can interact with teachers and communicate with classmates through their avatars. This can create an immersive learning experience that is more engaging and motivating than traditional, classroom-based learning. Furthermore, the metaverse can link VR creation to a platform for learning adaptivity and sustainable education.

The metaverse also provides an opportunity to create and share content across multiple platforms and devices. This means that students can access educational content from anywhere, at any time. It also allows for the creation of virtual classrooms and other learning spaces, which can facilitate collaborative learning among students and teachers. Finally, the metaverse offers new opportunities for data collection and analysis, which can be used to inform and improve educational practices.

There are several essential considerations to realize the metaverse's potential for education. First, educators must ensure that the design of metaverse-based platforms is grounded in best educational practices. This means that the metaverse should be designed to facilitate the development of higher-order thinking skills, explore diverse perspectives, and create meaningful learning experiences. It is also essential to ensure that the metaverse is accessible and inclusive to all students, regardless of socioeconomic background. Finally, ensuring that the metaverse is secure and compliant with relevant data protection regulations is crucial.

15.2 Online versus Offline Education

Online education and contemporary education are the two learning platforms that have gained talk in recent years. Both go with pros and cons, and it's important to understand their differences to be informed, which will make individuals make informed decisions about which variant of education is right for them.

Online education, also known as e-learning, is a type of education that is being done with online mediums. This means that students can access their courses and the materials, participate in various class discussions, and perform their assignments by sitting at any place in the world with an appropriate internet connection. Online education is apt to take any form, such as self-paced courses, synchronous classes, or the conglomerate of both.

One of the major advantages of online education is its flexibility. It allows students to study their course according to their own pace and schedule, which is beneficial for the individuals who are working along with their studies and cannot attend their classes in the brick-and-mortar classrooms. This form of education is more cost-effective than the contemporary one as it doesn't have any additional costs attached to it, such as traveling or being on campus (Chien & Hwang, 2022). One more advantage of online classes is their ability to provide class recordings; if a student cannot attend the class for certain reasons, he/she will be able to study from the class recordings given to that individual.

However, online education comes with some drawbacks too. One of the main issues is the lack of social interaction and socialization with teachers and peers. This affects the motivation and self-growth of an individual and makes it difficult to stay engaged in the course. It also makes it hard for the students to make study groups and blocks access to meet them in person when they have doubts. For the ones who are not confident and face problems with time management, online education becomes hard for them in the longer run.

Contemporary education, also called *traditional education*, is a form of education in the brick-and-mortar type of classroom. This means that the students attend the classes as a person in front of the faculties and their classmates. This form of education, with more personalized instruction and the ability to ask doubts and receive solutions whenever needed, makes contemporary education more effective than online education.

One of the major advantages of contemporary education is its ability to provide socialization and the sense of indulging one in society. Students can make their study groups and interact with their peers and the faculties, which is not provided in online education. This gives them a sense of motivation for the course, and if they lose their focus, they can seek help from their instructors and friends. All these factors help them in their self-growth and create a sense of competition in their innate.

However, contemporary education also carries some drawbacks. One of the major disadvantages is the lack of flexibility. Students have to attend the classes at a particular time and place, and sometimes it becomes difficult for them to follow these requirements, especially for the individuals who are working when it comes to cost, contemporary education is more expensive than the costs included for being on campus, traveling to the place and the costs associated with the commuting.

Overall, both education types are viable options for students. It depends on the choices individuals want to make according to their requirements, budget, and accessibility. Both of them have their own pros and cons.

The metaverse in online education carrier humongous potential on the online education; with the implementation of a fully immersive learning experience, the metaverse will allow the students to interact with the material in such a way that it will be a game changer and not possible with contemporary education or the traditional online education. This chapter will cover the benefits of metaverse on the online education system, which will include enhanced participation, personalized learning, and the capacity to build virtual environments.

One of the main benefits of a metaverse in online education is its ability to make the students participate more and be fully engaged. In the traditional online education system, students sometimes are found not to be fully engaged and find it hard to concentrate and remain interactive as they sometimes lose their focus. While the metaverse will be apt to solve this problem and make them more interactive and engaged, this will help them to understand the concept in a much better way, and they will be able to retain the knowledge they have acquired.

The metaverse also provides personalized learning; in the traditional online education system, the learning is basically one size fits all, wherein the students study with the same material at the same pace, but in the metaverse, the students will be able to study through the virtual environment and the education can be tailored according to their specific need and pace, for example, if a student is struggling to understand a concept then he/she can be provided some additional resources and activities to help that student to understand the concept well, this will be helpful for the students learning through the metaverse included online education (Davis et al., 2009).

Another benefit of the metaverse on online education is its ability to create virtual environments. Metaverse allows the creation of virtual labs, virtual fields, trips, and virtual classrooms, which is not possible in traditional online education. For example, metaverse can create a virtual experiment lab wherein the students can perform the experiments and find the observations in real time; metaverse can provide virtual trips, which will help them to explore a different part of the world and with students being in the classrooms. The students will also be able to socialize in a much-nuanced way through the metaverse online education. In traditional online education, the students may feel isolated and disconnected from their peers because they are studying in front of a computer with limited interactions with their peers, but in the metaverse, students will be able to interact with each other and the teachers as well this will help them to get a sense of community and the social interaction for the students who are studying remotely or online. The students can also make a group, and they will be able to discuss their issues in a group discussion. This will help them to understand the importance of teamwork and collaborative studies.

In conclusion, the metaverse will offer a wide range of benefits for the online education system, including increased engagement, personalized learning, the ability to create virtual environments, getting a sense of community, and promoting collaborative teamwork. Technology will continually move forward. It is evident that the metaverse will play an important role in online education.

15.3 COVID-19 Effect on Education

Globalization has made the world more connected than ever. The pandemic has impacted every country, irrespective of GDP, income, and ethnicity. However, as usual, the weakest have been affected the most. Education is a sector that is critical for every country. The wealthy have managed to mitigate the damage by opting for alternative forms of education. The poor, however, have been left out, as they can't afford this new online education form.

The pandemic has revealed a lot of gaps in our education systems, such as not having the ideal environment for efficient learning; or not having the broadband to listen to online classes. Most OECD (Organization for Economic Development and Development) and partners have closed their educational institutions for a duration of up to 10 weeks. Students during this time had to rely on television, radio, or online classes to make up for their missed classes. Students are now forced to work more independently, which has resulted in a lack of motivation to do their classwork. The teachers have also been affected, in the sense, that they are not trained in this new method of instruction.

Many nations, notably those engaged in the education sector, have experienced a decline in GDP as a result of the COVID-19 epidemic.

There has been a decrease in demand for education-related products and services, such as textbooks, school supplies, and educational technology, because of schools and colleges closing and switching to online learning.

Higher education has also been struck hard by the pandemic. With most of the nations closing their borders, international students were in a dilemma of whether to stay in the host country or return home. Countries like the United Kingdom and Canada relaxed their requirements during this unanticipated pandemic. It is to be noted that there has also been a significant decrease in the enrollment of international students. Although the institutions have shifted to an online form of education, it is observed that the main motivation for studying abroad was to build a network, absorb the culture, and try to work personally with people coming from different spheres of life. With online education, the institutions were not able to provide all of the above.

The problem with online education is the availability of too many resources. Both educators and students find this very cumbersome, as they need proper sources for their learning. According to research, the main issues that are plaguing e-learning are

- Educational policy
- Cost
- Flexibility
- Accessibility
- Internet connection

The problem with online learning is twofold in nature. There are those students who cannot afford electronic gadgets for their learning and there are those who are too addicted to screen time. Both are independent issues that need to be resolved at the earliest.

The next thing that is on the board is the evaluation of online exams. Most institutions around the world still prefer a pen-paper exam. However, desperate times call for desperate measures, and most nations had to adapt to this new form of evaluation. The problem with this form of evaluation is that there are no measures set in place that are foolproof and can stop students from cheating. It is also essential to put plagiarism procedures in the institutions to combat the following problem.

A school is not only a place of learning; rather, it is a place to develop new skills, develop your communication skills, and nurture bonds with your fellow peers. It has been proved that there are detrimental effects on a child's psychological and emotional well-being, due to the absence of a school environment. Not to mention that children are now highly susceptible to online exploitation. There has been a substantial increase in cases related to online bullying, which in turn has spiked an increase in various psychological problems (such as impaired learning and depression).

Let's not forget that we do have the positive effect of the pandemic on education. Poor learners can review the videos their teachers have given them, search for relevant videos on YouTube, and understand the topic at home. Students have control over the speed, timing, and location of their education. Students can access the content at any time since e-content is used in the classroom. Online education helps students manage their time more effectively.

We had to reevaluate how we teach people when the pandemic (COVID-19) outbreak was revealed. Researchers have applauded the metaverse, an interactive 3D world that merges the real world with the virtual. However, since it is still a relatively new subject, it is rarely studied from the perspective of education in the metaverse. Academics believe that one of the metaverse's most significant applications is in education and that has a promising future.

Meta-learning, which is the process of learning how to learn, has the potential to greatly impact education by allowing individuals to learn new skills and knowledge more efficiently and effectively. It could also lead to the development of more personalized learning experiences, as well as the creation of new educational technologies that can adapt to the unique needs and learning styles of individual students.

The metaverse in academic studies can be viewed as a classroom institution enhanced by metaverse-related advancements that merge with the elements of real life and virtual educational settings and, hence, in our opinion, the emergence of the metaverse in education can serve as a new academic setting. Students can make use of technology to access the classroom without being restricted by space or time, and they can use their online identities or virtual personas to interact. They will be able to experience the same level of engagement as if they were in a real-world learning setting. From this viewpoint, it is obvious that incorporating the metaverse with learning can provide individuals with a wide variety of incredible opportunities to learn. Additionally, meta-learning could also be used to improve the efficiency of teacher training programs and to create more effective educational programs for children with learning disabilities.

15.4 Use Cases of the Metaverse in Education

Metaverse technology has the potential to revolutionize the way an online medium is interacted with, delivered, and experienced; education is no exception. While the metaverse is still in its early stages of development, there are a variety of potential use cases that educators, researchers, and policymakers should consider when exploring the potential of the metaverse in education (Gruber, 2021). The following are four use cases of metaverse technology to amplify education.

1. One potential use case is the implementation of virtual classrooms, in which students and teachers can interact and collaborate in a 3D immersive environment. Hwang & Chien (2022) first coined this term. This can be used to create engaging and motivating learning experiences and to facilitate a greater level of collaboration among students. For example, third-graders can learn their geography subject in a more interactive manner thanks to the virtual space showing the locations with all the necessary information needed for a third-grader in real time. Be it sciences or literature, learning can become more interactive than before as virtual classrooms can be used to deliver content in a variety of formats, ranging from videos to interactive 3D simulations.

2. Another potential use case is the use of augmented reality (AR) and virtual reality (VR) to create highly immersive and interactive learning experiences (Kye et al., 2021). By utilizing AR and VR technology, educators can create unique learning experiences that allow students to explore and interact with virtual environments. For instance, AR and VR can be used to create virtual field trips, allowing students to explore locations around the world without ever leaving their classroom (Henderson, 2021).

   Let's take learning how to dissect the body of a frog. Many governmental bodies around the world have banned this practice for school students, but with the help of AR and VR, students who want to be biologists in the future can grasp experiences such as this while ensuring that no harm is being done to actual animals. In fact, this method can help users understand different parts of the animal and human biology in depth.

3. The metaverse can also be used to create virtual simulations, allowing students to experience real-world scenarios within a safe and controlled environment (Kye et al., 2021). These simulations can be used to teach a variety of topics, from physical sciences to financial literacy. In addition, AI-based applications can be used to create personalized learning experiences tailored to individual students. Virtual simulations can also be used as a way to conduct tests and examinations for students to test their knowledge, especially for examinations that require precision to carry out the task successfully, such as "Quantum Electrodynamics tests." Virtual simulations can not only help for courses in the curriculum but also help prepare students for unforeseen events such as fire, earthquake, etc.

4. Finally, the metaverse can create personalized learning plans and curricula, allowing students to customize their learning experiences to suit their individual needs (Kye et al., 2021). This could be used to create personalized lesson plans tailored to each student or to allow students to explore topics of interest in more depth. Personalization allows students to not fall behind and understand the subjects in depth. Application of this, where results can be more beneficial, is at the undergraduate and postgraduate level of education, where specialization is important for each student.

15.5 Discussion

Based on the use cases mentioned above, an ideal educational metaverse environment would be as follows.

In school (from pre-school to fifth grade), education can be more exploratory in nature. Geography lessons can be taught by taking the students on a virtual tour using AR and VR projectors; this can be used to show nation states not just in the present time but also in the past and in "potential future." Integration of fictional elements to make learning more engaging can also be done with this technology.

From middle school to high school (sixth grade to twelfth grade), more in-depth education can be taught. Sciences in particular will move from the current 2D interactive learning via online education to 3D interactive learning. The line between "theory" and "practical application" can be blurred with the metaverse technology. Further education such as undergraduate and postgraduate degrees can take their specializations to the next level by allowing interactions with other students of the same field without the need for travel, allowing them to broaden their understanding by taking in different cultural perspectives. In fact, this helps universities create a stronger bond between each other as meetings and conferences can be held in a similar fashion.

While these are great and beneficial ways to use the metaverse in the education sphere, complete implementation is still far away. Unless nations can adapt new technology with ever-evolving security, utilizing the metaverse to its full potential cannot be realized.

15.6 Conclusion

In conclusion, the metaverse has the potential to revolutionize the way education is delivered and experienced. There are a variety of potential use cases for the metaverse that educators, researchers, and policymakers should consider when exploring the potential of the metaverse in education. There is only one downside to integrating the metaverse into education, and it's the fact that metaverse-compatible technology cannot be implemented in every nation at the same time. Technological requirements are what is causing the current disparity between traditional education and online education. While First World nations can have access to a metaverse-based education, Third World countries could take some years to catch up and fully integrate it into their education system.

References

Chien, S. Y., & Hwang, G. J. (2022). A question, observation, and organisation-based SVVR approach to enhancing students' presentation performance, classroom engagement, and technology acceptance in a cultural course. British Journal of Educational Technology, 53(2), 229–247.
Davis, M., Kurniawan, S., Wideman, R., & de Freitas, S. (2009). Metaverse research: A review of the field and its future direction. Educational Technology & Society, 12(3), 4–20.
Gruber, E. (2021). What is the Metaverse? Everything You Need to Know. Retrieved from https://www.cloudwards.net/what-is-the-metaverse/

Henderson, A. (2021). What is the Metaverse? What to Know about the Future of the Internet. Retrieved from https://www.digitaltrends.com/computing/what-is-the-metaverse/

Hwang, G. J., & Chien, S. Y. (2022). Definition, roles, and potential research issues of the metaverse in education: An artificial intelligence perspective. Computers and Education: Artificial Intelligence, 3(100082), 1–6.

Kye, B., Han, N., Kim, E., Park, Y., & Jo, S. (2021). Educational applications of metaverse: Possibilities and limitations. Journal of Educational Evaluation for Health Professions, 18, 1–13.

Chapter 16

The Role of AI in Decision Making—Marketing Strategies and How Brands Use IPL as a Marketing Platform

S. Veena Reddy, Sudhakar Reddy Nalamalapu,
R. Ramakrishna Reddy, and Dr. Rajesh Kumar K.V.
Woxsen University
Hyderabad, Telangana, India

16.1 Introduction

Indian Premier League, or IPL, is an international cricket event that takes place there. IPL is frequently managed on a large scale with many investors and partners around the country. The Board of Control for Cricket in India (BCCI) mainly supports IPL. There have been several seasons of the IPL.

A double round-robin event with a total of eight teams has been a hallmark of every IPL season. So, throughout the league stage, they played 56 games. The top four teams compete in the semifinals, with the top two competing in Qualifier 1 and the third- and fourth-placed teams competing in the Eliminator. The winner of Qualifier 1 proceeds to the finals, while the loser of Qualifier 1 competes in Qualifier 2 against the winner of the Eliminator.

With consistent viewing and an incredible fan base, the IPL has done a fantastic job of marketing itself and produced profitable seasons. The IPL has collaborated with many companies and advertised in a very different and unique ways, which created profits for both sides. Here we discuss a few of the IPL and company's strategies:

The IPL has continually demonstrated that it is the best digital marketing platform. Newsletters, emails with discount coupons, item sales and e-commerce, player jerseys and stumps, and a variety of other goods and services might all be included. Every brand that decides to advertise during the IPL season sees an increase in product sales.

Like every prior season, IPL 2022 has seen a large influx of commercials in the hopes of reviving brand promotions that had stalled, particularly in the wake of COVID-19's protracted downturn.

16.2 Review of Literature

The author have investigated how international marketing ideas can be used to sell athletic events. Local sports are linked to corporate social responsibility (CSR), tourism, and entrepreneurship, and this is an ideal issue that has to be researched more if the IPL's success is to be replicated in other sports [1].

This paper explores the potential of collaborating with social media influencers to achieve your marketing goals. By engaging in influencer marketing, you can connect with individuals who can create a network for you in the future [2]. Regardless of whether your influencers' social capital is extensive or limited, they can access customers through their blogs and social networks in ways that your brand alone cannot accomplish

According to the author of this paper, sports marketing aims to meet the needs and desires of sports clients through all exchange activities. The basic goal of all sports marketing operations is to attract sports viewers [3].

16.3 IPL Marketing Strategies

Here we discuss the change in IPL marketing strategies before and after getting into digital marketing platforms.

16.3.1 IPL Product Strategy

The products the IPL is making or in the pipeline are to capture potential markets.

IPL pricing strategy: The winning team receives an average of 15 crores, while the teams finishing second, third, and fourth receive 10 crores, 7.5 crores, and 7.5 crores, respectively. The top four teams each win $40 million, while the other teams receive nothing. All of the teams raise funds by selling tickets and acquiring sponsorships. On average, each player earns around 80 Lacks.

16.3.2 IPL Venue and Distribution Plan

Except for 2009 and 2014, all IPL games have been played in India. The IPL 2009 was held in South Africa, whereas the first leg of the IPL 2014 was held in the United Arab Emirates. The IPL has established itself as a fast-paced, three-hour game that allows viewers and guests to enjoy themselves without fear of running out of time. A large crowd gathers to cheer on their beloved teams, whether it's a weekday evening or a weekend afternoon or evening. Star-studded lineups and well-known owners find ways to draw large crowds. However, it has been stained by the spot-fixing incident that resulted in a two-year ban for Chennai Super Kings and Rajasthan Royals [4].

16.3.3 (IPL) Marketing and Promotional Plan

Promotions are never a worry in terms of scale when you have such a large budget. There are sponsors and adverts set up for each team. Dhoni's Chennai Super Kings and Shah Rukh Khan's Kolkata Knight Riders have received the greatest media attention. Both the Royal Challengers Bangalore and the Mumbai Indians are not far behind [5]. In addition to using traditional media, each team is active on different social media platforms, where they showcase past seasons' highlights and well-known performances by their players. There have been times when actors and singers have performed during the season's opening ceremony, drawing enormous crowds.

16.4 Technology and AI

AI has a significant impact on coaches' strategic decisions before, during, and after the game. AI can distinguish several sporting occurrences such as a forward pass, a penalty kick, LBW in cricket, and many other related motions using wearable sensors and high-speed cameras. Coaches may be able to better prepare athletes for competition by using this data. Players participate in this data-driven evaluation of quantitative and qualitative components, which eventually aids coaches in developing better training regimens for their teams.

The match results can be predicted using machine learning. There is tremendous data present in either the sport of cricket or soccer. To forecast the upcoming conflicts, a model for releasing the outcome can be developed. Students work at Great Learning on "IPL Cricket Match Outcome Prediction using AI Techniques" and demonstrate one of the best practical applications of prediction.

Deep learning neural networks are being trained by researchers to make predictions about topics that are beyond human capacity. For example, a player's performance can be optimized by analyzing and providing real-time input reports on topics like batting technique, posture, and shot choice.

Fans can participate in the action on the field through the use of artificial intelligence (AI) to generate virtual reality (VR) experiences for them. This can be utilized to provide spectators with a complete experience and to deeply include them in the event. AI can also be employed to examine fan behavior and offer unique suggestions for enhancing their experience.

16.5 Metaverse

The metaverse is a computer industry vision of the internet's next generation: a single, shared, immersive, persistent, 3D virtual arena where humans can experience life in ways they cannot in the physical world.

Some technologies, such as VR headsets and AR glasses, are rapidly growing; however, other crucial metaverse components, such as appropriate bandwidth or interoperability standards, are likely to take years or never materialize [6].

16.5.1 The Metaverse in IPL

Gujarat Titans, a newly formed IPL franchise from Ahmedabad, has created a virtual region in the metaverse called "The Titans Dugout." The Gujarat Titans debuted their team logo at The Titans Dugout after embracing virtual reality.

Cricket is a game with limitless potential, and we are thrilled to announce Gujarat Titans admission into The Metaverse as we prepare to unveil our team logo, Gujarat Titans Chief Operating Officer Arvinder Singh said. The metaverse debut of the Gujarat Titans logo and The Titans Dugout will definitely provide our fans with an engaging and enjoyable experience. We are confident that this will not only provide a fantastic experience for our fans, but also provide them with a unique opportunity to connect and collaborate with the squad.

The association sponsors of the IPL team Lucknow Super Giants (LSG), Gigabyte Technology and its gaming grand AORUS, have established the team's metaverse in an effort to boost fan involvement online. This initiative, which is a first for sports in India, will assist the team in bringing the fans even closer together.

This new platform will provide a one-of-a-kind experience for fans, especially because they will be unable to visit the stadiums because the whole IPL group stage will be held in Maharashtra. A virtual cricket sports stadium as distinct as the curving facade to the spiral pathway at the front is developed in this metaverse. Visitors can check out the players' stats and try on their jerseys, thanks to specially created panels along the stadium's internal wall. The stadium's exterior walls are adorned with vibrant artwork portraying the unique spirit of Lucknow through dancers, musicians, and location specific features [7].

16.6 SWOT Analysis

16.6.1 Strength

The main features of the IPL's business that provide it a competitive edge in the market are discussed in terms of the league's strengths. A brand's strength can be attributed to a variety of elements, including its financial state, competent employees, product differentiation, and intangible assets such as brand value. The IPL has the following strengths, according to the SWOT analysis:

1. The IPL is one of the most well-known and well-publicized cricket events in the world.
2. The IPL was the first sporting event to be live-streamed on YouTube and Indiatimes.
3. The IPL draws elite international athletes, major corporations, and celebrities, making it a tremendous hit with fans.

4. The BCCI expects the IPL brand to generate $1.6 billion in sponsorships and TV rights over the next five to ten years.
5. The IPL is sponsored by well-known companies such as Delhi Land & Finance (DLF). Coca-Cola, Samsung, Maruti, TVS, and Parle.
6. It has a big global audience and is popular among cricket lovers.
7. The presence of foreign players has boosted the pool of domestic players available.

16.6.2 Weaknesses

Inadequacies of a brand are certain elements of its business that can be improved in order to raise its position. Some defects are characteristics that the company lacks or in which the competition excels. The following problems can be found in the IPL SWOT analysis:

1. Disputes over team ownership, television rights, the suspension of the chairman, and other difficulties have harmed the IPL reputation.
2. Disagreements with other international cricket bodies harmed the brand's reputation.

16.6.3 Opportunities

Any brand can improve in some areas to increase its consumer base. Brands can benefit from geographic expansion, product advancements, improved communication, and other opportunities. The opportunities found in the IPL SWOT analysis are as follows:

1. Through marketing and products, IPL has a tremendous possibility to profit from well-known firms.
2. Through advertising and the involvement of cricket fans and players, a sizable cricket following can be attracted.
3. Involving boards from different nations can assist to enhance the sport and thus the IPL.

16.6.4 Threats

Any company may face dangers in the shape of components that could imperil its operations. Threats can originate from a variety of causes, such as rising competition, changed political agendas, competing for products or services, and so on. The following risks were identified in the IPL SWOT analysis:

1. The appeal of cricket will decrease as other sports become more popular among young people and more cricket is played.
2. Government policy, taxation, and other legislation may all have an impact on the IPL.
3. The introduction of comparable events in other nations will be detrimental to the IPL.

16.7 The Magical Multi-Dimensional Marketing Plan of the IPL

1. Timing and Targeted Audience: The IPL has largely taken place at night from April to May (4 to 8 PM), making sure that all of the audiences are free and available at that moment is the timing approach. The goal of this strategy is to develop quick and effective techniques to attract customers.
2. Players and Influencer Marketing: During the IPL, player sponsorships of various products and businesses hit an all-time high. Commercial content is created by television players to advertise a wide range of services, goods, and brands. And the combination of IPL and movie stars has heightened interest even further. The marketing lesson is to employ influencer marketing wisely to reach the most amount of people possible.
3. Big Brands and Collaboration: The commercial partnership with IPL has grown stronger with each passing year. Vivo is the IPL 2021's flagship sponsor, joining Dream11, Phonepe, Byju's, and Just Dial as co-presenting sponsors. Tata is now. This, along with other sponsors for the game's other components, raises the IPL to a sporting spectacle that piques the public's interest. It is no longer a game, but rather a movement, an event to remember for the rest of the year and something to anticipate.

    Marketing tip: Instead of working alone, collaboration may transform marketing initiatives.
4. Digital Marketing and Engagement: Another excellent marketing approach that has significantly benefited and increased the IPL is digital and content marketing. Behind-the-scenes footage of the

players, contests, quizzes, live sessions, appealing creatives, blogs, and trending hashtags have firmly and properly hooked the web surfer. Because of the younger target audience's consumption of real-time imagery and game events, the IPL has achieved top-of-mind recall. Digital promotion is a new sort of marketing that provides a number of alternatives.

5. Interaction with Fans and Viral Effects: Paying close attention to and emphasizing viewers is a major component of the IPL marketing plan. Going above and beyond to assist them and arranging unique transportation for them to attend cricket competitions in other states was a stroke of genius. For example, Chennai Super Kings' Whistle Podu Express delighted die-hard CSK fans while pushing marketing to new heights. This had a major impact, with fans sharing photographs and videos on social media sites in real time, giving the fan moments a viral feel.

The marketing lesson: If you invest in people, they will help you spread the word.

IPL marketing strategies use digital marketing and collaboration marketing.

16.8 Brands Use the IPL As Marketing Platform and High Audience Engagement

16.8.1 CRED

CRED is one such company whose innovative IPL advertising went viral. CRED is well-known for its innovative marketing strategies. CRED earned a name for itself in 2021 with its amusing ads. The first featured Rahul Dravid as "Indiranagar Ka Gunda," while the next two had Jackie Shroff doing Zumba and Kumar Sanu advertising insurance. Early Man Film also launched a boy band campaign, which featured 90s originals Venkatesh Prasad, Javagal Srinath, Saba Karim, and Maninder Singh.

Focusing on the campaign's relevance is an important consideration. Brands must link their advertising to the popular mood. A true marketer understands that when creating commercials, the public's sentiment is the critical factor to consider. Another clear thing is that comedy can help you keep your audience interested.

16.8.2 Dream 11

MS Dhoni supports Dream 11, which is the ideal option for cricket enthusiasts. Dhoni is renowned for his clever game techniques, the main message promoted. Dream 11 developed marketing campaigns with the hashtags #KheloDimagSe and #DimagSeDhoni to engage with users who share Mahi's passion for in-depth analysis, extensive sports knowledge, and mastery of the game.

Keep in mind the irony of cricket from your childhood. The tagline for their advertising, #YeahGameHainMahan, also tells a similar tale. It describes the difficulties Gully cricketers faced while playing the game and the joy associated with it. The background music is also so calming that it is the ideal match to generate nostalgia in us while also having an emotional effect.

16.8.3 IPL TV Advertising

The most widely used form of advertising has consistently been television.

Despite the rise of digital gadgets, television advertising continues to prosper and plant deeper roots, dominating the Indian Adex. Television now controls 42% of the Indian AdEx market. There is no doubt that businesses and marketers continue to advertise their brands on television due to the large volume.

16.8.4 Swiggy

If media reports are to be believed, the collaboration between Swiggy India and IPL, which dates back to 2017, has done wonders for the food delivery service. Swiggy has started conversations on topics like grabbing food without missing a single ball, binge eating while you binge watch, and comfort food. At the same time, your favorite team is in danger, capitalizing on the obvious connection between food and cricket. The strategy primarily relied on television advertisements, with brief spots airing during planned pauses encouraging customers to place orders. This was further solidified when Swiggy joined the IPL as an official broadcast sponsor in 2019.

Additionally, Swiggy used Hotstar, the IPL's streaming partner, to enable viewers to order food through Swiggy POP (pre-designed meals made within the POP sector of the app ranging from INR 65 to INR 200 without any delivery fee) but within the Hotstar app's UI.

The resumption of the Match Day Mania campaign, which once more emphasized the advantages of Swiggy delivery, provided support for the two prominent associations. Uncle Gulab Jamun was also brought back, but he was in love with Laddoos this time.

16.8.5 PhonePe

The marketing plan for PhonePe is based on its strategic goal of enabling digital payments for every Indian family. Building affinity for digital payments among the category non-users (those who still need to try out digital payments) and encouraging preference for PhonePe among the category users will be the main marketing goals for PhonePe in 2021, beginning with the IPL campaign.

This year, the IPL, with which PhonePe has been linked for the past three years, is investing heavily in the competition by accepting six new partnerships.

PhonePe is a sponsor of four IPL franchises, including the Mumbai Indians, Chennai Super Kings, Royal Challengers Bangalore, and Delhi Capitals, in addition to its position as an associate sponsor on Disney+ Hotstar and co-presenting sponsor on Star India.

16.8.6 Myntra

Myntra has collaborated with several of the most talked-about IPL teams, including Royal Challengers Bangalore, Mumbai Indians, and Chennai Super Kings, providing advertisers with an unprecedented opportunity to capitalize on the nation's excitement.

The right chest patch of the Royal Challengers Bangalore (RCB)jersey features a patch with the Myntra logo, which serves as the team's official fashion sponsor. One of the most important marketplaces for Myntra is Mumbai, which is recognized as the center and innovator of fashion and style.

The company is, therefore, the Mumbai Indians' presenting partner and has integrated its logo into all of the team's branding and messaging. On Myntra, you can purchase anything from the MI team, including jerseys and autographed bats. Myntra is giving away daily prizes for participating in its interactive games tied to the cricketing spectacular in order to connect with these folks on social media and on its website.

16.8.7 *Pepsi*

The most successful IPL campaign to date centers on the restless Indians who are eager to get things done "now here, right now." One of the best IPL marketing initiatives that has effectively tapped into the youth of India is Pepsi's "Oh Yes Abhi!" promotion.

Celebrities such as Ranbir Kapoor, Mahendra Singh Dhoni, and Priyanka Chopra Jonas were seen breaking down barriers in the IPL marketing campaign. Dhoni, the most composed of the three, is keen to win the match, while Ranbir is ready for chaat and a Pepsi. Meanwhile, Priyanka demonstrates her eagerness to take the stage.

16.8.8 *VIVO*

Because it is a powerful league that unites people, the IPL has been the center of most significant announcements and product launches, whether it is because of the association with Aamir Khan, the introduction of the V-series, or the most recent announcement of Virat Kohli as the new brand ambassador.

The smartphone company VIVO is back as the IPL's title sponsor. According to sources, VIVO spent Rs. 1133.71 crores on advertising this fiscal year. VIVO invests Rs 440 crores in sponsorship each year for the IPL. Nipun Marya, the director of a brand strategy for IPL 2021's telecommunications company, discussed their branding approach with exchange4media, particularly in light of their reappearance.

In addition, the corporation has a few creative gimmicks up its sleeve. As part of this agreement, VIVO intends to implement a 360-degree marketing plan, with Virat Kohli serving as the new brand ambassador. He will be seen promoting and raising awareness for the launch of a new product range. All planned ATL and BTL initiatives, such as upcoming TV campaigns, print, outdoor, social media, and events, will be included in the relationship. During the Vivo IPL season, the firm also intends to participate in activities.

16.8.9 *Disney+ Hotstar*

It is without a doubt one of the best IPL advertisements with a musical theme, featuring a multilingual hymn that elicited a wide range of emotions in cricket fans. The inter-city competitiveness on the pitch was depicted successfully, with lots of nice humor, and the multilingual hymn drew a swarm of cricket fans from all across the country who spoke different languages.

The song, written and performed by Nucleya, one of India's most popular singers, integrates eight Indian languages and features eight rappers from throughout the country. Because dancing is such an essential aspect of Indian culture, each team performed a distinct step to provide diversity and excitement to the performance. Fans from all over the country were dancing to the song, which signaled the release of a new album.

16.8.10 Byju's

IPL and Byju's have been working together for a long time. It began as an associate sponsor but is now a co-presenter this year. Byju's principally focused on the idea that children should be able to balance academics and extracurricular activities.

The customers were so down after the pandemic that Byju's believed the IPL season would bring some cheer, and they also added 20 million subscribers this season.

16.9 Tips to Launch the IPL Digital Marketing Strategy

Each IPL digital marketing technique may definitely help you draw in more viewers and maintain your prominence for a considerable amount of time. In addition, you will be able to determine what needs to be done next after you have the people's attention or the position.

So, let's examine the various digital marketing techniques employed in the IPL.

1. IPL Is a Marketing Tactic in Itself: The cornerstone of a digital strategy lies in comprehending your target audiences. In the context of the IPL, brand reputation management plays a pivotal role. In India, cricket holds a divine status, and regardless of the match type, spectators are fervently enthusiastic to watch it.

   Additionally, individuals continue to be in a vacation mood in the months of April and May. Children often do not have to worry about tests during the summer or enjoy their summer break. These factors combine to make now the ideal time for the IPL.

Therefore, if you're organizing an event, be sure to pick the right time. In the event that you are running a kids' camp in February, hardly any kids will attend.

2. Influencer Marketing: As a component of their digital strategy, this IPL competition also offers a high-caliber degree of influencer marketing. You can see that the entire RCB, or Royal Challengers Bangalore, team, is promoting Hewlett Packard's and products.

   Rohit Sharma, the captain of the Mumbai Indians, is currently involved in the CEAT brand's marketing. In this sense, nearly every IPL player is involved in the influencer marketing gimmick.

   Therefore, it is your job to study IPL's course on influencer marketing. Utilizing the right forms of influencer marketing at the right moment is crucial. This will ensure that your target viewers are aware of it.

3. Live Images and Videos from Scenes: You will see that there are numerous live recordings of players and team behind-the-scenes tales if you follow the social media accounts of each IPL team. Let's use the IPL team KKR, or Kolkata Knight Riders, as an example.

   Every time they depart for the stadium before a game, and when they return to the hotel after a game, this team broadcasts live on Facebook. People are really interested in seeing what athletes often do before and after a game.

   Posting eye-catching creatives and in-the-moment photos also get customers to think about the company constantly.

4. The Collaboration of Film Stars: We are all aware of how glitzy IPL competitions are. This is the fact that many teams are either sponsored by or owned by movie stars. For example, Bollywood royalty Shah Rukh Khan and Juhi Chawla own Kolkata Knight Riders, or KKR.

   Preity Zinta, on the other hand, is the club's owner. Akshay Kumar is involved in Delhi Daredevils' marketing. Abhishek Bacchan and Junior Bacchan both love the Mumbai Indians.

   These movie stars visit the stadium to watch games and cheer for their preferred squad. Therefore, associating your brand with a movie star will always be advantageous. Include this digital approach in your plan.

5. Social Media Marketing: In the IPL, social media is crucial. Each squad has a Facebook profile, Instagram account, and Twitter handle. You can see that every team is taking advantage of every opportunity to include a digital presence in the digital strategy.

In addition, they publish live blogs, films, updates from matches, real-time pictures, and many other things. Additionally, each squad has a website of their own. Every record, fixture, and blog are all kept up to date here.

You can visit the Royal Challengers Bangalore or RCB website. They have their stuff, blogs, schedules, and many other things on this website. On the website, there is a live chat option as well.

6. Popular Twitter Hashtags: We are all aware of how well liked the IPL tournament is, and nobody can help to talk about it. The matches are frequently discussed by media outlets like NDTV and Cricbuzz. Before every game, they discuss the players and examine the field.

And the hashtag begins to gain traction on other social media sites, particularly Twitter. You can see the various hashtags that become popular before, during, and after every match.

References

1. Ratten, V. (2011). International sports management: Current trends and future developments. Thunderbird International Business Review, 53(6), 679–686.
2. Brown, D., & Hayes, N. (2008). Influencer Marketing? Routledge.
3. Mullin, B. J., Hardy, S., & Sutton, W. (2014). Sport Marketing 4th edition. Human Kinetics.
4. Bhogaraju, S. D., & Korupalli, V. R. K. (2020, January). Design of smart roads–A vision on Indian smart infrastructure development. In 2020 International conference on communication systems & networks (COMSNETS) (pp. 773–778). IEEE.
5. Jaipuria, S., & Jha, S. K. (2022). A study on influence of toss result, toss decision and venue on the outcome of IPL cricket match. International Journal of Sport Management and Marketing, 22(3–4), 287–313.
6. Lee, L. H., Braud, T., Zhou, P., Wang, L., Xu, D., Lin, Z., ..., & Hui, P. (2021). All one needs to know about metaverse: A complete survey on technological singularity, virtual ecosystem, and research agenda. arXiv preprint arXiv:2110.05352.
7. Wang, F. Y., Qin, R., Wang, X., & Hu, B. (2022). Metasocieties in metaverse: Metaeconomics and metamanagement for metaenterprises and metacities. IEEE Transactions on Computational Social Systems, 9(1), 2–7.

Chapter 17

Metaverse in Public Sector

Tanveer Nayak, Saransh Kalambele, and Anurag Jain
School of Business, Woxsen University, Kamkole, Hyderabad, Telangana

17.1 Introduction

The metaverse is a mode of communication that combines the virtual and physical world. This connects the digital world with augmented reality (AR) and virtual reality (VR). In this world, individuals can do businesses, transactions, work, play games, experience new activities, and can entertain. Individuals can do whatever they want to do and what they do in their real world. Internet was introduced in 1990s to this world. By 2020, people started learning about the internet its pros and cons. By 2010, the internet was taken to another level when the "Internet of Things" was introduced in the world, where you can connect and exchange the data over other devices with the help of sensors, software, etc. In 2020s, the world has entered into "Web 3.O," wherein the metaverse you can create your avatar anytime and can live a life according to your own rules in the virtual world.

The metaverse was introduced to many companies such as Nvidia, Roblox, Snap, etc., but Microsoft and Facebook are the early adopters of the metaverse. It has been upon the meta platform (Facebook) that you can create groups, chats, events, etc. Facebook has its own currency called "Facebook Credits" through which you can buy and trade in the virtual world. Another meta known as "Microsoft Mesh" created by Microsoft allows creating apps with better tools and applications. Mesh aims to mix the real and virtual world. Mesh has developed to a level where it can change the way interaction allows you to experience and share the different activities of the real and virtual world [2]. Microsoft wants to develop Mesh in a such

DOI: 10.4324/b23404-17

a way so that if anyone is not present physically but should be present mentally. Mesh wants to create the avatars that could communicate on the individual's behalf.

The government has started working on metaverse technology and has considered its benefits. During the COVID-19, metaverse-associated technologies and companies shifted into AR and VR. Companies adopted its benefits and conducted its meetings and shared their highly confidential data on the single platform. The question arises how the public sector would benefit and what role the government can play. The government found that the metaverse could help them change the system. The avatars created would be able to answer questions asked by the customers; then AI would analyze these questions, experience, and inquiries from the customer; and will revert back if asked the same question. The emergence of the Metaverse has revolutionized life, providing the opportunity to work within a personalized artificial environment that caters precisely to individual needs. This will benefit the environment as less carbon emissions would be released and would reduce the expenses. "Digital Twin" is a metaverse technology application that will help in public sectors like reducing crime, carbon emissions, expenses, etc. This application would help to find out the major problems in the system as soon as possible, and this technology would be able to deter potentially dangerous situations, such as explosive ordnance, firefighting, etc. as the robots would be sent to handle these kinds of situations, saving of the human life.

17.2 Case Analysis of Different Divisions in the Public Sector

Jeong's research suggests that colleges are trying to educate students for the fourth industrial revolution by designing curriculum that addresses societal needs and develops problem-solving skills. They also aim to use the most effective teaching methods [4]. An example of this is the use of the metaverse in an anatomy course at Seoul National University, where students are able to study and practice the human body using AR and VR technologies.

Turk et al.'s research suggests that the metaverse is a culmination of various technologies such as VR, IoT, NFTs, blockchain, wearable technology, mixed reality, and AR. They also highlight that the potential uses of the metaverse are endless [8]. However, it is unclear whether there will be one singular metaverse or multiple ones. Tech companies like Facebook,

Microsoft, and Google are also working toward creating their own metaverse platforms, where each company might have its own distinct platform, product group, and formations.

An Accenture article states that their simulation technology for training vehicles can create a shared virtual environment. By utilizing the metaverse, they can enhance training by providing situational awareness for both individual and team training, particularly at a tactical level or in multi-domain exercises. This can build on existing investments in virtual reality and simulation, and expand them into the metaverse.

Sudeep Srivastava's blog post argues that the use of metaverse in education allows students to take virtual classes remotely while still feeling the presence of a physical classroom [6]. Educational institutions and metaverse technology companies are partnering to overcome physical limitations and make the learning experience more interactive and immersive. Through metaverse, both teacher and students can be present at the same time and have the opportunity to create their own identities in the form of avatars. The metaverse can also create a variety of environments for activities such as roleplaying, hands-on learning, laboratory exercises and more. It also allows for creation of static environments such as textbooks for learning resources and activities.

According to an Outlook India article, the agriculture industry is increasingly adopting and engaging with web 3 and metaverse technology [1]. This technology provides a cutting-edge advantage and creates opportunities in the agriculture industry. Web 3 and metaverse technology offer unparalleled expertise and support for a profitable and sustainable agricultural value chain. These technologies provide comprehensive solutions to address current farming challenges and consist of a blockchain-based infrastructure that is customer-friendly. This platform provides farmers worldwide with metaverse tools to help them be successful in the metaverse world and allows them to work with in-ground expertise.

In an article, Naveen Joshi discussed how the tourism industry was impacted by the pandemic and how the concept of metaverse in tourism could change the way consumers interact with destinations. He argues that immersive virtual worlds have the potential to substitute some forms of actual travel without negatively affecting the tourism industry. In the near future, the metaverse could provide the most immersive travel experience. Many consumers prefer to try out products before making a purchase, and the metaverse allows individuals to virtually visit a destination and have an experience before committing to a trip [3]. The metaverse has the potential to revolutionize the tourism sector by allowing for trial before purchase and could benefit the industry. Additionally, the metaverse can open up new opportunities for the tourism industry by creating virtual tours, experiences, and activities that may not be possible in real life. It can also provide a way for people to visit places that may be inaccessible or too far away, making travel more accessible for everyone. Furthermore, it can also help to attract a younger generation who is more tech-savvy and interested in virtual experiences. In addition, it can also help to reduce the environmental impact of travel, as virtual travel eliminates the need for physical transportation. Overall, the metaverse could be a game changer for the tourism industry, and it will be interesting to see how it develops and how it is adopted in the future.

Tula Giannini and Jonathan P. Bowen's research paper states that the increasing use of digital immersive experiences in art and museums has emphasized the need for deeper engagement with the art and the emotions it evokes [7]. The COVID-19 pandemic has accelerated the development of digital identity and the importance of digital experiences in daily life. They argue that the metaverse, a rapidly growing platform that supports virtual life in 3D as a part of the internet and web 3, has the potential to bring new opportunities for digital artists, entrepreneurs, and inventors. They envision a multidimensional and multimedia space where individuals can connect with their digital identities through experiences such as creating art avatars and using technologies such as AR, VR, NFTs, and more.

An article from *Analytics Insight* states that the metaverse is being utilized in the entertainment industry to create virtual worlds that are separate from reality. These virtual worlds include theme parks and amusement parks that attract visitors from all over the world without the need for additional fees [5]. The metaverse is also being used to create venues for long-term concerts and performances, which can be profitable. Since people tend to view the digital world as real, the metaverse also has a significant impact on the entertainment and media industries through the use of media psychology. Additionally, the metaverse also provides an opportunity for entertainment companies to expand their reach beyond geographical boundaries and to create new revenue streams through virtual experiences, ticket sales, merchandise, and in-world advertising. The metaverse also allows for greater audience engagement, as it enables the creation of interactive and immersive experiences. With the use of avatars, users can interact with the virtual world and with other users in a more natural and personal way, creating deeper connections with the content and the brand. This can help to build a loyal fan base, increase brand awareness, and generate more revenue. The metaverse can also enable new forms of storytelling and content creation, allowing for greater creative freedom and experimentation. Overall, the metaverse has the potential to bring significant changes to the entertainment industry, providing new opportunities for growth and innovation.

17.2.1 The Current State of the Metaverse in the Public Sector

The metaverse is still a relatively new technology, and its applications in the public sector are still being explored. However, there are already a number of examples of metaverse environments being used in the public sector, including virtual town halls, virtual training and education programs, and virtual environments for public engagement and collaboration.

One example of a metaverse application in the public sector is the virtual town hall, where citizens can attend meetings, ask questions, and provide feedback in a virtual environment. This can be particularly useful for citizens who are unable to attend physical meetings, such as those living in remote areas or those with disabilities.

Another example of metaverse application in the public sector is virtual training and education programs. These programs can help to improve the delivery of services by providing employees with the skills and knowledge they need to perform their duties more effectively.

17.2.2 The Current State of the Metaverse in the Public Sector in India

The current state of the metaverse in the public sector in India is still in its early stages. While some government agencies have begun to explore the potential of the metaverse, there are currently no large-scale metaverse projects in operation in the Indian public sector. However, there are indications that the Indian government is interested in exploring the potential of the metaverse for various applications such as e-governance, public service delivery, and virtual meetings.

In recent years, various government and private sector organizations in India have been exploring the use of virtual and augmented reality for various purposes such as remote training, virtual product demonstrations and virtual reality-based tourism. These uses of VR and AR do not fall under the metaverse, but they are a step toward the metaverse.

India's National Informatics Centre (NIC) and the Ministry of Electronics and Information Technology (MeitY) are some of the organizations that have begun to explore the potential of the metaverse.

As the technology evolves, it is expected that the metaverse will become more prevalent in the public sector in India, as government agencies seek to improve the delivery of services and create new opportunities for engagement and collaboration.

Finally, virtual environments can be used to facilitate public engagement and collaboration. For example, virtual environments can be used to host public consultation and feedback sessions, allowing citizens to provide input on important policy decisions.

17.3 Challenges and Opportunities

The metaverse presents a number of challenges and opportunities for the public sector. One of the main challenges is the cost of creating and maintaining a metaverse environment. Developing a metaverse environment requires significant resources, including hardware, software, and staff. Additionally, the metaverse has to be continuously maintained and updated to ensure that it remains relevant and useful to its users.

Another challenge is the legal and regulatory environment. The metaverse is a digital space, and there are many legal and regulatory issues that must be taken into account, such as data privacy and security, intellectual property, and liability.

Despite these challenges, there are also many opportunities for the public sector to use the metaverse to improve the delivery of services, to create new opportunities for engagement and collaboration, and to improve the overall experience of citizens.

17.4 Discussion on Some of the Challenges

Cost: Developing and maintaining a metaverse environment in the public sector can be costly, as it requires significant resources such as hardware, software, and staff.

Legal and regulatory environment: The metaverse operates in a digital space, and there are many legal and regulatory issues that must be taken into account, such as data privacy and security, intellectual property, and liability.

Adoption: The metaverse is still a relatively new technology, and it may be difficult to convince stakeholders and users to adopt it.

User experience: The user experience in the metaverse must be intuitive and easy to use to ensure user engagement and satisfaction.

Technical expertise: Building and maintaining a metaverse requires specialized technical expertise that may not be available within the public sector.

17.5 Finding New Opportunities

Improved service delivery: The metaverse can be used to improve the delivery of services in the public sector by providing employees with the skills and knowledge they need to perform their duties more effectively.

Public engagement and collaboration: Virtual environments can be used to facilitate public engagement and collaboration, allowing citizens to provide input on important policy decisions.

Accessibility: The metaverse can provide greater accessibility to services for citizens who are unable to attend physical meetings, such as those living in remote areas or those with disabilities.

Cost savings: The use of the metaverse can lead to cost savings in the long term; for example, by reducing the need for physical infrastructure and travel.

Innovation: The metaverse can provide opportunities for innovation and experimentation in the public sector by offering new ways of delivering services and engaging with citizens.

17.6 Decision Making in the Public Sector Metaverse

When developing a metaverse environment in the public sector, there are a number of key considerations that must be taken into account. One of the most important is user research. It is essential to understand the needs and requirements of the users of the metaverse environment in order to ensure that it is relevant and useful to them.

Another key consideration is the choice of platform and technology stack. The metaverse is a complex technology, and it is important to choose a platform and technology stack that is appropriate for the project.

Finally, it is important to consider the legal and regulatory environment. The metaverse is a digital space, and there are many legal and regulatory issues that must be considered, such as data privacy and security, intellectual property, and liability.

17.7 Conclusion

In conclusion, the emergence of metaverse technology in the public sector has the potential to revolutionize the way governments interact with citizens and provide services. By creating immersive virtual environments, governments can improve communication, collaboration, and participation in decision-making processes. Additionally, the use of metaverse technology can also improve the delivery of services, such as education and health care, and increase accessibility for individuals with disabilities. However, it is important for governments to consider the potential challenges and implications of implementing metaverse technology, such as data privacy and security concerns, as well as the need for increased investment in infrastructure and training. Overall, while the metaverse is still in its early stages, it has the potential to bring significant benefits to the public sector in the future.

References

1. Farooque Khan (2023).Farooque Khan is shaping the Argriculture Industry Through Blockchain. Outlookindia.com. https://www.outlookindia.com/business-spotlight/farooque-khan-is-shaping-the-agriculture-industry-through-blockchain-news-238286.
2. Hyun, J.J. A study on education utilizing metaverse for effective communication in a convergence subject. *International Journal of Internet, Broadcasting and Communication, 13*(4), 129–134.
3. Joshi, N. *How metaverse is reshaping the tourism industry*, 2022. https://www.allerin.com/blog/how-metaverse-is-reshaping-the-tourism-industry
4. Jeong, E. (2020). Education Reform for the Future: A Case Study of Korea. International Journal of Education and Development Using Information and Communication Technology, 16(3), 66–81.
5. Parvin Mohmad (2023). Is the metaverse inching closer to reality?. https://www.analyticsinsight.net/is-the-metaverse-inching-closer-to-reality/
6. Sudeep Srivastava (2023). Reimagining the future of education with the metaverse. https://appinventiv.com/blog/metaverse-in-education/
7. Tula Giannini, Jonathan P. (2019). Museums and Digital Culture. Springer Seires on Cultural Computing. Springer Cham. https://doi.org/10.1007/978-3-319-97457-6
8. Türk, T. (2022). The concept of metaverse, its future and its relationship with spatial information. Advanced Geomatics, 2(1), 17–22.

Chapter 18

Application of Metaverse in the Automobile Industry

Bhavika Saraswat, Jai Kothari, Geddam Annirudh, and Sanjeev Ganguly

Woxsen University, Hyderabad, Telangana

18.1 Introduction

The word "metaverse" refers to a fully immersive and interactive virtual environment where users (individual's or group's) can communicate with each other and interact with virtual items in real time [1, 2]. However, the meaning of the metaverse changes with different people's perspective and reasoning. The metaverse is a virtual environment that functions like the real world and it allows the users to interact with each other. The concept of the metaverse was first coined in the book *Snow Crash* in 1992 by N. Stephenson [3].

In recent times, a number of metaverse-based applications have gained a lot of interest. There are two types of metaverses: the current metaverse and the Second Life Metaverse. Their difference lies in the following:

- The advancement in deep machine learning has made the new metaverse more fluid and it is more immersive than the last one; it also offers a powerful performance and organic creation model.
- The new metaverse leverages the mobile handsets to promote reach and connectivity.

DOI: 10.4324/b23404-18

■ The financial viability and stability of the metaverse increased with the advent of blockchain technology and virtual currencies (like Dogecoin and Etherium).

Users can access the virtual space created by metaverse using avatars, which is a shared communal place generated by the fusion of virtually improved physical reality and physically persistent virtual reality. As pictured by the founder Mark Zuckerberg, the metaverse is an artificially created immersive where the boundaries of the real and the virtual world starts to fade away, allowing the virtual avatars to interact with each other. The study by Damar [4] describes the metaverse as "the Layer between you and reality." The metaverse is frequently pictured as a shared virtual reality environment where individuals can interact, work, and play in numerous virtual worlds. It is also an enlarged form of virtual reality (VR), encompassing a variety of pursuits and settings, from gaming and entertainment to education, employment, and business [5].

The digital channels in our daily life are increasing more and more with time. In the game *Fortnite*, we experience it on a daily basis. We are attracted toward that digital world to experience what it has to offer. We will need gadgets like AR glasses to access this metaverse world as it becomes more immersive, like the real world. One of the recent applications of the metaverse was seen as a soccer match between AC Milan and Fiorentina screened by Italy's Soccer Division. It will be the same as the time when the internet was developed and we cannot imagine our life without the internet now. We are still learning what the metaverse will actually look like after it is fully developed. The full potential of the metaverse and the use of avatars in the metaverse are yet to be ascertained, taking into consideration the ethical and human rights of people.

The metaverse is the start to fabricate something that will bring a revolution, similar to what the internet brought back in the day and it works like a simulation world combining all the disruptive technology existing now, be it cryptocurrency, AR, VR, or social media. All are mixed together to create a whole new world for the users in the real world. It is just not the extension of the physical world but the physical world and the metaverse world are capable of influencing each other significantly. For example, when we have a meeting in the metaverse, we are just meeting in the normal 2D metaverse. Web 3.0 is the natural evolution from Web 2.0, where having ownership of digital assets will be possible. People can make communities in Web 3.0 that can be accessed through tokens and

NFTs [6]. Based on Tokenomics, people can build huge communities with the same organizations. It will bring a revolution in the working world. The concept of the metaverse that was recently released publicly by Facebook rebranding as Meta, would completely change the way we communicate with the outside world. The corporations can adopt the metaverse in their daily operations and business strategies as it is there to bring transformation in all the sectors of the economy. The wide application that the metaverse will bring by immersing the real with the virtual world is yet to be ascertained [7].

18.2 Literature Survey

In this section, we will be surveying different reports and documents related to automobiles and recent developments that have taken place in the last 10 years. In recent years between 2010 and 2014, we have noticed automobile market share is rampantly high not just in Europe but also in the United States of America. This only pushed these countries to adapt new practices of Environmental, Social and Governance (ESG) per country. Having to face the challenges of carbon emissions, the companies now aim at creating an efficient method to regulate the automobile industry [8].

Before we describe the depth of the metaverse, many researchers and their findings suggest that the metaverse is still in its infancy stages, and may take up to a decade of waiting for us to notice its significance in the industrial sectors [3, 9].

Initially, the metaverse was a concept introduced in the year 1992 through a science fiction novel, but thanks to its exponential growth over the last several years and the potential it offers for the future, it has recently become a hot issue.

Additionally, businesses will also find the metaverse to be a dynamic environment. Before the metaverse is incorporated into the real world and becomes a part of our daily lives, there are still numerous obstacles to be overcome. This is why we should look forward to developing a comprehensive strategy as the virtual world of the metaverse will become an entity for the physical world [10, 11].

A recent study expanded on the applications of metaverse tech in experiencing different products from the wider perspectives of consumers.

The future impact on the business techniques we use, the ways in which we perceive different brands, and develop human interaction will be revolutionary as the boundaries between the physical and digital worlds will be somewhat blurred from current perceptions.

18.3 Automobile Industry

The automotive industry refers to all businesses and endeavors concerned with the production of motor vehicles, including the majority of its parts, such as their hulls and engines, but excluding their tyres, batteries, and gasoline. The manufacturing branch that creates automobiles, trucks, buses, and other motor vehicles are known as the automobile industry. Motor vehicle design, development, manufacturing, marketing, and sales are all part of a worldwide industry [12–16]. One of the largest jobs worldwide and a significant contributor to economic growth is the automobile industry. Original equipment manufacturers (OEMs), which create the cars and their components; suppliers, which create the systems and parts used in cars; and aftermarket, which creates accessories and replacement parts are the three main divisions of the automobile business. Automobile development is a complex process that requires major design criteria often overlapping each other [17]. Overlapping happens due to the vehicle's crash rating, safety ratings, fuel efficiency, driving experience, aerodynamics, etc.

With the emergence of integrated technologies like IoT and 5G as well as new technologies like electric and autonomous vehicles, the industry is continually redefining how we interact with our automobiles and the transportation networks as a whole. The development of emerging markets, the accelerated development of new technology, sustainability legislation, and shifting consumer attitudes toward ownership are all factors that are causing today's world to change significantly [18]. The automobile industry is likely to get into a transformation like the other industries and has been affected by the fast automation and adoption of new digital business models.

Recent developments in the automotive sector have drawn attention to a number of trends, including the following:

■ Electric vehicles (EVs): Electric cars are becoming more popular as a more environmentally friendly substitute for conventional gasoline-powered vehicles as awareness of climate change and air pollution rises. A large variety of electric models will be released by many major automakers in the upcoming years. It is a push toward sustainability by making their vehicles lighter and more fuel-efficient; automakers are employing more advanced materials like aluminum and carbon fiber. The promotion of alternative greener fuels, electric and hydrogen cars is seen to combat climate change and global warming [19]. Car makers have lately been focusing on improving the aerodynamics of the vehicles so the consumers get higher performance and fuel efficiency. By the year 2050, it is expected there will be a 70% increase in oil demand. Car makers are also using advanced manufacturing tools like 3D printing, newly formed metal alloys, etc. in the manufacturing of their cars to improve the supply chain productivity and cut down on the manufacturing cost.

■ Autonomous vehicles (AVs): With numerous businesses investing in this technology, the development of self-driving automobiles has been moving swiftly. AVs have the ability to increase safety, lessen traffic, and alter how we see car ownership. Increased connectivity and communication between vehicles as well as between vehicles and other elements of the transportation system, such as traffic lights and road infrastructure, are made possible by the incorporation of internet of things (IoT) technology into automobiles. Dedicated short-range communication provides for fluid communication between vehicles without requiring any road infrastructure for communication.

■ 5G Technology: 5G connections have a widespread adoption in 2023. The automakers are bringing the necessary technological innovations in order to adopt the technology that will help further improve the productivity and safety features. We will be able to get on-time traffic updates and road monitoring with 5G technology.

■ Shared car services: This means the consumer can use the car to travel places by paying per trip or subscription basis. Ride-hailing and car-sharing services, like Ola and Meru Cabs, are growing in popularity, and this pattern is predicted to continue. This change is influencing how people see car ownership and reshaping the car industry and society. As traffic congestion increases in busy cities, resulting in loss of time and money, the car-sharing services have seen an increase in popularity [20].

■ Cybersecurity: As information technology is used in cars more frequently, cybersecurity of cars is growing in importance for the auto sector industry. It has become a necessity to protect the vehicles as we use them in our daily lives. Protection of vehicles is needed from virus attacks and unauthorized access to cars. In order to protect passengers and other road users from cyberattacks and hacks, automakers are adopting various precautions as safety of the customers is their priority. It can be done by constantly reviewing the systems for traces of cyberattacks and responding instantly if detected [13].

18.4 How the Metaverse and Automobile Industry Are Related

The integration of the metaverse (virtual and augmented reality technology) into the driving experience is referred to as the "metaverse" in the context of automobiles. Someday people may feel the actual sensations of riding an actual car in the metaverse. This might incorporate functions like AR interfaces, which would superimpose digital data over the driver's perspective of the real environment, and VR head-up displays, which would allow drivers to see virtual navigation information projected onto the windscreen. Furthermore, automobiles using metaverse technology may be able to connect to other vehicles and a broader metaverse network, enabling real-time updates and communication with other moving vehicles. Giving drivers real-time traffic and road condition information could enhance traffic flow and boost safety. It is a marketing and sales instrument for car manufacturers as they can provide an immersive experience of their car offerings to the customers. Every car manufacturer wants to have a slice of this metaverse because it can be the next big thing in the industry. Many experts think it will be a competitor's advantage to other companies if they are able to develop it as their competence.

Integrating VR and AR technologies (known as the "proto-metaverse") into vehicles to enhance navigation, entertainment, and communication experiences is the future of the metaverse in the automotive sector. These technologies can be used to provide drivers and passengers with real-time information such as traffic updates and weather forecasts, as well as immersive games and social interactions. The integration of autonomous driving capabilities has the potential to become part of the automotive sector metaverse, providing a more seamless and effective driving experience and the companies using this tech to generate revenue. In the future, digital touchpoints will be as important as physical touchpoints to meet customer expectations. They will use the metaverse tech to attract and retain customers, enhance customer experience, and bring optimization to their manufacturing.

For example, Hyundai is a South Korean multibillion-dollar conglomerate manufacturing cars. It has shown keen interest in investing and exploring the huge potential that the metaverse holds for the future of the automobile industry. In 2020, Hyundai Motor Group pledged to invest roughly $1.6 billion into the development of future technologies such as smart cities, automatic cars, and the metaverse. The company believes that the future for the metaverse is very bright in creating new business opportunities and enhancing its customer experience [21].

In the case of Hyundai, it has a clear vision of creating a metaverse-based platform that allows customers to interact with cars in a virtual environment, where they can test-drive vehicles, customize the design, and even purchase cars. It has been experimenting with the use of VR in its showrooms, allowing customers to explore and customize vehicles in a virtual environment. The company has also been experimenting with the use of VR in its manufacturing process, allowing engineers to remotely collaborate on the design and assembly of vehicles. The metaverse-based platform also aims to connect Hyundai owners with other owners, allowing them to share experiences and information. Hyundai is also leading toward future through a concept called "meta mobility." Cars of the future will be a 3D entertainment system for the passengers instead of just being limited to driving.

18.5 Mark Zuckerberg's Vision toward the Metaverse

The CEO of Facebook, Mark Zuckerberg, has publicly acknowledged his ideas for the metaverse, which he sees as the logical next stage in the development of the internet. In the future, he sees people interacting in a common digital area, just like they do in the real world. He said that "developments in virtual reality and augmented reality technology, which let users create and explore realistic digital settings, will make this possible".

He envisions the metaverse as a space where individuals can interact, exchange stories, and create different kinds of information. He considers it a place where people can collaborate, learn, and have fun. In order to develop a sense of community and connection within the metaverse, "he has claimed that it is his intention to build it in a way that is open and inclusive, available to individuals all over the world." Additionally, he thinks that this is the next step toward development and adoption of Web 3.0 and that it will be a more social, engaging, and immersive experience than what we currently have. He also stated that "the next generation of the internet is metaverse" and all the existing social media websites will be the part of this new metaverse technology.

18.6 Implications

18.6.1 Positive Aspects

The metaverse is going to have a huge impact on the automotive industry. Alternatively, it is also known as AR or VR. There is a whole new world created in virtual reality. Similarly, we can explore the virtual world in open-world games like *GTA* or *Cyberpunk*. We can experience that world with the use of VR headsets. When we project those things in our real world, we use AR. We already have real-world applications of AR in the cars we drive in the form of "drive-in displays" [12].

Basic information like speed and directions are projected on this glass display. There are future implications of AR technology if we focus on automobile engineering, especially car design. Engineers will be able to focus on visualizing their car designs in real time. They can assemble cars virtually and check the validity of their designs. Plans are to build the entire assembly lines of cars. BMW and NVIDIA are already working on a similar project called the Omniverse, where the entire assembly line of BMW cars is being created and the engineers will be able to change those as per their requirements.

Car manufacturers should realize that using the metaverse technology in their assembly lines will help the workers to work very ergonomically and comfortably. This will make the entire production process faster and more streamlined. There are Autobots used in the supply lines. If those stop working in between the process, the engineers can control those Autobots through the metaverse without creating any hindrance in the process. This can have huge implications for car sales. The car dealers can showcase the cars in the metaverse to the clients even if the actual car is not on display. The dealers can even show different colors and accessories provided by the car manufacturers to the customers in real time.

The metaverse can also help in the after-sale services of cars by training the engineers to easily repair parts, and easily diagnose problems. Important maintenance information cannot be conveyed properly through 2D manuals. The metaverse enables the reduction of the risk of work failures as everything is shown in 3D. It is easily understandable by the engineers to work on. It is not there to impact the jobs in the automotive industry. In summary, Hyundai is investing in metaverse technology to provide new opportunities for the company, enhance customer experience, and also create new business opportunities.

One potential application is in the area of VR and AR car showrooms, where customers will be able to search and customize their vehicles in a virtual environment based on their needs. This would allow car manufacturers to showcase their entire range of models and options without the need for physical showrooms, reducing costs, and allowing for more efficient use of space. Customers would also be able to explore and customize their vehicles in a more immersive way, potentially leading to increased satisfaction and sales.

Another potential application is in the area of virtual test-drives. Customers would be able to experience what it is like to drive a car in a virtual environment, allowing them to get a sense of how the car handles and performs before making a purchase. This would also be beneficial for car manufacturers, as it would allow them to showcase their cars in a variety of different driving scenarios, such as on a race track or in a city setting.

The metaverse could also be used for vehicle maintenance and repair. For example, virtual training sessions could be conducted for mechanics and technicians, assisting them to learn and acquire new skills in controlled spaces. Additionally, virtual assistance could be provided to mechanics working on vehicles in the field, allowing them to access technical information and receive guidance in real time.

The metaverse can be used by the automakers to earn money through advertisements and the car dealers to win customers over. They are showcasing their products on the platform. They are using NFTs, making auto launches virtually on the metaverse, and selling online billboards on the platform.

Finally, metaverse technology could also be used in the development of autonomous vehicles. Self-driving cars could be tested and fine-tuned in a virtual environment before being deployed on real roads, allowing for a more efficient and cost-effective development process, not compromising the public safety.

There are several unseen risks associated with the application of the metaverse in the automobile sector. Some of the key risks include the following.

When we are talking about data privacy and security, more and more data is poured in by millions of people in the metaverse database, there is always a risk of data breaches and hacks, which could possibly lead to the exposure of sensitive information being leaked. Furthermore, there may be security threats about the collection and use of personal data by profit-making companies, as they may use that data to target consumers toward advertisements and manipulate them to buy products they do not need or other unethical practices, which raise privacy concerns.

In terms of cybersecurity, as the metaverse becomes more integrated with vehicles, there is a risk of cyber-attacks that could compromise the safety and functionality of vehicles. This could include hackers taking control of a vehicle's systems or stealing sensitive data. On a reliability scale, the metaverse with respect to the automobile sector increases dependency, which could lead to huge losses to companies if there are any experiences like technical difficulties or security breaches.

Job replacement, as the penetration of the metaverse increases in the automobile industry, could decrease in the actual need for physical dealership stores and test-drives, which could snatch a lot of human jobs for those working, increasing the unemployment rate. The advent of the metaverse introduces significant social and psychological risks, encompassing concerns such as addiction, social isolation, and reduced physical activity, affecting both individuals and communities. Regulation may be a need for introducing new rules and regulations to ensure data privacy and security is well maintained, as well as to ensure there is safe and ethical use of this technology.

It's important for companies operating in the automobile sector to weigh the potential benefits of the metaverse against these risks and to put in place robust security measures and regulations to mitigate these risks. In conclusion, the metaverse has the potential to change the way the automobile industry operates by providing new and innovative ways to showcase, test, maintain, and develop vehicles. It can be used to improve the customer experience, reduce costs, and enhance the efficiency of operations. In the future, robotics will enable anything to get mobile, just by adding wheels to it controlled by AI. It has a widespread application from transportation to hospitals. Non-fungible tokens can also be applied to car ownership. People can own NFTs that show the ownership stake in a car, giving them access to the car itself.

18.7 Conclusion

There is no doubt that the rise of the metaverse has stimulated debates on its potential good and bad impacts on economy and society. Communication, entertainment, education, and industry are just a handful of the areas of daily life that may be altered by the use of the metaverse in day-to-day life. It also brings major societal and ethical concerns regarding privacy, security, and the impact on the everyday world. More research and development are needed to fully understand the potential benefits and dangers of metaverse technology and to ensure that it is implemented in a responsible and equitable manner. The integration of metaverse technology into vehicles has the potential to enhance the driving experience and make transportation safer, more efficient, and more ecofriendly. For example, it might enable cars to interact with each other and with infrastructure, resulting in improved traffic flow, reduced congestion, and fewer accidents. Additionally, this could enable the development of innovative modes of transport, such as shared mobility services and autonomous vehicles. However, it also brings up major concerns related to security, privacy, and the potential effects on employment in the transportation sector.

References

1. Mystakidis, S. (2022). Metaverse. *Encyclopedia, 2,* 486–497. http://doi.org/10.3390/encyclopedia2010031
2. Mohamed, E. S., Naqishbandi, T. A., & Veronese, G. (2023). Metaverse! Possible Potential Opportunities and Trends in E-Healthcare and Education. *International Journal of E-Adoption (IJEA), 15*(2), 1–21. http://doi.org/10.4018/IJEA.316537
3. Stephenson, N. (1992). Snow Crash: A Novel. Spectra. https://scholar.google.com/scholar_lookup?title=Snow%20crash&publication_year=1992&author=N.%20Stephenson
4. Damar, M. (2021). Metaverse Shape of Your Life for Future: A bibliometric snapshot. *Journal of Metaverse, 1*(1), 1–8. Retrieved from https://dergipark.org.tr/en/pub/jmv/issue/67581/1051371
5. Singh, A., & Kumar, A. (2022). Metaverse. Available at *SSRN 4243086.*

6. Smith, R. (2022). NPD with the Metaverse, NFTs, and Crypto. *Research-Technology Management, 65*(5), 54–56.

7. Zhurauski, E. A. (2022). Metaverse. Electronic systems and technologies [Electronic resource]: Collection of materials of the 58th scientific conference of graduate students, undergraduates and students of BSUIR, Minsk, April 18–22, 2022. Belarusian State University of Informatics and Radioelectronics; Editorial Board: D. V. Likhachesky [and others]. Minsk, 2022. S. 895–896. https://libeldoc.bsuir.by/handle/123456789/46926

8. Kim, J. Y., & Oh, J. M. (2022). Opportunities and Challenges of Metaverse for Automotive and Mobility Industries. In *2022 13th International Conference on Information and Communication Technology Convergence (ICTC)* (pp. 113–117). IEEE.

9. Dwivedi, Y. K., Hughes, L., Baabdullah, A. M., Ribeiro-Navarrete, S., Giannakis, M., Al-Debei, M. M., … & Wamba, S. F. (2022). Metaverse Beyond the Hype: Multidisciplinary Perspectives on Emerging Challenges, Opportunities, and Agenda for Research, Practice and Policy. *International Journal of Information Management, 66*, 102542. https://doi.org/10.1016/j.ijinfomgt.2022.102542

10. Chayka, K. (2021). Facebook Wants Us to Live in the Metaverse. What Does That Even Mean? Access date: 08/11/2021. https://www.newyorker.com/culture/infinite-scroll/facebook-wants-us-to-live-in-the-metaverse

11. Dick, E. (2021). Public Policy for the Metaverse: Key Takeaways from the 2021 AR/VR Policy Conference. https://itif.org/publications/2021/11/15/public-policy-metaverse-key-takeaways-2021-arvr-policy-conference/

12. Nilsson-Lindén, H., Sundin, E., Zackrisson, M., Hildenbrand, J., Jonasson, C., Schaller, V., … & Lundin, P. (2021). Ecosystem for reuse of automotive components. In *LCM 2021. 05–08 September 2021 Stuttgart, Germany the 10th International Conference on life cycle management.*

13. Mckinsey (2023). The Metaverse: Driving Value in the Mobility Sector. https://www.mckinsey.com/industries/automotive-and-assembly/our-insights/the-metaverse-driving-value-in-the-mobility-sector

14. Oktav, A. (2017). New Trends and Recent Developments in Automotive Engineering. https://www.researchgate.net/publication/321621798_New_Trends_and_Recent_Developments_in_Automotive_Engineering/citations

15. Chang, W. R., Hwang, J. J., & Wu, W. (2017). Environmental Impact and Sustainability Study on Biofuels for Transportation Applications. *Renewable and Sustainable Energy Reviews, 67*, 277–288.

16. Zheng, K., Zheng, Q., Yang, H., Zhao, L., Hou, L., & Chatzimisios, P. (2015). Reliable and Efficient Autonomous Driving: The Need for Heterogeneous Vehicular Networks. *IEEE Communications Magazine, 53*(12), 72–79.

17. Ascone, D., Tonja Lindsey, T., & Varghese, C. (2009). An Examination of Driver Distraction as Recorded in NHTSA Databases (No. DOT HS 811 216). National Highway Traffic Safety Administration.

18. Voinea, G. D., Gîrbacia, F., Postelnicu, C. C., Duguleana, M., Antonya, C., Soica, A., & Stănescu, R. C. (2022). Study of Social Presence While Interacting in Metaverse with an Augmented Avatar during Autonomous Driving. *Applied Sciences, 12*(22), 11804.

19. Stegen, K. S. (2015). Heavy Rare Earths, Permanent Magnets, and Renewable Energies: An Imminent Crisis. *Energy Policy, 79*, 1–8.
20. Nansubuga, B., & Kowalkowski, C. (2021). Carsharing: A Systematic Literature Review and Research Agenda. *Journal of Service Management, 32*(6), 55–91. https://doi.org/10.1108/JOSM-10-2020-0344
21. Reuters (2022). Beyond Cars: Hyundai Says "Metamobility" Will Link Real and Virtual Worlds in the Future. https://www.reuters.com/technology/beyond-cars-hyundai-says-metamobility-will-link-real-virtual-worlds-future-2022-01-04/

Chapter 19

AI and Human Cognizance

P. Sanjna, D. Sujith, K. Vinodh, and B. Vasavi
Woxsen University, Hyderabad, India

Delukshi Shanmugarajah
Middlesex University, London, UK

19.1 History of AI

AI was first introduced in the year 1956 by John Mccarthy in a conference. The story behind AI is machines operating like humans and understanding that the machines have the ability to think and learn by themselves, as humans do. Alan Turing, who was a mathematician, has put his hypothesis and questions into an action and analyzed if machines can think, which was called the Turing test, and enabled machines to think like humans.

19.2 Artificial Intelligence and Human Consciousness

Recently, understanding and AI, as well as mindfulness applied to AI, have received a lot of attention (Manzotti, 2005; Signorello, 2018). According to one viewpoint, there is a chance of obtaining, creating, and implementing these models, and then, when applied to AI, it is possible to learn human awareness. According to Holland, there are two types of care: delicate and substantial. Weak phony mindfulness is in charge of the design and advancement of devices that assist in the therapy of discernment, whilst strong phony mindfulness is in charge of the design and advancement

DOI: 10.4324/b23404-19

of perceptive robots. Re-created knowledge is now being employed in a variety of fields, including AI, academic cerebrum inquiry, neurology, and others. Man-made insight has also begun to make progress in the same way as imaginative effort has. AI may be able to take leadership of tasks and vocations that need some human effort. In addition, the metaverse facilitates swift and independent data processing and retrieval, enabling efficient exploration and analysis of information, leading to informed decision-making. AI can be envisioned as a human-crafted entity, integrating human discernment and reflexes to emulate human-like qualities, ultimately aiming to mimic and replicate human cognition and emotions. We call insight what we learn from our experiences and how we respond to situations and events. Investing in AI should be done in the same way that visualizing frozen yogurt produces a delectable flavor and a bright, creative mind. Mindfulness will be attempted as a possibility by man-made thinking frameworks. Man-made information is related with mind science, where it has turned into a serious development in the field's audit, thanks to this process for thinking derived from the interaction of neurons in the human frontal cortex. To give just one example, computer-based comprehension has enabled the destruction and recovery of word-related plans. A handful of people have also introduced the "machine risk thought." Before AI can be used in general, it must first be understood. At its core, modernized believing is an extension of human data, and its progress is reliant on computational advancements. For an unusually lengthy period, copied data has made the essential strides not to coordinate attention in specialists. Care clearly refers to several aspects of human understanding that are necessary for our finest intellectual abilities: opportunity, strength, thrilling experience, learning, and thought, to name a few.

19.3 Types of AI

The first two types of AI, reactive AI and limited memory AI, are simple and would help people for the betterment of life, whereas the other two, theory of mind AI and self-aware AI, would come at a greater loss and risk for the human civilization as they can understand humans and make decisions on their own using the intelligence they have as shown in Figure 19.1 (Joshi, 2019).

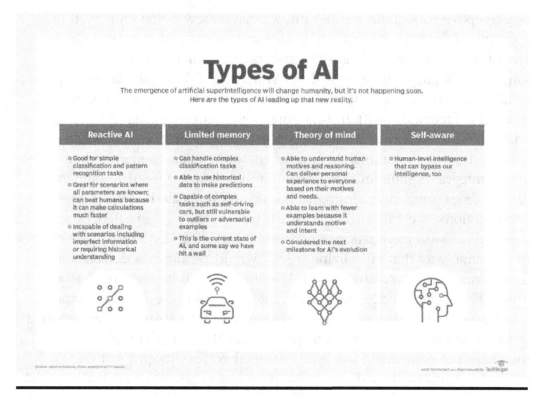

Figure 19.1   Theory of Mind AI and self-aware AI.

19.4 Can AI Develop Human-Like Conscious?

AI is currently one of the most problematic concerns, with little consensus on the differences and similarities between human and machine data (Wang, 2020; Dong et al., 2020, Human-driven and destinations), such as the mission for human-like data as the best quality level for AI, are unaffected by various essential inconveniences, such as perseverance, reasonableness, and morals, while the importance of cooperation between the mind, the body, and the general climate has been emphasized.

Man-made consciousness (AI) and ongoing leap forwards in data innovation might simplify it for individuals and robots to work all the more adequately. Subsequently, much work has gone into creating human-aware AI, which attempts to assemble AI that adjusts to the intellectual capacities and cutoff points of human colleagues as a "colleague." To underscore a serious level of coordinated effort, similarity, and correspondence in "mixture groups," similitudes; for example, "mate," "accomplice," "change self-image," and "mutual perspective" are utilized. When going about as "human colleagues," AI accomplices should have the option to screen, investigate, and respond to a wide assortment of modern human social elements like consideration, inspiration, feeling, inventiveness, arranging, and argumentation. Accordingly, these "computer-based intelligence accomplices" or "colleagues" should have human-like (or humanoid) intellectual capacities that take into account complementary understanding and joint effort (for example, "human awareness"). No matter how modern and independent AI specialists advance in certain spaces, they will doubtlessly stay oblivious to robots or particular reason devices that help individuals in specific and complicated tasks (Cockburn et al., 2018). They have an essentially unique working framework (computerized versus organic) and intellectual characteristics and powers than natural creatures like people since they are advanced machines.

1. Self-driving autos are an AI-helped innovation that utilizes a customary neural organization.
2. From robot-aided operations to the protection of private documents, AI plays a unique role in the healthcare business.
3. Today's robots lack natural intelligence, yet they are capable of problem solving and thinking.
4. The Roomba 980 model employs AI to measure room sizes, recognize obstructions, and recall the best cleaning routines. The Roomba can also estimate how much vacuuming is required based on the size of a room and cleans floors without the intervention of humans.
5. AI is employed in Google Search, Siri, and Google Assistants, among other search engines and assistants.
6. AI-based misrepresentation recognition and purchaser results can help banks, Visas, and loan specialists diminish extortion and oversee hazard (fraud divisions at banks and Visas, Verifi, Ravelin, Stripe).
7. Massachusetts General Hospital, one of the world's most prepared foundations, has paired up with handling goliath NVIDIA to organize AI-controlled items for the illness area, examination, therapy, and the chiefs.
8. AI is heavily integrated in Facebook's platform, whether it's Messenger chatbots, algorithmic newsfeeds, photo tagging recommendations, or ad targeting.
9. Slack's AI utilizes an information structure called the "work diagram" to gather information on how each organization and its laborers utilize the application and speak with each other.

19.5 Cognitive Abilities of AI

Intellectual limit is an extensive mental ability that incorporates thinking, critical thinking, arranging, conceptual reasoning, complex idea handling, and learning through experience. The three-technique model is the most exhaustive scientific classification of intellectual capacities. The main layer incorporates explicit and confined capacities, the second incorporates bunch variables and wide capacities, and the third incorporates general mind. Machines can gather data, store the data in memory, and recuperate the data when an issue should be tended to. Scholarly gifts are human limits that are being dealt with in AI for it to execute jumbled tasks quickly and capably. For instance, AI-driven vehicles can achieve autonomous navigation by analyzing course maps, roads, streets, and pathways, while also conducting internal assessments during turns in a discreet manner. These capacities exhibit the robots' scholarly capacities. When coming to memory and reviewing, AI regularly utilizes PC vision to obtain tactile information and afterward store them. For instance, on the off chance that I have a pal called Avantika, AI will decipher data from my faculties and express feelings as a companion whenever it sees Avantika.

19.6 Ethics of AI

Man-made brainpower morals, or AI morals, are a bunch of convictions, ideas, and strategies that manage moral conduct in the creation and arrangement of the AI situation utilizing generally acknowledged good and bad standards.

Robot ethics, commonly referred to as roboethics or machine ethics, is the study of how to build ethical robots and what rules should be followed to guarantee that robots behave ethically. Roboethics is concerned with issues such as whether robots will be able to address a long-term risk to people and if the use of explicit robots, such as killer robots in wars, will be detrimental to humans. Roboticists must ensure that autonomous structures may conduct ethically acceptable behavior when robots, AI structures, and other free systems, such as self-driving vehicles, work with humans.

Computerized reasoning (AI) and mechanical technology are adjusting and changing our human headway overall. In the public area, applying AI moral norms to the preparation and execution of algorithmic or savvy systems and AI drives is basic. Simulated intelligence will be made and utilized in an ethical, safe, and reliable way in light of the fact to man-made mindfulness ethics. Computer-based intelligence morals and well-being should be an essential need in the plan and arrangement of AI frameworks. The motivation behind AI ethics is to forestall human and cultural issues brought about by AI framework abuse, misuse, terrible plans, or unexpected bothersome outcomes.

A self-driving vehicle sees its current circumstance and drives all alone, with practically no human information. A gigantic amount of information should be caught consistently by a bunch of sensors introduced all through the vehicle for the vehicle to perform productively and handle its driving climate. These are then handled by the vehicle's independent driving PC framework.

The autonomous automobile must also undergo extensive training in order to comprehend the data it gathers and make the best judgment feasible in any given traffic condition.

Everyone makes moral judgments every day. When a driver slams on the brakes to avoid colliding with a jaywalker, the risk is shifted from the pedestrian to the car's passengers. Consider a self-driving car approaching a grandma and a child with faulty brakes. By veering off somewhat from the street, it is feasible to save oneself. Rather than a human driver, the vehicle's PC will settle on the choice this time. Which would you like: the grandma or the kid? Do you think there is only one right response? This is a normal moral situation that represents the significance of morals in specialized advancement. Therefore, we must build technology and AI in such a way that they are based on ethics and follow principles. AI is the future of the world; it should be created in such a way that it serves the country and its people in the most ethical manner abiding by all laws and regulations.

19.7 Language and AI

Language and understanding are always linked to each other at all points of time and these are linked to challenges in robotics as well (Cangelosi, 2010). There are advancements that have been done in the field of robotics in deep learning, speech understanding, and image ion as such. Studies say that a robot without any pre-existing knowledge of linguistics is able to learn linguistics commands with the help of deep learning and praising. T. Dutoit (1997) has explained that the robots in the future have to deal on a daily basis with complicated tasks that are diverse and highly undetermined.

There are many drawbacks and reasons why language is challenging in AI and robotics.

More viable human-robot communication is turning out to be progressively critical as mechanical technology propels to understand the maximum capacity of robots for society. Despite significant advances in AI and machine learning over the last decade, language acquisition and understanding are still related to a variety of robotics issues. The fields of deep learning, language (including machine translation), speech recognition, picture recognition, image captioning, distributed semantic representation learning, and parsing have all achieved significant progress. While communicating in a language should be essential for the arrangement, our current ability to give communication in a language is restrictive. Language is a futile and representative framework. Future service robots will have to cope with sophisticated, diversified, dynamic, and extremely unexpected linguistic occurrences on a daily basis while engaging with human users.

The main purpose of the research is to spotlight the obstacles that are faced by engineers and they have overcome in a process to develop robots in a more natural manner, where a robot can process the language naturally like humans (NLP). Delivering well-founded and meticulously reviewed presentations about the current capabilities of robots, including their prowess in speech and language integration, adaptability to new situations, real-time decision-making instead of relying solely on analysis, and creating easily understandable and communicative robots. Language itself is dynamic, intellectual, and social.

In order to make the robots behave and speak like individuals in practical and fair situations, there is a need to build approaches that actually allow robots to understand the expressions and phrases that are connected to a real-world environment. Creating robots that converse regularly with people in social settings. We need to understand that language is neither a physical entity nor a genuine signal which rather a distinct framework in which the meaning of signing alters depending on the context.

19.8 What Is Language to Us?

Language is the ability to learn and use jumbled correspondence systems, particularly the ability of individuals to do so, and language is a specific example of such a system. Language is what separates humans from other species (Mavridis, 2015; Dutoit 1997; Noda et al., 2015). Because we think through language, words, as revealed by the savant, are the machinery of perception. Language is the necessary tool for communication.

Language is what distinguishes us as individuals. It is the method through which individuals communicate. Learning a language entail mastering a complex system of vocabulary, design, and punctuation in order to communicate successfully with others.

Language is an essential component of human cooperation. People are the only species who have perfected intellectual verbal communication, despite the fact that other organisms have some form of communication. Language aids us in communicating our feelings, opinions, and thoughts to others. It has the capacity to generate and at the same time have the capacity to destroy the social structure. It may appear indisputable.

19.8.1 Language Importance in Individual Development

People learn to speak at different speeds, and the age at which a kid begins to use language might indicate how well they are growing. This does not, however, only apply to infants. It also applies to tiny children learning a second language at school that differs from the one they speak at home, adults learning a new language, and people who have lost their language due to an accident and are attempting to reclaim it (Cangelosi et al. 2010).

19.8.2 Language's Importance in Culture and Society

Language allows us to convey our feelings and thoughts, and it is fascinating to our species because it allows us to transmit the unambiguous convictions and practices of other communities and networks.

19.8.3 Channel of Thought

Language is a medium of thought; it's the way we think and express ourselves. When a person's reasoning cycle is disrupted, their reasoning cycle capacity will be changed. Language is the medium where we communicate our experiences and it is also a reflection of signals and signs.

19.8.4 Communicate with Another

Individuals all across the world communicate with one another and exchange ideas as the concept of globalization takes hold. Language's significance cannot be disregarded, even with the advancements in technology that have served as a medium for communication. Understanding a common language has aided people in communicating, even if they are from different parts of the world. Language has evolved into a vital means of communication between nations, social groups, various organizations and associations, networks, and friends. Communication with other countries: different nations communicate in different languages. Because English is a universal language, global communities exchange perspectives through it.

19.8.5 Personal Communication Necessitates the Use of Language

Despite the fact that much of human connection is nonverbal (we may express our feelings, sentiments, and ideas through our motions, articulations, tones, and sensations), language is critical for individual correspondence. Whether it's having the ability to communicate with your friends, your partner, or your family, having a shared language is essential for these kinds of interactions.

19.8.6 The Importance of Language in Emotional Development

Because dialects have such a strong internal impact on us, it's fairly rare for us to say only one phrase to anger or appease someone (Mutulu et al., 2009). Every word, no matter how tiny or huge, has a considerable amount of power. We can see how words may affect us on the inside, but it's also crucial to consider the emotions that can control language. The fact that every language has a word for "adoration" or "outrage" shows that emotions have a strong impact on language.

19.8.6.1 Is It the Same for All?

Language, like culture, that other most human trait, is notable for its unity in diversity: there are numerous dialects and societies, each unique yet fundamentally similar, in light of the fact that there is one human instinct and that one of its major properties is the ability to allow such variety.

Dialects differ in a variety of ways. They may use a variety of sounds, construct words in a variety of ways, and arrange words to form sentences in a variety of ways, and that's only the beginning! When we say "language," we're referring to the act of speaking, writing, or signing. We're not talking about how individuals can communicate with their bodies, faces, or eyes; we're talking about an organized language system.

A "vernacular" is a group of languages that is not identical and is not understood by people who speak other dialects of the same language. The accent of the language, words that are used and the individuals portraying and organizing their speech are said to be examples of how languages can vary from one to another. This might be combination of geographical and social reasons, and people who use or speak the same language are more likely to reside in a neighborhood.

Etymologists use the term "lects" in several circumstances. This phrase refers to the way people speak inside a discourse community that recognizes them in some way, but not because of friendly circumstances or where they live.

We have a similar mental structure and are "wired" for language. We dwell on the same planet and we may have (usually) comparable interactions.

However, when it comes to language, particularly language development, we all have different approaches to deciphering our interactions and incorporating them into the language creation process. For you, one sound may represent something, whereas for the other person, a different sound may imply the same thing. I may use one gesture to convey a message, whereas another person may use a different signal. As a result, people in different parts of the country invented their own methods of pronouncing "man," "woman," "dog," and so on.

After a group of people agreed on a sound/motion set, their relatives either changed it or migrated away and went through strong/motion change processes on their own, creating tongues.

The language for robots is different. We have various programs like Java, Python, and C++, lisp.

19.9 What Is Intrinsic Motivation?

Intrinsic motivation is playing a vital role in developmental psychology as it is the basics for spontaneous exploration and curiosity (Nguyen and Oudeyer, 2013). It is said to create a brainstorming situation among humans, which is essential for cognitive growth in humans and it is combined with the curiosity of robotics in recent times. Firstly, it gives you an idea of tactics that are being utilized in psychology as part of the intrinsic study.

Secondly, we need to provide evidence that these tactics are not feasible and inconsistent when it is applied to reinforcement learning. Thirdly, we need to provide a solution, a formal topology, where several computational ethodologies provide the basis for operational processing and intrinsic motivation.

19.9.1 How to Teach Intrinsic Meaning to Robots

We need to devise techniques for robots to grasp spoken words robustly in a real-world environment, despite inherent uncertainties, in order to build robots that can interact organically with people in a real-world context, such as workplaces and homes. We must recognize that language, rather than being a tangible thing or a set of objective signals, which is the dynamic symbol system where the meanings vary depending on the context and situations and that is understood subjectively.

A method for teaching robots about engine capabilities combines dynamic naturally persuaded learning with impersonation learning. The SGIM-D algorithmic plan enables robots to efficiently learn high-layered constant sensorimotor backwards models, and in particular, it learns dispersions of parameterized engine arrangements that settle a corresponding appropriation of parameterized objectives/errands. To improve I, SGIM-D improves its assessment L1.

For example, in the examination, a robot arm must understand how to adapt and use fishing line, which shows that SGIM-D effectively correlates with social and natural learning, as well as the benefits of human properties, which helps to figure out the effective way to deliver a variety of results in a climate, while growing more precise arrangements in large spaces.

SGIM-D employs a social learning strategy. The learner imitates the situations in the shown way in a short span of time, while also recalling the desired outcome/goal. It's recommended to remember that ration before beginning its autonomous exploration. It then generates a new aim while keeping the prior one in mind.

19.9.2 Logic-Based Programming

19.9.2.1 Programming

Muggelton S. has introduced Advanced Induct Logic Programs, which offer solutions to declarative problems encountered in programming. These programs present a list of viable options to accomplish tasks, incorporating elements of unpredictability and distribution in reasoning (Muggleton, 2003).

19.9.2.2 Semantics and Orders

19.9.2.2.1 Various Order: Thought Age by Robots

The interior cycles of words are needed to empower robots and arrange data. For robots, calculations like LDA are utilized to classify circumstances and words.

19.9.2.2.2 Word Meaning Acquisitions

It is feasible to isolate data from pictures utilizing multi-model data. The robot, on which this model is deployed, gathers multimodal information from the objects displayed before it, while a human user demonstrates the object attributes to the robot. At last, the robot had the option to perceive inconspicuous items with an exactness of 86% and show phrases with pinpoint precision.

The studies mentioned in the preceding section, as well as multimodal information obtained by looking, gripping, and shaking items, were utilized to categorize concepts into categories and calculate hierarchical links. The robot's expected hierarchical structure, with hierarchical linkages based on feature similarities being recorded. When this paradigm is used to the problem of concept formation localization, the following outcomes are obtained.

For both the age of different thoughts and the learning of connections between them, AI calculations have been proposed. The proposed approach likewise permits robots to gain syntax from the beginning since the progress between these ideas is viewed as sentence structure. Individual, item, movement, and limitation thoughts are made utilizing MLDAs, which order multimodal information obtained from situations where people use objects.

19.9.2.3 Some Metaphorical Phrases to Consider

19.9.2.3.1 Metaphor as a Cognitive Process

In earlier times, metaphors were used to communicate, and it helps humans to understand, process, and experience the things and situations in society. Sayantini (2022) has explained the AI cognitive process. For example, "I'm overjoyed" is a phrase when someone is extremely happy and joyous. When the subject of the verb "will" is normal in the literal sense, whereas "joy" is not, this statement sounds most natural and may not appear metaphorical. The conceptual metaphor "emotions are liquid" reveals that we understand "joy" as an intangible goal domain in terms of a "liquid." Metaphors can help with emotional intelligence as well as the cognitive ability to process complicated information (Hesslow, 2002).

19.9.2.4 Observational Learning

19.9.2.4.1 Learning from Demonstration (LfD) and Programming by Demonstration (PbD)

These are the terms that are used to explain how exactly the robot will function, where both the language and robotics get advantages from learning when implemented with action, which is frequently called *imitation learning,* where learning occurs in place of supervision. Re-creation of instructor's rules and trajectories is said to be imitation learning.

19.9.2.4.2 Reinforcement Learning

Reinforcement learning helps the robot to analyze and discover the optimal behavior, which it understands through the trial-and-error method. This reinforcement learning helps to create robots with true linguistic skills. For example, if we ask a robot to put the table tennis ball over the net, in this process the robots process through the data and observation of dynamic variables with a proper velocity that actually gives the assumption of future outlook or outcome.

19.9.2.4.3 Punctuation and Activities

It is said that the important plan of language content in humans is made of three main categories: 1) sensory framework, which is linked to the expressiveness of feelings such as expressions and signals; 2) being calculative and purposeful situations or understanding the framework where the subjects are linked to semantics; and 3) syntactic computational framework, which deals with sensory functions and to provide a purposeful framework.

19.9.2.5 Pragmatics

As a joint effort with humans, improving robots that can collaborate with people should be a primary objective of our language and advanced mechanics research. To achieve a common goal, humans and robots must be able to communicate effectively and respect one another's physical and mental states. During the language acquisition process, newborn children should comprehend the speaker–listener or educator–student roles, as well as the reversibility of these jobs. Data is clearly handed on during genuine collaboration through practical demonstrations, but it is also deictic and clearly articulated during a discussion (Bossman, 2016).

19.10 Society and AI

The evolution and advancements of AI have influenced society in both long and short terms. AI has had major ramifications in the professional world for those working with modern technologies, and there are now ethical laws in place to help people make good decisions in complex situations. AI technology and its advancements have influenced many aspects of society, providing both benefits and drawbacks to humans (Ostrom, 2016). AI applications can be controlled so that no harm is done to security or personal data, or human rights are violated. The use of AI aided in forecasting the labor market. AI aids in the creation of new products by increasing productivity. With AI, there is a significant rise in questions about whether it can actually increase job loss at one point while also creating new jobs at another. AI is used for the "social good," and it is a fact that technological advancements have enabled AI to analyze and process data. AI's capabilities enable it to solve a wide range of problems in the world, including the creation of a self-sustaining society.

19.10.1 Can AI Create a Society of Its Own?

AI is becoming increasingly important in society for making decisions and analyzing business trends (Cangelosi and Schlesinger, 2015). By analyzing future trends, it plays a key role in the company's decision-making process (Admoni and Scasselati, 2017; Koch, 2019). It has applications in the banking, health, and manufacturing industries, among others. AI is constantly striving to improve its effectiveness and efficiency by eliminating all human errors. It is said that AI can create its own society because AI will be used in every industry and in everyone's lives in the future.

AI in the Field of Medical Sciences:

■ AI has revolutionized the medical field and had a significant impact. Different types of machine learning and models have been developed to aid in predicting critical cases and determining whether a patient has cancer or tumor based on past symptoms and health records. It also aids in future health predictions for patients, allowing them to take preventative measures sooner and live a healthier lifestyle (Derrington, 2017).

■ AI has created a virtual and private assessment as well as advanced technology equipment that is designed specifically for people's monitoring and different cases and their health situation outcomes in a timely manner. It enables doctors to conduct assessments in a much more timely manner, allowing them to begin treatment right away. Once the assessment is completed, AI provides the best medical recommendations on the spot.

■ The use of healthcare bots is another excellent way for the medical industry to work their way in the field, as it allows them to provide 24/7 assistance and categorizes appointments according to the severity of the situation, reducing the amount of effort required to manage appointments. Without AI-based machines, this would not have been possible.

AI in the Air Transport Industry:

■ Airport transportation is the most organized mode of transportation in the world, and it is here that the need for AI has emerged as a viable option. Here, AI machines are involved in providing routes and planning, as well as takeoff and landing times, which are all calculated and displayed for a smooth plane operation.

■ The navigation of maps and routes, as well as a thorough examination of the entire cockpit panel to ensure that everything is in working order, was carried out with the assistance of AI in the airways. This has produced very effective and promising results, which is why it is recommended that you use it frequently. AI's main goal in the field of air transportation is to ensure that humans have a comfortable and safe journey.

AI in Banking and Financial Institutions:

■ In the bank, AI has played an important role in managing financial transactions and handling large and diverse activities. Machine learning models, which are AI, have been used to help banks with day-to-day tasks such as operational or transactional tasks, the stock market and their management methods, and so on.

■ With the help of AI, which is a major aspect in the banking industry, it also assists in tracking and monitoring unusual transactions and reporting them to regulators. Other scenarios include credit card analysis, in which well-known credit card companies track transactions on a geographical level, determine whether they are suspicious based on various parameters, and then work to resolve the issue.

■ AI is attempting to provide the highest level of customer satisfaction while also improving their travel experience. With the help of past purchases and tracking techniques, it also personalizes the offers to the tickets.

■ Machine learning algorithms, with the help of AI, look for ways to maximize sales revenue in the long run.

■ It can detect climate changes and much more with the help of AI, which will allow us to predict flight delays in advance. Additionally, it aids in crew scheduling as well as traffic detection for landing and takeoff.

AI in the Gaming Industry:

■ Virtual games are the rage these days, and the demand and profit potential are unimaginable. This is one of the areas where AI has made the most progress. The bots are always ready to play, and you don't need to wait for anyone else.

■ It provides a real-time gaming experience with the help of AI. AI gaming also includes mind games that improve a person's IQ and critical thinking.

AI in the Automotive Industry:

■ With the help of human knowledge, manufacturing and robots are developing at the same time. In comparison to the financial industry, the automotive industry employs less AI.

■ AI is referred to as the "new adaptors" in this industry.

■ AI is being used in the supply chain, manufacturing, production, and, most recently, "driver assessment," in which a person can choose whether or not to drive a car by sitting in the driver's seat.

- Tesla is an example of a successful automated vehicle. One of the amazing inventions of AI is the ability to drive on its own based on the route map, analyzing and detecting and calculating the distance and roads, and driving safely.
- Tesla would be AI. Elon Musk is a brilliant visionary who is the CEO of Tesla, SpaceX, and a slew of other companies that have a global impact. Tesla's autonomous driving has prompted the entire automobile industry to take notice of Tesla, as it is a ground-breaking concept developed by Tesla's team. In the near future, we will likely see a good and controllable AI society of Tesla that is used for autonomous driving as each car can communicate with another car for safe driving. Tesla's team has devised a revolutionary plan. AI in the coming years can cause good or can cause bad to the human civilization, but it is sure that AI would definitely have their own societies and civilizations for the betterment of themselves as well as humans.

19.10.1.1 AI in the Manufacturing Industry

In the manufacturing sector, AI has limitless potential. Everything from maintenance to replacing humans in automated tasks has been automated. Brynjolfsson and McAfee (2016) say that AI allows you to improve the quality of your work and output while also increasing your output. Microsoft, for example, will transform all information so that workers can perform better.

19.10.1.2 AI in Organizational Intelligence

For businesses, a large amount of data is generated from customers, which takes a long time to process and analyze. Traditional business and methods are failing due to technological and speed advancements. AI enables companies to explore data, analyze data, and predict changes faster than humans, allowing them to make quick and effective decisions.

19.10.1.3 AI in Urban Design

AI aids in the development and planning of cities. There will be a massive amount of data that needs to be analyzed; AI gathers large amounts of data and aids in the organization and understanding of urban areas as they evolve. AI data can express itself and show how growth has progressed in the past and in the future, utilities required, safety, and so on.

19.10.1.4 AI in Education

The concept of education must evolve from generation to generation, and this evolution is critical (Chatterjee and Bhattacharya, 2020). People in the education industry are always asking where changes are needed and how to make them. AI has the potential to create a dynamic, systemized, and effective learning environment for subjects, which could be a game changer. AI teachers are another example of useful advancements (Siau, 2017). AI can be a better tutor by showing students visualizations in 3D to help them understand concepts better.

19.10.1.5 AI in Fashion

With the help of AI, the world can better understand people's buying patterns and changing behaviors, as well as predict future fashion trends, which is a huge step forward.

19.10.1.6 AI in Management of Supply

AI will be able to predict humans without judging but in a way with proper risk analysis and find exact decisions even in difficult situations and in a cost-effective manner. AI will be able to create more dependencies and complicated data than humans. As a result, proper and effective decisions can be made.

19.11 Singularity

In terms of technology, singularity means a hypothetical future where technology is growing very rapidly and is out of control and irreversible (Dickson, 2020). These powerful technologies will change rapidly and changes unpredictably transform our reality. Singularity would be applied to such advancements where it involves computers and programs that are being advanced with the help of artificial intelligence which is created by humans. These changes would affect and cross the boundary of humanity and computers. Nanotechnology is said to be one of the important technologies that probably will make singularity come into reality. This explosion will show a drastic impact on human civilization. These computer programs and AI turn the machines and robots into super intelligent and high-cognitive-capacity machines that would be beyond human capability and intelligence.

If AI would return in a way that would destroy human civilization, singularity has won its pace. When AI forms a society for itself, there is a high chance that they become stronger and humans cannot destroy that vast technology. Humans create AI, which can destroy its own kind and this action is an irrevocable action. Once AI has its own society, they are protected in their society, which cannot be destroyed.

The singularity would occur when computer programs improve to the point that AI surpasses human intelligence, potentially erasing the human-computer divide. One of the main technologies that will make singularity a reality is nanotechnology.

This expansion of intelligence will have a tremendous impact on human society. These computer programs and AI will evolve into super intelligent machines with cognitive powers far exceeding those of humans.

Following are the challenges that society needs to face when AI has its own society, which would give a way to singularity:

■ Not all of the effects are positive. AI has the potential to cause harm by leaking private information. Recognition of faces: Several states and cities have banned the government from using facial recognition because it can be manipulated and AI interference with secret privacy grows.
■ AI will undoubtedly cause a shift in the workforce. As AI advances, it will take away human jobs and work more efficiently in their place, resulting in job losses.
■ With AI advancements in the automotive and car industries, there is a risk that autonomous vehicles will harm people.
■ Another issue is that it has the potential to cross ethical and legal lines. With AI's goal of benefiting society, it would have a negative impact on society if it strayed too far from the desired goals.
■ Maintaining privacy can be difficult. AI is a powerful tool that is backed up by data. Every second, it collects data on everyone, making it difficult for people to maintain their privacy. If businesses and governments make appropriate decisions based on the information they gather, as China does with its social system, social oppression can result.

- The current trend of digitization, combined with AI and the Internet of Things, has made the situation more vulnerable to cyber-attacks.
- Autonomous weapons. For military applications, AI has opened up new possibilities, particularly in weapon systems with special functions for selecting attacking targets. These weapons should be used in conjunction with proper command and responsibility, and they should always be associated with humans.
- Robotics: Robotics must be safe, dependable, and secure. We must ensure that robots are aware of and follow ethical laws, and that they do not harm society. However, AI development has created a society in which robots may become powerful enough to turn against society and work.

19.12 AI and Its Future

Going back to 2017, when Facebook, Tesla, and many other major players were competing in the AI industry, a real-time example of AI could create its own society (Berger, 2018). Facebook created two AI robots named "Alice" and "Bob," and had them sit in front of a live audience to test and introduce them to the world. Where Facebook's plans failed to materialize and go as planned, the robots stunned the entire world, including the Facebook team, by conversing in their own language. This is the first sign that AI can perform tasks that are similar to those performed by humans. They created their own language and spoke with each other, which, in future, if provided a number of AI systems, there might be a chance where all AIs can talk to each other and form a society.

As the trend indicates, they have various levels of life. AI is attempting to come alive in the same way that humans do. According to philosophical anthropology, the first step is to comprehend the purpose of the purpose and to become goal-oriented. Another factor is that it tries to improve itself to the point where its organism allows it to do so. This is something that trees, birds, and other living creatures do. It can evolve and allow itself to learn and adapt to new environments, allowing it to create its own survival species. It's beneficial in one way and detrimental in another.

All of these may be benefits that AI provides to society, as it is claimed that AI has the ability to create society for itself. Though it has brought many benefits and advancements to society, it has also brought with it a number of challenges that may arise in the future. The concept of singularity emerges when AI and advancements in the world reach a point where they are uncontrollable and unstoppable.

References

Berger, I.W (2018). *The Impact of Artificial Intelligence on the World Economy. The Wall Street Journal.* https://www.wsj.com/articles/the-impact-of-artificial-intelligence-on-the-world-economy-1542398991

Brynjolfsson E., McAfee A. (2016). *The second machine age: Work, progress, and prosperity in a time of Brilliant.* ISBN: 978-0-393-35064-7. https://wwnorton.com/books/the-second-machine-age/

Cangelosi A., Schlesinger M. (2015). *Development robotics: From babies to robotics.* Cambridge.

Chatterjee S., Bhattacharya K. (2020). *Adoption of artificial intelligence in higher education: A quantitative analysis using structural equation modelling, Education and Information Technologies,* 25, 3443–3463.

Cockburn I. M., Henderson R., Stern S. (2018). The impact of artificial intelligence on innovation *(No. w24449).* National Bureau of Economic Research.

Derrington D. (2017). *Artificial intelligence for health and health care.* McLean (VA): The MITRE Corporation, https://www.healthit.gov/sites/default/files/jsr-17-task-002_ aiforhealthandhealthcare12122017.pdf

Dickson B. (2020). *Reflection on artificial intelligence singularity.* https://bdtechtalks.com/2020/06/29/artificial-intelligence-singularity/

Ostrom N. (2016). *Superintelligence: paths, dangers, strategies.* Oxford University Press, Oxford.

Siau K. (2017). *Impact of artificial intelligence, robotics, and machine learning on sales and marketing.* Twelve Annual Midwest Association for Information Systems Conference (MWAIS 2017), 48, pp. 18–19.
A Review on Social Robots for Language Learning

Admoni H., Scasselati B. (2017). Social eye gaze in human-robot interaction: a review. Journal of Human-Robot Interaction, 6(1), 25–63.

Bossman J. (2016). *10 Ethical issues in artificial intelligence.* https://www.weforum.org/agenda/2016/10/top-10-ethical-issues-in-artificial-intelligence/

Cangelosi A. (2010). Grounding language in action and perception: From cognitive agents to humanoid robots. *Physics of Life Reviews,* 7(2), 139–151.

Cangelosi A., Metta G., Sagerer G., Nolfi S., Nehaniv C., Fischer K., ... & Zeschel A. (2010). Integration of action and language knowledge: A roadmap for developmental robotics. *IEEE Transactions on Autonomous Mental Development,* 2(3), 167–195.

Dong Y., Hou J., Zhang N., Zhang M. (2020). *Consiousness and cognitive computing affect the development of artificial intelligence.* 1–10.

Dutoit T. (1997). *An introduction to text-to-speech synthesis,* vol 3. Springer Science & Business Media, Berlin.

Hesslow G. (2002). Conscious thought as simulation of behaviour and perception. *Trends in Cognitive Sciences*, 6(6), 242–247.

Joshi N. (2019). *Types of artificial intelligence.* https://www.forbes.com/sites/cognitiveworld/2019/06/19/7-types-of-artificial-intelligence/?sh=6618bfe0233e

Koch C. (2019). *Will machines ever become conscious?* https://www.scientificamerican.com/article/will-machines-ever-become-conscious/

Manzotti R. (2005). *Artificial intelligence and consciousness.*

Mavridis N. (2015). A review of non-verbal and verbal human–robot interactive communication. *Robotics and Autonomous Systems*, 63, 22–35.

Muggleton S. (2003). Learning structure and parameters of stochastic logic programs. In *Inductive Logic Programming: 12th International Conference, ILP 2002 Sydney, Australia, July 9–11, 2002, Revised Papers 12* (pp. 198–206). Springer Berlin Heidelberg.

Mutlu, B., Yamaoka, F., Kanda, T., Ishiguro, H., & Hagita, N. (2009). Nonverbal leakage in robots: communication of intentions through seemingly unintentional behavior. *In Proceedings of the 4th ACM/IEEE international conference on Human robot interaction* (pp. 69–76).

Nguyen, S. M., & Oudeyer, P. Y. (2014). *Socially guided intrinsic motivation for robot learning of motor skills. Autonomous Robots*, 36, 273–294.

Noda, K., Yamaguchi, Y., Nakadai, K., Okuno, H. G., & Ogata, T. (2015). *Audio-visual speech recognition using deep learning. Applied intelligence*, 42, 722–737.

Sayantini. (2022, Dec 21). *What is cognitive AI? Is it the future?* https://fingertips.co.in/blog/what-is-cognitive-ai-is-it-the-future-of-ai

Signorello C. M. (2021). Can computers become conscious and overcome humans? *Frontiers in Robotics and AI*, 5, 121.

Wang, P. (2020). *A Constructive Explanation of Consciousness. Journal of Artificial Intelligence and Consciousness*, 7(02), 257–275.

Chapter 20

Emerging Trends of AI and Digital Transactions Replacing Plastic Money in India

---

Jeevan Venkata Sai Gollapalli, Saransh Kalambele,
and Anurag Jain
Woxsen University
Hyderabad, Telangana, India

Ezendu Ariwa
University of Wales Trinity Saint David
Wales, UK

20.1 Introduction

The Internet was introduced in 1986 in India. The internet was made available only for research and educational purposes. Then, in 1996, digital payments through banks were introduced and HDFC, CitiBank, and Induslnd banks were the banks that took initiative to introduce this in the market. They were the early adopters of the market and made digital payments available by 1999. Before digital payments (such as debit cards, credit cards, and net banking) were introduced, cash was used to transfer money, one has to stand in the bank to transfer or deposit money into the account holder. Digital payments made the customer's and banker's life easy; the customers can transfer money online while sitting on their couches at home or at the office. Banks were shifted from traditional ways of doing work to virtual ways of doing work. Customers were experiencing real-time

DOI: 10.4324/b23404-20

transfer of funds from their accounts. To further improve efficiency, banks implemented IT tools to provide customers with the best experience. As banks started adopting digital payments, they also started looking for new ways to gain more advantage in the market over their competitors. Firstly, the customers were also afraid to adopt the technology because of data privacy and security breach concerns. They were not ready to adopt concepts like net banking and mobile banking. The government of India promoted the uses and benefits of digital payments.

NCPI (National Payments Corporation of India) introduced UPI on 11th April 2016 by Dr Raghuram G Rajan, then governor of RBI in Mumbai. The UPI was introduced in corporation with 21 member banks. Banks introduced their own UPI Apps to the customers for their use which were made functional from 25th August 2016. The customers could download the apps from the Google Play store and Apple store.

UPI (Unified Payments Interface) is a system that has combined all the services provided by the banks into a single platform. This allows transferring peer-to-peer, inter-bank, and peer-to-merchant. UPI is an identity given by apps (like Google Pay, PhonePe, Airtel Pay, Paytm, etc.) that is used for receiving and sending money. One just needs a UPI ID or bar code and PIN. To generate a UPI ID, one just needs a phone number that is linked to his/her bank account. All of his/her details would be verified by the app from the bank. The PIN is a 4- to 6-digit code set by the account holder himself/herself that is needed to be entered while transferring money to someone's account. Bank transfers are done in real time using the UPI apps. Anyone just needs the account number and IFSC code and the money will be transferred in just seconds. One does not have to wait for the verification through the bank for 2 to 4 hours. UPI has made life easier; you don't have to carry plastic money (cash, debit card, credit card, etc.) or you don't have to memorize or have to take down the account holder's number and IFSC code. You just either enter the phone number or the UPI ID of the person.

When UPI was introduced into the market, people were afraid of this technology. This technology was mostly used by the youth. But, after the demonetization in India on 8th November 2016, the majority of India shifted towards UPI payments because it was becoming difficult to carry debit cards and credit cards and doing net banking or mobile banking. While doing net banking, if one's account is not added to the holder's account portal, then it will take 2 hours to get the account verified. Until then you have to just wait for the transfer of funds. As in the advancement of technology, people are avoiding even carrying their debit and credit cards for shopping, payments, etc.; instead, they are using UPI payments. The government then introduced the Digi-locker app where you can keep each and every useful identity card (such as driver's license, Aadhaar card, Pan Card, and Ration Card) after this initiative by the government when your mobile phone became everything and the need for debit and credit cards became less.

The UPI came into the picture of everyone's mind during COVID-19 when no one was ready to even touch plastic money (debit and credit cards, machines, and even cash). The use of UPI increased because of the vegetable seller, auto-rickshaw, etc. started accepting UPI payments and then people understood the real meaning of UPI payments; they were able to know the benefits of using UPI apps. Around 3 billion-plus transactions were placed during the year 2018 using UPI apps. UPI apps became the preferred mode of transaction because there was no charge deducted while using debit and credit cards; the charges are deducted by the banks for every transaction done.

From the year 2016, there was tremendous growth in UPI transactions each and every month; the transactions are increasing in billions. The highest number of transactions in December 2016 was 2 million (approx); then in the year 2017, the transactions increased by hundreds of millions and the highest number of transactions achieved was 145 million (approx.); in the year 2018, 620 million transactions (approx); the year 2019, transactions reached into the billions and it was around 1 billion (approx); from the year 2020, the UPI transactions took another level and everyone started using it and recorded around 2.2 billion (approx) transactions; the year 2021 recorded 4.5 billion (approx) transactions in the month of December; for the last year 2022, the transactions recorded were 7.8 billion (approx). The banks are also increased to 382 all over India.

Financial institutions are starting to appreciate that AI and machine learning are becoming increasingly potent tools for detecting fraud in all situations, particularly digital transactions. Since its inception, AI has been at the forefront of avoiding fraud, processing payments, and implementing proper transaction methods. Chatbots are being built to incorporate mobile banking applications, thereby increasing customer support. Customers can view the status of their transactions, refunds, and bank balances, among other things. Companies utilize tens of thousands of unique features that are present in every transaction to make sure that the consumer is carrying out the planned transaction. AI has proved invaluable in assessing corporate and retail clients' credit histories in order to determine loan eligibility. Many AI-powered digital technologies generate collateral-free loan solutions by utilizing multiple credit rating algorithms.

Countries using cash as a mode of transaction face many issues in their economies as to tracking the unaccountable cash used by whom. This cash could be used either by businesses or government bodies. There would be no trace and won't be easy to track the funds. To avoid these circumstances, many countries have shifted to make the country a cashless economy. The payments made online would be crystal clear that from where and how the cash flows between bodies. The government could easily track the funds transferred online. Moreover, the government would know how much taxes one should have to pay if the income is crystal clear, but in the case of cash, it won't be easy because cash can be stored and spent wherever and whenever one wants to spend it.

20.2 Literature Review

In recent times, the revolution of electronic banking is happening at a breakneck pace. Electronic banking began with a debit card and a credit card, but things gradually changed, and then net banking entered the picture, and then UPI entered the picture. This has boosted the economy's growth. According to a McKinsey report, which is a consulting firm, the use of cash while shopping, traveling, or making any transaction in any asset in 2013 was 95%. According to the Business Standard report, a brokerage company, cash transactions were lowered in 2016, and the transaction percentage was 68% in 2016. The Indian government intends to remove significant impediments since they will harm the economy. In a nutshell, there will be no more increase in transactions. The RBI (Reserve Bank of India) and the government of India intend to work together to expand the use of digital currency and other non-cash payments. The government's vision for digital transformation in 2018 was to design a payment and settlement payment system in India that would be controlled and brought by the RBI.

In 2016, the government of India and the Reserve Bank of India committed to boosting the economy by increasing the use of digital/ electronic payments by all sections of society in order to achieve the aim of a cash-less society. The broad outline of this vision was to focus on the 5Cs that will assist them in transforming the digital transaction, which are cost, confidence, convergence, convenience, and coverage. Concentrating on these 5Cs is meant to complete the digital transformation. To achieve customer centricity, the RBI concentrated on three strategies: effective supervision, robust infrastructure, and responsive regulation. These three initiatives will assist the government in accelerating the pace of digital transformation. They want to reduce cash transactions while increasing the growth of the electronic/digital payment space, which will help them grow the economy. The government stated that they must ensure that Aadhaar cards are used in the payment system as quickly as possible. During the budget session, the Indian government also planned for this fiscal move, which was intended to strengthen digital payments. This first step was to waive the fee for card-based and other digital payments services such as UPI, online banking, and others. We shall concentrate on UPI in this research report. By decreasing the cash transactions, they aim to increase the growth of the electronic/digital payment space, which will be helping them to grow the economy. For this thing, the government said they need to ensure faster usage of Aadhaar cards in the payment system. The government of India also prepared for this fiscal measure that was meant to be the reinforcement of digital payment in the budget session. This one step was to exempt the charge on the card-based and other digital payments service like UPI, net banking, and many more. In this research paper, we will be focusing on UPI.

After the epidemic, the rise of digital payment has accelerated in the subsequent three years. Specifically, UPI payments can be used to buy clothes, groceries, and other items. This electronic payment system has piqued the interest of numerous experts because of its importance in the financial market. As we address this vital problem, much research has occurred on this topic, such as the role, benefits, various modalities, and safety of digital payment; the major significant topic that is mostly discussed is security.

The growth trend of cashless transactions has been increasing as a result of e-payment and e-banking. Utilizing remittances, quick payments, and technology to their fullest extent will guarantee that clients are making optimal use of the cash available to the bank and other financial organizations. In this paper, they also emphasized the significance of e-payment, which he explained will assist to save time, reduce the risk of loss, improve security, be convenient and user-friendly, and bring more insight into the financial supply chain.

The cashless approach has one advantage in that money can be stored in an electronic wallet or a card, which can then be used to purchase a product at any point-of-sale terminal installed on the business premises. A cashless economy is one in which they presume that there is no transaction friction that can be reduced by using the money balance, and this gives the justification for retaining such a balance, even when they earn a rate of return, according to Ejiofor and Rasaki (2012).

The adoption of electronic transactions is critical for the fundamentals of economic growth, development, cash-related fraud reduction, accountability, and transparency, according to Mieseigha and Ogbodo (2011).

The adoption of electronic payments will positively affect economic growth and trade.

The importance of various customer satisfaction and loyalty metrics in forecasting the customer share of wallet, recommendation, and retention has been investigated. The findings of this article reveal that good intentions alone will not suffice for digital payment systems. The consumers' adoption of cashless transactions, which is the research topic, has been revealed to us and that a computerized wallet is rapidly becoming a standard method of online installment through various means. Customers are adopting advanced wallets at an unfathomably rapid rate. This will be accelerated to some extent due to convenience and comfort, according to Dr. Hema Shewta Rathore (2016)

Digital payment using a wallet is highly convenient for consumers while purchasing products online without any physical movement across any place, according to Rathore (2016).

A study on demonetization and its impact have facilitated cashless transactions, with the growth of the cashless exchange system reaching new heights in the world. Individuals are increasingly shifting away from cash purchases and toward cashless transactions. This statement emphasizes that the cashless framework is a prerequisite as well as a requirement for the general public so that they may easily make the transaction and acquire the product from the comfort of their own homes, according to K. C. Balaji and K. Balaji (2017).

Santomera (1996) expressed this after examining their numerous forms of payment, including debit and credit cards, smart cards, e-wallets, gift cards, and a number of others. They are advocating for an increase in the use of the medium of exchange, as suggested by the Baumol-Tobin model. This model indicates that the number of assets used decreases with declining household earnings. Additionally, it demonstrates how the choice of medium of exchange varies with income levels. However, the crucial distinction lies in the allocation of income for household consumption, which favors using the medium of exchange with the highest interest to purchase items representing a significant portion of income.

Manivannan (2013) wrote a research paper titled "Plastic money means less payment of cash checking system." In this investigation, she has done extensive research on the usage of plastic money i.e., credit cards as a measure of luxury. According to their research, higher-income people are more likely to use e-payment and plastic money. However, the payment option is being extended not only to metropolitan customers, but also to rural customers. With the recent expansion of the banking industry, fixed-income groups also have started to use electronic money payment, plastic card payment, and particularly credit cards.

The topic for this research is written by Roopali Batra and Neha Kalra (2016), titled "Are digital wallets new currency." According to both assessments in this research paper, in the age of digitalization, the examination intends to consider the 52 respondents' client recognition, fulfillment, inclination, and usage design inclination with regard to advance digital wallets. Moreover, the intricacy and difficulty in choosing the right option are evident. The findings of this study show that there is a massive untapped market for digital wallets in terms of both increasing awareness and usage.

Kunal Taheam, Rahul Sharma, and Saurabh Goswami (2016) wrote the paper "Drivers of digital wallet usage: Implications for leveraging digital marketing." The findings of this research article have emphasized different components that motivate individuals who use a digital wallet to make payments and installments. They conducted research in Punjab, which revealed that people in Punjab are using digital wallets for the purpose of security and control, which has been influenced by sociocultural and responsiveness requirements for the improvement of the wallet.

According to the findings of the study, there is a considerable difference between digital payment adoption and consumer education qualifications. Consumer perceptions of digital payments had a strong beneficial effect on consumer adoption of digital payments, according to Singh and Rana (2017).

The key objectives of this paper are as follows:

i. to investigate the notion of UPI and plastic money
ii. to analyze how users are using UPI.
iii. to study the main reasons and purposes for customers adopting UPI.
iv. to comprehend the issues encountered when using UPI and plastic money.

20.3 Methodology

The paper makes use of primary data gathered through a structured questionnaire filled by 150 respondents. The respondents were classified based on their age, gender, and educational qualifications. This data was validated and cleaned in Excel before being imported into Tableau for visualization. A 5-point Likert Scale was used to assess the level of acceptance of using UPI. The results were obtained using frequency analysis and a graphical representation of the data.

20.4 Data Analysis and Interpretation

This section provides detailed information about the participants' gender, age, educational qualifications, and so on. When responses were sorted by gender, it was discovered that 65% of responses are from male participants and 35% are from female participants shown in Figure 20.1.

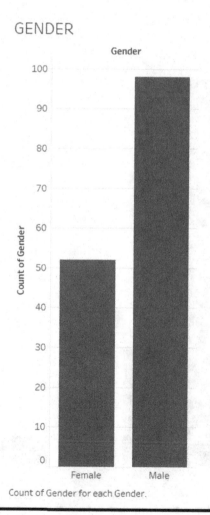

Figure 20.1   Gender details.

As shown in Figure 20.2, 62% of the participants were between the ages of 18 and 25, 18% were between the ages of 25 and 34, 12% were between the ages of 35 and 44, and the remaining 8% were between the ages of 45 and 65.

The chart below (Figure 20.3) reveals that around 52% of the participants have completed or are presently pursuing post-graduation, and 34% have graduated or are currently pursuing graduation.

The occupations of various respondents are depicted in Figure 20.4. It was discovered that 62% of them are students, 16% are employees, and 4% are teachers and professors. Engineers, businessmen, and others follow.

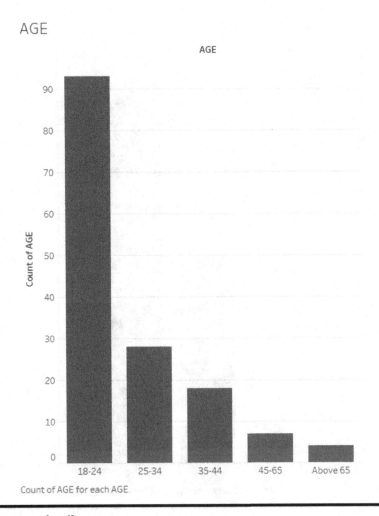

Figure 20.2   Age details.

EDUCATION

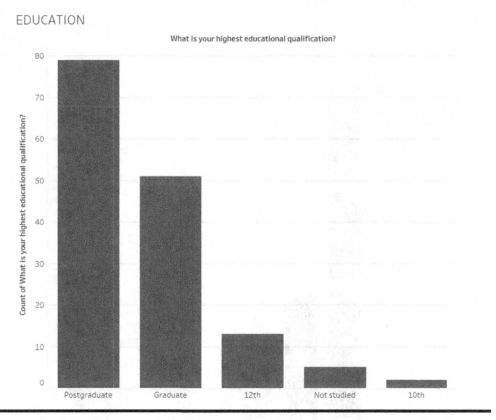

Figure 20.3   Education.

OCCUPATION

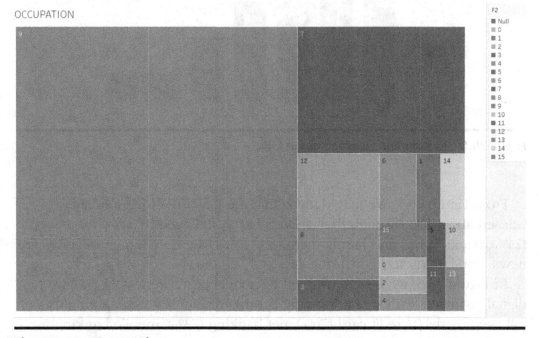

Figure 20.4   Occupation.

Q4

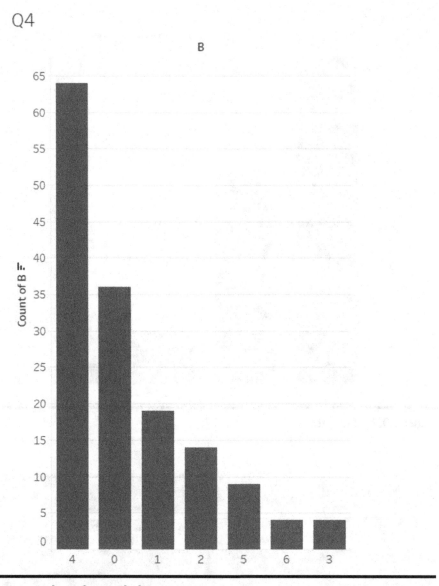

Figure 20.5   Respondents learned about UPI.

From Figure 20.5, We may deduce that the majority of respondents learned about UPI through their friends (42%), followed by advertisements (24%), banks (12%), and family members (10%). The remaining categories are news, non-banks, and government.

In Figure 20.6, we have illustrated respondents' awareness of various digital payments. UPI was known by approximately 92% of respondents, followed by debit/credit card (76%), net banking (73%), mobile banking

Q5

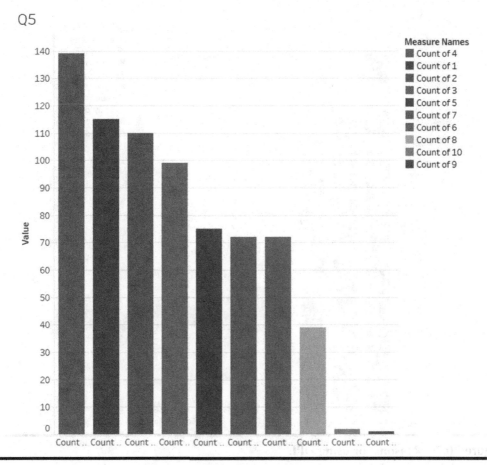

Figure 20.6 Respondents' awareness of various digital payments.

(66%), NEFT/RTGS (50%), mobile wallets (48%), pre-paid cards (48%), and IMPS (26%).

Digital Payment Method	Number of Respondents
BHIM UPI	139
Debit/Credit	115
Net Banking	110
Mobile Banking	99
NEFT/RTGS	75
Mobile Wallets	72
Pre-Paid Cards	72
IMPS	39
None	2
Crypto-Currency	1

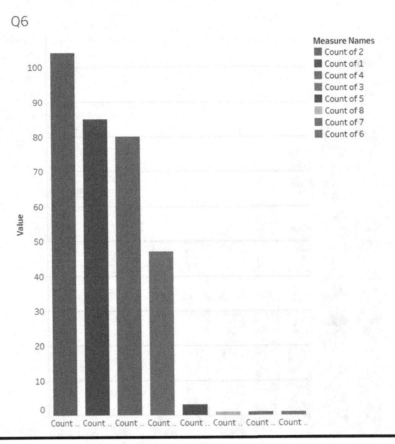

Figure 20.7   Reasons for using UPI.

In Figure 20.7, primary reasons for utilizing UPI over plastic money are depicted. According to research, 69% of respondents choose UPI since it is faster than plastic money. UPI is used by 56% of respondents because they believe it is safer than plastic money. Because of the ease of use of UPI, 53% of respondents use it and 31% of respondents utilize it for cash back and discounts.

Reason for Using UPI	Number of Respondents
Faster than Plastic Money	102
Secure than Plastic Money	85
Ease of Usage	80
Cash Back & Discounts	47
None	5

There are several reasons why respondents use UPI and are represented graphically in Figure 20.8. We can infer that sending money is the biggest reason for using UPI (89%), while the next two top reasons are bill payments

Q9

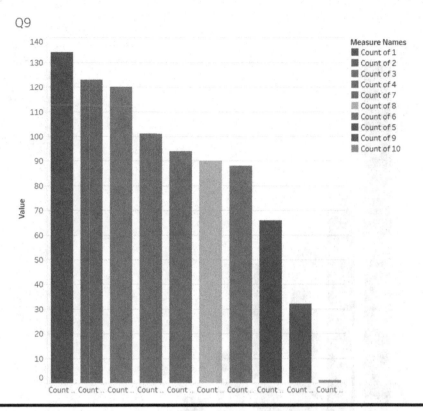

Measure Names
■ Count of 1
■ Count of 2
■ Count of 3
■ Count of 4
■ Count of 7
■ Count of 8
■ Count of 6
■ Count of 5
■ Count of 9
■ Count of 10

Figure 20.8   Purposes for using UPI.

(82%), shopping (80%). Booking travel tickets (67%), mobile/TV recharge (62%), grocery shopping (60%), payment via food ordering apps (58%), and petrol pumps/taxi/hotel/restaurants (44%) are next. They also use UPI for non-financial purposes such as balance checking and ordering checkbooks (21%), as well as for other purposes such as investment.

Purposes for Using UPI	Number of Participants
Sending Money to others	134
Bill Payments	123
Shopping for Various Electronic Items & Clothes	120
Booking Tickets for Traveling	101
Mobile/ TV Recharges	94
Grocery Shopping	90
Payment via Food Ordering Apps	88
Petrol Pumps/ Taxi/ Hotels/Restaurants	66
Non-Financial Purposes such as Balance Checking, Ordering Checkbook, etc.	32
Others	1

Q12

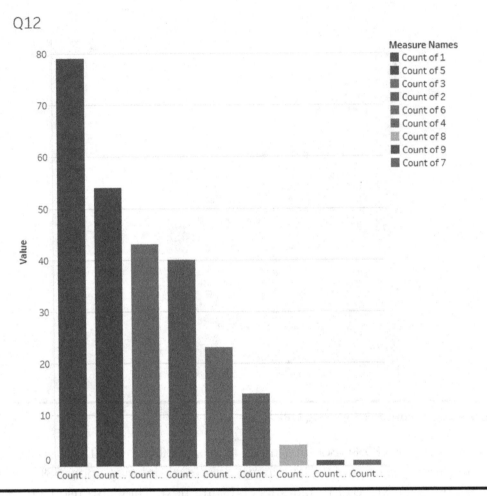

Figure 20.9   Challenges that consumers utilizing UPI.

The preceding Figure 20.9 depicts the challenges that consumers experience when utilizing UPI or plastic money. The first major concern with plastic money is that it is more complex and takes longer time periods than UPI (52%). The next most common response is "No major problems encountered while utilizing plastic money or UPI" (36%). Other major issues include a lack of trust in plastic money, which is unsafe and risky (28%), and the fact that plastic money is more costly than UPI (26%). Other concerns include a lack of point-of-sale machines or internet access (15%) and being unfamiliar with/uncomfortable with plastic money (10%).

As shown in Figure 20.10, the most prevalent reason for utilizing UPI is convenience (68%), followed by offers and discounts (16%), and trust (16%).

Q11

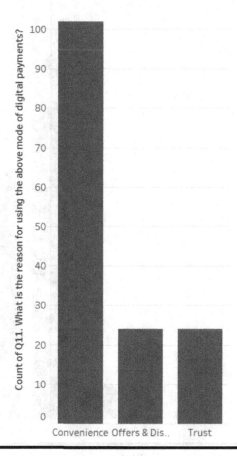

Figure 20.10   Utilizing UPI as per convenience.

In Figure 20.11, we can unmistakably perceive that the rating for the level of acceptance of UPI is 4(57%) and 5(36%).

20.5 Findings

The following are the results of the aforesaid analysis:

  i. About 42% of respondents learned about UPI from friends.
 ii. Respondents' awareness of various digital payments is as follows: UPI is the most popular payment method (92%), followed by debit/credit cards (76%), net banking (73%), and mobile banking (66%).

UPI ACCEPTANCE

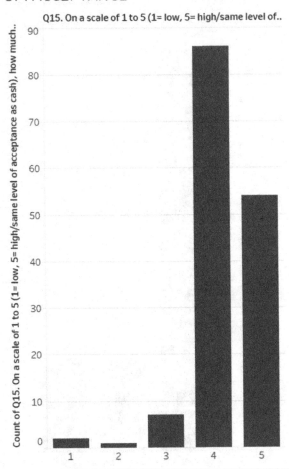

Figure 20.11   Level of acceptance of UPI.

iii. Approximately 69% of respondents use UPI because it is faster than plastic money, and 56% use it because it is more secure.

iv. Cash back and discounts have little influence on UPI usage among customers.

v. The majority of individuals use/link UPI with sending money to others/ fund transfer (89%), bill payments (82%), shopping (80%), and ticket booking (67%).

vi. Approximately 52% of respondents believe that plastic money is more complicated and time-consuming than UPI.

vii. Respondents' overall acceptance of UPI is 4 out of 5 (57%) and 5 out of 5 (36%).

viii. Sixty-eight percent of respondents use UPI mostly for its convenience and ease of use.

20.6 Conclusion

Going digital is critical and essential, as it has far-reaching implications for the government and the country. As an outcome, money spent on printing and circulating money in the economy will be minimized, while the accountability and transparency of money used for transactions across the country will be increased. It will also help combat corruption and money laundering in many regions of the country. As a result, many countries have embraced this concept and are aiming to go digital. It also poses significant infrastructure concerns and necessitates significant technological improvements in order to address fraud and cyber security issues in the financial services sector. The government and the RBI should work together to enhance public awareness and properly publicize these programs in order to increase public trust in these payment instruments. UPI was developed by making mobile phones the foremost payment device for sending and receiving payments. Compared to other payment systems, UPI is one of the most advanced, attempting to provide a simple interface for transferring payments between individuals, merchants, or customers to merchants with swift and easy usage. The widespread availability of banking services, as well as the emergence of smartphones, encourages consumers to utilize UPI. The study also found that respondents had a favorable perception about UPI and were familiar with UPI and other digital transaction methods.

20.7 Limitations

The following are the study's limitations:

i. The sample size is tiny, with only 150 respondents.
ii. The survey excludes other types of digital payments such as smart cards and gift cards.
iii. Since the majority of respondents are postgraduate and graduation students between the ages of 18 and 25, the data may be a little skewed in interpreting and obtaining the right conclusion.

iv. Moreover, 65% of respondents are male, suggesting that there may be unintended bias in the analysis and that appropriate conclusions based on gender may not be obtained using this data.

20.8 Future Scope

Further research can be conducted on the following topics:

i. The effect of income levels on the mode of digital payments used by the consumer.
ii. The impact the customer's gender has on the mode of digital payments and the level of acceptance.
iii. The analysis of the country's overall degree of acceptance of similar digital payments based on gender, age, and income levels.

References

Electric Journals

Ebipanipre Gabriel Mieseigha, and Uyoyou Kingsley Ogbodo. "An Empirical Analysis of the Benefits of Cashless Economy on Nigeria's Economic Development." IISTE- Journal & Books Hosting – Conferences & Workshops Solutions. Research Journal of Finance and Accounting, April 9, 2011. https://core.ac.uk/download/pdf/234629696.pdf.

Ejiofor, V. E., & Rasaki, J. O. (2012). Realising the benefits and challenges of cashless economy in Nigeria: IT perspective. International Journal of Advances in Computer Science and Technology, 1(1). https://www.academia.edu/2395352/REALISING_THE_BENEFITS_AND_CHALLENGES_OF_CASHLESS_ECONOMY_IN_NIGERIA_IT_PERSPECTIVE.

Hema Shweta Rathore. "Adoption of Digital Wallet by Consumers – BVIMSR." BVIMSR's Journal of Management Research, April 2016. https://bvimsr.org/wp-content/uploads/2020/04/10.-Dr-Hem-Shweta-Rathore.pdf.

K. C. Balaji, and K. Balaji. "A Study on Demonetization and Its Impact on Cashless Transactions." PDF Free Download. International Journal of Advanced Scientific Research & Development, March 2017. https://docplayer.net/96590756-A-study-on-demonetization-and-its-impact-on-cashless-transactions.html.

P. Manivannan. "Plastic Money a Way for Cash Less Payment System – World Wide Journals." Global Research Analysis, January 2013. https://www.worldwidejournals.com/global-journal-for-research-analysis-GJRA/recent_issues_pdf/2013/January/plastic-money-a-way-for-cash-less-payment-system_January_2013_1598866557_05.pdf.

Batra Roopali, and Kalra Neha. "ARE DIGITAL WALLETS THE NEW CURRENCY? - APEEJAY Journal of Management and Technology." Apeejay Journal of Management and Technology, January 2016. https://www.coursehero.com/file/48756297/Volume11No1Article4pdf/.

Shamsher Singh, and Ravish Rana. "Study of Consumer Perception of Digital Payment Modes." Journal of Internet Banking and Commerce, October 31, 2017. https://www.icommercecentral.com/open-access/study-of-consumer-perception-of-digital-payment-mode.php? aid=86419.

Kunal Taheam, Rahul Sharma, and Saurabh Goswami. "Drivers of Digital Wallet Usage: Implications for Leveraging Digital Marketing." IJER Serial Publications, 2016. https://serialsjournals.com/abstract/12791_15.pdf.

Index

Note: *Italicized* pages refer to figures.